Media Law and Regulation in the European Union

National, Transnational and U.S. Perspectives

Media Law and Regulation in the European Union

National, Transnational and U.S. Perspectives

Emmanuel E. Paraschos

Iowa State University Press / Ames

To Janet, Sophia and Alexi

Emmanuel E. (Manny) Paraschos received his Ph.D. from the University of Missouri, Columbia. He served as a Fulbright professor in Scandinavia, where he taught at the Norwegian Institute of Journalism, and as dean of the European Institute for International Communication in Maastricht, The Netherlands. Dr. Paraschos has lectured widely in Europe and in the United States and has been a reporter and an editor in his native Greece and in the United States, as well as a United Nations correspondent in New York. He is presently a professor of mass communication at Emerson College, Boston, Massachusetts.

© 1998 Iowa State University Press, Ames, Iowa 50014
All rights reserved

Authorization to photocopy items for internal or personal use, or the internal or personal use of specific clients, is granted by Iowa State University Press, provided that the base fee of $.10 per copy is paid directly to the Copyright Clearance Center, 27 Congress Street, Salem, MA 01970. For those organizations that have been granted a photocopy license by CCC, a separate system of payments has been arranged. The fee code for users of the Transactional Reporting Service is 0-8138-2807-4/98 $.10.

⊚ Printed on acid-free paper in the United States of America
First edition, 1998

Library of Congress Cataloging-in-Publication Data

Paraschos, Emmanuel E.
  Media law and regulation in the European Union : national, transnational and U.S. perspectives / Emmanuel E. Paraschos.—1st ed.
        p.   cm.
  Includes bibliographical references and index.
  ISBN 0-8138-2807-4
  1. Mass media—Law and legislation—European Union countries. 2. Mass media—Law and legislation—United States. I. Title.
KJE6946.P37   1998
341.7′57′094—dc21   97-30366
Last digit is the print number: 9 8 7 6 5 4 3 2 1

Contents

Preface, ix

1

The European Union: Purpose, History, Organization, Membership, 3

Introduction, 3

The History of the European Union, 6

The E.U. Organization and Procedures, 19

The European Union and the Mass Media, 24

Notes, 26

2

Philosophical and Legal Foundations, 27

Transnational Freedom of Expression Covenants, 27

Constitutional Provisions of the E.U. Member Nations, 34

Media and the European Court of Human Rights, 44

Notes, 57

3

Personal Protections, 59

Defamation, 59

Privacy, 70

Right of Reply, 78

Court Coverage, 83

News Source Protection, 87

Notes, 93

4

National Security, Public Order and Morality-Oriented Limitations, 97

National Security and Order, 97

Obscenity and Insult to Public Morals, 101

Blasphemy and Racism, 106

Notes, 112

5

Secrecy and Access to Information, 113

E.U. Regulations on Access, 115

National Frameworks, 118

Notes, 127

6

Broadcasting Content/Program Regulation, 129

The E.U. Directive (89/552/EEC), 133

National Frameworks, 140

Notes, 150

7

Advertising, 153

The E.U. Framework, 156

National Frameworks, 162

Notes, 172

8

Pluralism, Competition and Concentration, 175

The E.U. Framework, 181

National Frameworks, 183

Notes, 192

9

Self-Regulation and Ethical Considerations, 195

Media Ethics and the Council of Europe, 197

National Frameworks, 200

The E.U. Nations' Journalistic Codes of Ethics, 205

Notes, 245

Postscript, 247

Notes, 254

Bibliography, 255

Index, 263

Preface

Some of us who have spent a lifetime as students of international communication might have a tendency to view the recent popularity of global communication as little more than a nouveau chic topic of scholarly work. Whether the subject is news, advertising, mass media, the Internet or the telecommunications industry, the study of the transnational dimension of the communication processes is an old, challenging and fulfilling field of inquiry. Most of us have been attracted to it because of its intrigue, its Byzantine complexity, its vast and often unappreciated impact on people and public policy and, of course, because of our ignorance of it. But most important, perhaps, it is the feeling that studying it might help us communicate better and, eventually, understand more. Therefore we welcome the resurgence of the scholarly interest in this topic, regardless of its name or orientation—global or international.

Although typologies of the field historically took us from geographical units of study to philosophical and political categories of media systems, there was always an aura of mystery surrounding the legal parameters of media performance in other parts of the world. Many studies in the last two decades have provided glimpses of the laws that govern media behavior in specific regions of the world, but very few have offered a comprehensive look into these laws. Furthermore, in recent memory there has not been a study focusing on the legal limits of the mass media of a group of important nations such as the European Union.

This work attempts to fill that void. Although it focuses primarily on laws and regulations that concern freedom of expression and affect the news media (print and electronic) and the work of journalists, considerable attention has been paid to the rules governing those who own the media and those who help sustain them, the advertising industry.

Three main reasons motivated this work: One is the simple quest to see how these 15 capitalist, liberal and dynamic democracies of the traditional West protect and/or limit their mass media. The second emanates from the challenge of the unique supranational regulatory presence of the European Union, which, with the cooperation of its member states, has crafted its own legislation governing the same media. The third motivation is based on the potential for a constructive comparison between these laws and regulations and those prevalent in the United States.

Finally, the hope is that as the pages unfold, the reader will have an unusual view of the various peoples of the European Union—from the perspective of what they consider important enough to legally protect and control and how that differs from what is practiced in the United States. This comparison of values and principles from each side of the Atlantic should yield interesting and valuable results. Undoubtedly, lessons can be learned by either side, and, perhaps, the true value of this work ultimately may lie in its allowing the reader to discover the often subtle but fascinating differences that exist between these two worlds, even among legal provisions that are seemingly similar.

However, even as useful and provocative comparisons are made among rules, standards and philosophies, it should be pointed out that this book is not for lawyers or law students—it is for students of the law.

The first chapter discusses the history, function and organizational structure of the European Union and how it addresses media issues. The second chapter focuses on the philosophical and legal roots of media protection and control both within the European Union and the world's other major international organizations. It concludes with the press provisions of the constitutions of the E.U. member states and the precedent-setting media-related decisions of the European Court of Human Rights, whose rulings are binding on its member states.

Although European mass media have traditionally been unapologetically more partisan and less commercial than those of the United States, the common cultural foundation of Western Europe and the United States emerges clearly through laws protecting the individual (Ch. 3). With the exception of the "right of reply," which, unlike the United States, is by and large legally recognized both by the Union and its member states, defamation, privacy, news source confidentiality and court coverage tend to offer legal sanctuary to individuals in similar ways on either side of the Atlantic.

On the other hand, significant differences in culture and in the interpretation of the roles of media and government in contemporary society emerge clearly in the regulation of national security issues (Ch. 4), broadcasting (Ch. 6), advertising (Ch. 7) and media ownership (Ch. 8). In the case of the latter, however, the differences seem to become increasingly smaller as European media tend to follow more and more U.S. media patterns, which are characterized by capitalist goals and practices, such as transnational owners, mutually complementing horizontal and vertical media acquisitions and the continued expansion of non-media companies into media ownership.

But perhaps the clearest manifestation of influence by U.S. legal tradition on European media law can be found in the relatively recent Union adoption of the principle of the "right to know" or "freedom of information," or as it is known within the Union, "transparency" (Ch. 5). The strides that the Union and its member states individually have made toward more government openness, accessibility and accountability have surprised many.

Also surprising may be the popularity of some of the instruments of self-regulation available in E.U. member states, especially that of the press council, which, regardless of its lack of punitive power, still serves a significant cathartic, moral and safety-valve public function. There are virtually no surprises, however, in the codes of professional ethics observed in the E.U. member states. Domestic as well as international professional associations obviously are guided by principles similar to those held by professional associations in the United States (Ch. 9).

The research for this book began many years ago when, mainly through law professors, professional media associations, embassies' press attachés and scholarly law books and journal articles, I started collecting press laws from many parts of the world for lecture material in my international journalism courses. It was then that I first discovered an unexpected diversity among press laws in other countries as well as the excitement of analyzing the differences between them and those in effect in the United States.

The idea matured, however, during my tenure as the dean of the European Institute for International Communication in Maastricht, The Netherlands, between 1991 and 1994. It was then that I was able to witness how the European media, and those who work within them and in related fields, interact with the laws of their individual countries and those of the European Union. Although I had practiced journalism in both Europe and the United States before, my recent time there taught me to appreciate, again, the different ways in which mass media and journalism function and are treated in these two distinct types of society.

This re-learning experience, however, could not have been possible, and consequently, this work might never have been completed without the encouragement and expert assistance of many wonderful friends and colleagues. My sincere gratitude, therefore, goes to:

Dr. Dirk Voorhoof of the Law School of the University of Ghent, Belgium; Prof. Aalt Willem Heringa of the Law School of the University of Limburg, The Netherlands; Marie McGonagle of the Law Faculty of the University College Galway, Ireland; Dr. Ingrid Volkmer of the Department of Pedagogy of the University of Bielefeld, Germany; Dr. Nelson Traquina of the Department of Communication Science, Universidade Nova de Lisboa, Portugal; Jeroen Schokkenbroek of the Human Rights Media Section of the Council of Europe and Eija Poteri, documentarian at the Finnish branch of the Nordic Documentation Center for Mass Communication Research, University of Tampere, Finland, for helping with the texts of their native countries' laws, as well as Dr. Don Perret of the foreign languages program at Emerson College for his assistance with the French text and graduate assistant Paola Colombo for her help with the Portuguese text.

Also my heartfelt appreciation goes to Dr. Dwight Teeter, dean of the School of Journalism, University of Tennessee; Sandra Coliver, law program director of Article 19, the International Centre Against Censorship, London; and Dr. Kyu Ho Youm, professor at the Walter Cronkite School of Journalism and Telecommunication at Arizona State University, for their insightful suggestions at various stages of the manuscript and/or their encouragement throughout the project.

I am also specially grateful to Spyros Pappas, former director general, and the librarians of the European Institute of Public Administration, Maastricht, The Netherlands, for their help in accessing E.U. archives, and Jan Bierhoff, managing director, and the staff of the European Journalism Center, also of Maastricht, for pointing me to the proper resources of many E.U. countries. Special thanks are due the Text and Academic Authors Association for supporting my research with one of its grants and the respective national professional associations and members of the Department of Journalism and Mass Communication of the University of Tampere, Finland, for providing and/or translating the codes of ethics.

Finally, I owe an inestimable debt of gratitude to my wife, Janet Nyberg, for her understanding, continual encouragement and expert manuscript editing, and my children, Sophia and Alexi, for their patience throughout the long process of writing this book.

Media Law and Regulation in the European Union

National, Transnational and U.S. Perspectives

The European Union: Purpose, History, Organization, Membership

Introduction

The summer of 1989 was not a good one for Jack Valenti, president of the Motion Picture Association of America. Almost 50 years earlier he had helped defeat the Germans and the Italians in World War II. Now he was fighting them again, but this time he also had to fight the French *and* the British *and* the Dutch *and* the Spaniards and many other Europeans: The European Union was about to pass a piece of legislation that would require its member states to limit non-European television programming, which was primarily American, to no more than 40 percent of their programming. That summer Valenti fought the good fight, but this time he was on the losing side—on October 3, 1989, the European Union passed the Directive on Transfrontier Television, which called on its members to reserve more than half of their television programming for "European works." It was the first time that Europeans challenged so directly, so collectively and so unabashedly the American audiovisual entertainment machinery that had so successfully dominated European markets since World War II. The message of the Old World was unwelcome news in the New World.

Valenti responded by saying that the Europeans "threw a grenade into our area, and the pin's pulled out," and U.S. Trade Representative Carla Hills called the directive a sign of the rebuilding of "fortress Europe."[1] *The New York Times* followed suit by calling the agreement an "absurd effort to regulate public taste,"[2] and *The Boston Globe* saw it as an act of "cultural protectionism."[3]

Jacques Delors, the socialist European Commission chairman, however, who saw it in much the same way as most of the other European Union leaders, put it in a different perspective:

Culture is not a piece of merchandise, like other things. There will not be protection of the European market, but neither will there be laissez-faire. I say to the United States, "Do we have the right to exist, to perpetuate our traditions?"[4]

France's Foreign Minister for European Affairs, Edith Cresson, who later became prime minister of France and the E.U. Commissioner on science, research, development and education, was more caustic:

What will remain of our cultural identity, if audiovisual Europe consists of European consumers sitting in front of Japanese TV sets showing off American programs?[5]

But behind the simplistic "we" vs. "they" battle cries of these European and American combatants, their unrepentant provincialism and their occasional reliance on aggressive patriotism, there lay huge financial concerns with even larger political implications.

During the five years preceding the directive's passage, the pressures on the commission were immense. On one side there were the cultural purists, accompanied by the new European audiovisual entrepreneurs and their multinational conglomerates. On the other, there were the Americans, who were trying to protect their nation's second foreign-trade-deficit-reducing industry, and some of Europe's broadcasting executives, especially those from small countries, who were fighting the quotas because they would deprive them of access to inexpensive and popular American programs that normally cost them one-tenth of the price of producing them domestically. It was truly a case of "The Television Europeans Love, and Love to Hate."[6]

But even some, including Americans, thought the European Union move was inevitable. A senior Hollywood studio executive said, "The rape and pillage can only go on for so long."[7] Others, such as the Danes, thought it unfair for "government to tell us what to schedule," while the pessimists had no doubt that "European rubbish will be no better than American rubbish."[8]

In any case, despite the intense lobbying and the risk of causing an irreparable rift within the Western Alliance, the consensus held and sent a clear signal to the United States, that even on mass communication matters, where American superiority had been traditionally conceded worldwide, the Union was willing to make a stand to protect its peoples' interests, be they cultural, financial or political. The Union had "arrived"—and the relationship between these two capitalist giants would never be the same again.

The Union's arrival on mass media matters coincided precisely with the arrival in Europe of the technological revolution that precipitated, especially among the European electronic media, a series of significant developments, such as their liberation from traditional government ownership and operation, privatization, transfrontier and transcontinental transmission, print-electronic media alliances and, probably most important, commercial sponsorship to a degree that was never before seen in Europe. Media commercialism was an especially large challenge for most of these proud welfare states, where egalitarianism and not competition seem to be the governing social rationale. However, all these new media-related phenomena had a clear common element: their foundation on economic, as well as cultural, principles. Thus the door was opened for the former "economic community" to legally bring almost all of the media activities, directly or indirectly, under the Union's purview.

But where the collective power of the Union governs on issues related to competition, trade and finance, individual national authority specifically has been reserved for the legal regulation of a vast area of media behavior issues, such as defamation, privacy, court coverage, national security, obscenity, racism, government access, etc. However, even in these areas of regulation that seemingly have nothing to do with commercial or competitive interests and everything to do with each nation's cultural definitions, tolerances and sensitivities, national authority has been eroding and is being superseded by the Union's ubiquitous legal arm. The most common avenue through which the Union can claim jurisdiction over such culturally driven issues is the transfrontier movement of messages, which makes them a commodity that can be regulated by the Union. Another regulatory avenue is the Union's commitment to the protection of human rights, the policing of which requires legal vigilance and punitive action against those who disseminate messages that are violative of those rights. In short, good Union citizenship requires the presence of and adherence to more and more common rules of behavior, a practice which, in effect, continually weakens national jurisdictions and replaces them with the collective conscience of the Union and its rule enforcement. This process has been affecting both "Europhiles" and "Euroskeptics," except that for the former it represents a dream and to the latter a nightmare. The Union has arrived indeed.

The History of the European Union

The Formative Years

The idea of a European union had been around for centuries. It did not gain momentum, however, until the end of World War II when the battered Europeans started to think that the dreadful war experience might have been avoidable, that a united Europe might have had a better chance against the Nazi war machine, or even more optimistically, that Hitler might never have emerged as a leader of a member nation of a European union. In fact, it was in 1944, even before their liberation, that Belgium, The Netherlands and Luxembourg decided to formulate the Benelux Union (which eventually became effective in 1948).

Another factor that gave additional impetus to the concept of a united Europe at the time was the emergence of Communism as a crude and powerful adversary in the area. One month after the February 1948 Communist invasion of Czechoslovakia, the Western European Union defense agreement among the Benelux countries, France and the United Kingdom came into being.

One thorny issue in this "unity" debate was how to solve the "German problem." One side argued that the punitive provisions of the 1919 Treaty of Versailles should not only be retained but expanded, thus ensuring that Germany remained weak. The other side argued that Europe, with a new enemy in sight (USSR and its satellites within mainland Europe), needed Germany's contribution to a European defense and could ill afford the reimposition of a forced economic marginalization of that country. In short, the liberal thinking of the time was that, this time around, it might make more sense to incorporate Germany into a united Europe scheme so that her political, social, economic and military growth might be better monitored and guided.

It is significant to note that the architect and chief proponent of this new idea was Jean Monnet, an articulate and efficient Frenchman whose country had waged three savage wars against Germany in the last 70 years. Before World War I Monnet spent time in England as a distributor of his family's brandy, and during World War I he served on the Inter-Allied Maritime Commission, an international committee that coordinated the economic contributions of France and the United Kingdom to the war effort. Between the two wars he became Deputy Secretary-General of the League of Nations, but in 1939 he was asked by the French government to resume his role as coordinator of the economic development effort of France and the United Kingdom. In fact, it was Monnet who devised the Franco-British Union plan that Churchill proposed in 1940 in an effort to delay France's surrender to Germany. Monnet spent the rest of the war years in the United States and Britain overseeing financial aspects of the Allies' war effort.

After the war ended, Monnet's vision of a united Europe, including Germany, seemed to gain momentum. His thoughts were validated in a speech Churchill gave at Zurich University in 1946, in which he talked about a "partnership between France and Germany" as being essential to the effort to rebuild the "European family" or the "United States of Europe."[9]

The vehicle that gave Monnet the opportunity to advance his proposals was the controversy over Saarland, the overwhelmingly German coal- and iron-rich region lying between France and Germany that the French had unsuccessfully tried to annex in the past. The French objected to Germany's being given full access to that region's resources because they were afraid that the German economy would, again, develop a tremendous economic advantage over its neighbors.

First, Monnet gained national recognition for his 1947 plan that modernized French industry and agriculture (setting government-approved financial goals, a 48-hour work week, etc.) and then, as a member of the 1950 de Gaulle government, he began working closely with French Foreign Minister Robert Schuman, whose family was from Alsace, a region neighboring Saarland, and who also was eager to end the dispute between France and Ger-

many. The Monnet plan that Schuman presented to the French
government was based on the principle that the French and West
German steel and coal industries should be placed under a single,
independent, supranational administration, the High Authority,
which would guide their development. The mission of the proposed organization was further refined to include the pooling of
coal and steel resources of member states in order to consolidate labor forces, products and services. The idea satisfied enough of the
French concerns while it allowed Germany to re-enter the European family as an equal partner. Several neighboring countries
found the concept attractive enough to participate: Belgium, The
Netherlands, Italy and Luxembourg joined France and Germany in
the signing of the European Coal and Steel Community (ECSC)
agreement in Paris in 1951. Jean Monnet was named its first president.

With the ECSC in operation, Monnet tried to fulfill the rest of
his dream by inviting the six Paris Treaty signatories to join in a
military alliance called the European Defense Community (EDC).
After a long and bitter discussion in the French National Assembly,
the EDC was voted down and Monnet was forced to conclude that
the way to European unity was through economic rather than military cooperation.

After declining a second term as the ECSC president, Monnet
established the Action Committee for the United States of Europe
(ACUSE), which consisted of members from all the major political
parties of the six ECSC partners. ACUSE's efforts paid off when the
foreign ministers of the six partners met in Messina, Italy, in 1955
and appointed a committee, headed by Belgian Foreign Minister
Paul-Henri Spaak, whose charge was to draft plans for the creation
of a common (customs- and tariff-free) market, and common policies on transportation and energy (atomic and conventional). The
committee's proposals, which relied heavily on the ECSC model,
became the basis for the 1957 Treaty of Rome, which established
the European Economic Community (EEC) and the European
Atomic Energy Community (Euratom).

On July 1, 1967, the ECSC, the EEC and Euratom merged into
the European Community (EC), which would operate through a
Commission (the body that initiates and enforces decisions); a
Council of Ministers (the legislative and decision-making body);
the Assembly, or European Parliament (the legislative advisory
body); the Economic and Social Committee (a consulting body);

and the Court of Justice (the decision-interpreting body). The foundation of the European Union had been laid.

The Normative Years

French President Charles de Gaulle, West German Chancellor Conrad Adenauer and EC Commission President Professor Walter Hallstein (a former Adenauer aide) were EC's early protagonists. But it was the warm personal relationship between de Gaulle and Adenauer that propelled the EC to a remarkably productive first decade: trade among member states tripled that of member states with non-member states, and the removal of internal tariffs as well as the erection of external tariffs were completed ahead of schedule.

The dominance of the EC by France and West Germany was evident in the negotiations that followed the Rome Treaty concerning the EC's Common Agricultural Policy (CAP). It took five years for member states to agree on CAP, and the result was a policy that was based on free-trade principles benefiting West German industry and protectionism benefiting French farmers. The dominance of those two countries in the 1960s inhibited the creation of a common foreign policy, because the smaller countries were unwilling to cede any more power to their larger partners.

De Gaulle's leadership, in particular, had a significant impact on the community. He twice vetoed (to the astonishment of his partners) British applications for membership, mainly because he saw Great Britain as being allied more closely with the United States than with Europe, and he caused the eventual resignation of Hallstein after they clashed on the issue of Community rights versus individual state rights. When de Gaulle realized that on certain issues he might be outvoted, he boycotted (through the "empty chair" policy) several EC meetings until the 1966 Luxembourg compromise, which allowed members veto power on certain issues. Hallstein saw that as a considerable weakening of the commission's power and resigned.

Georges Pompidou, who succeeded de Gaulle in 1969, and the new West German Chancellor Willy Brandt followed a less nationalist line in their EC dealings so that the United Kingdom, Denmark and Ireland were added to the original six partners in 1973—the Community population reached 255 million.

Complications due to the enlargement of the Community and

the recession following the 1973 Yom Kippur war (which precipitated the quadrupling of petroleum prices) caused considerable
discomfort to the Community. Member states faced serious unem-
ployment, inflation and deficit problems, and the Community's
inability to devise a common energy policy exacerbated the situation.

Despite its significant economic problems, the EC decided at its
Paris summit to continue its supranational economic programs by
establishing the European Regional Development Fund, which
aimed at bridging the gap between the Community's more- and
less-developed members. In the same meeting it was also decided
to establish the European Council (explained later in this chapter)
and to allow for direct popular election of the members of the European Parliament as a necessary outgrowth of the Community's
commitment to the principles of pluralistic democracy.

The appointment of Roy Jenkins, a prominent British Labor
Party Member of the Parliament and an articulate Europhile, gave
new momentum to the EC and enhanced the Community's international role by concluding a new General Agreement on Tariffs
and Trade (GATT) and signing agreements with many developing
nations. Jenkins also was responsible for creating the European
Monetary System (EMS), a credit, exchange and intervention vehicle through which the EC could minimize currency fluctuation
and facilitate fiscal cooperation among member states. Part of EMS
was the European Currency Unit (ECU), a compilation of portions
of each of the EC member currency units.

The EC was facing new problems as Greece was admitted in
1981: The new British Prime Minister, Margaret Thatcher, complained bitterly about the alleged disproportionally high U.K. contribution to the EC and the lack of accountability of EC institutions to the member states; the United States and Japan were
leaving Europe behind technologically; the CAP financing was
draining the Community's resources faster than anticipated; and
no member was willing to expedite decision-making by returning
to a majority-vote system as envisioned in the Treaty of Rome.
Most of these issues began to be addressed during the French presidency under Francois Mitterand in 1984, and a new blueprint of
the Community's operation emerged through the Single European
Act of 1987.

The Community's protectionist agricultural policies came to

haunt it again after the admission of Spain and Portugal, as world prices fell and the dollar declined sharply in 1986–87. New Commission President Jacques Delors then proposed a new funding system for the Community that relied not on value-added tax (VAT) but on a portion of the country's gross national product (GNP). The main part of the new formula called for an increase in a national contribution from 1.4 percent of VAT to 1.2 percent of GNP (equivalent to 1.9–2.0 percent of VAT).

The momentum toward more unified monetary, social and foreign policies received a new impetus under the ambitious Eurocrat Delors. The 1988 Hanover summit reappointed him with instructions to prepare a plan for European Monetary Union (EMU), and the 1990 Dublin summit proposed an expansion of the Single European Act, a task that was assigned to the Intergovernmental Conference on Political Union. Those two plans culminated in the Treaty on European Union negotiated in December 1991 in Maastricht, The Netherlands, and signed there two months later.

The Treaty of Maastricht is based on three "pillars." Pillar 1 details the plan for Economic and Monetary Union and supplements the Community's powers with regard to education, training, research, technology and the environment. Pillar 2 defines the organizational structure and procedures of a Common Foreign and Security Policy. Pillar 3 addresses social issues such as immigration, employment, judicial and police cooperation, combating drug addiction and fraud, etc. The treaty also took bold steps toward establishing European citizenship and enhancing the powers of the European Parliament by allowing it co-decision and veto powers in certain areas.

As much as the Treaty of Maastricht accomplished for the European Union, it did not solve the Union's major organizational problem, the tug-of-war between the E.U. central authority and its individual member governments. This continuous battle has resulted in an extremely complex governing mechanism, which generally focuses on accommodating the ever-changing needs of "subsidiarity," that is, deciding which issues should be placed under the aegis of national governments and which under the central authority of the Union. The answer, in the best E.U. tradition, seems to be couched in terms, rules and processes that satisfy all the partners any time each wishes but almost never everyone at the same time!

Despite this perpetually "unstable equilibrium," as former EEC Commission President Roy Jenkins (1977–81) used to call it,[10] and all the historical, cultural and philosophical differences on governing among its members, the European Union has been a large and largely positive force in the life of Europeans. Its influence, in fact, has reached well beyond the original economic aspects of the Union (mainly the free movement of goods, capital, services and people among member states) and today is beginning to address many social, political and even cultural dimensions of the lives of Europeans. In one respect, therefore, the E.U. founding fathers should be resting well: What they envisioned emerging out of the ashes, chaos and despair of World War II, based more on hope and less on experience, has made an impressive start. For the first time in their history, European nations have in place the mechanism to resolve major differences among themselves through peaceful means.

What started as a proactive search for a defensive political scheme that would ensure that war never returned to Europe, however, has evolved into a supranational organization with executive, legislative and judicial branches and a menu of jurisdictions that range from monetary to television programming policies. By focusing on their commonalties rather than on their differences, post–World War Europeans discovered, albeit often reluctantly, that a central collective, supranational authority might indeed be the most efficient way to identify common concerns, implement solutions and consolidate product and services standards that affect the lives of 350 million people. And despite the notorious political paralyses that grip the Union every time there is an international crisis, more ambitious Union proponents still dare to envision an eventual single monetary unit and a common foreign policy.

The Union's Members

Perhaps the main reason behind the European Union's organizational complexity and apparent slow decision-making processes, in addition to the magnitude of its responsibility, is the diversity— in history, traditions, methods, values and goals—of the member states that safeguard this supranational apparatus and even staff it.

The 12 signatories of the Treaty of Maastricht were joined on

January 1, 1995, by Austria, Finland and Sweden. Norway, which had also negotiated its entry at that time, did not join, following a country-wide referendum that disapproved of the government's intentions. It was the second time since 1972 that Norway had planned to join but its voters rejected the plan.

Following is a brief look at the chief member-state characteristics that are salient to this study:

Austria (admitted in 1995)

One of the European Union's newest members, Austria is a presidential parliamentary democracy of approximately 8 million people, the vast majorities of whom are Germanic (99 percent) and Roman Catholic (89 percent). Most Austrians (56 percent) work in the service sector, while 35 percent work in industry (steel, machinery, autos, glassware, paper and electrical and optical equipment) and commerce and 8 percent in agriculture (grains and potatoes, cattle and pigs) and forestry. Austria's main trading partner is the European Union (approximately 70 percent of its imports and 68 percent of its exports).

Austrians have the highest per capita Gross Domestic Products (GDP) in the European Union, approximately $21,000 per year, and a 99 percent literacy rate. There is one television set per 2.8 persons, one radio set per 1.6 persons, one telephone per 1.8 persons and 445 newspaper copies per 1,000 persons.

Belgium (admitted in 1958)

Belgium, one of the six founding partners, is a parliamentary democracy with a constitutional monarch. It is one of the most densely inhabited countries of Europe and has a population of a little more than 10 million. Although three-quarters of Belgians are Roman Catholic, the ethnic division between the Flemish population (55 percent) and the French Walloon population (33 percent) has been a source of severe linguistic, cultural, economic and political strife over the years.

Two-thirds of Belgians (the highest proportion in the Union) are employed in industry (steel, glassware, textiles, chemicals), commerce (50 percent of its production is sold abroad), service and transportation, and 2 percent are employed in agriculture. The literacy rate is 98 percent, and the approximate per capita GDP is $17,300 per year. Three-quarters of Belgium's export and import deals are with E.U. states. There is one television set per 4.2 persons, one radio set per 2.2 persons, one telephone per 1.9 persons and 213 newspaper copies per 1,000 persons.

Denmark (admitted in 1973)

Denmark is a constitutional monarchy with a homogeneous population of a little more than 5 million, almost all of whom are ethnic Scandinavians and Evangelical Lutherans. Half of the Danes work for industry (machinery, electronics, textiles, furniture), commerce and the service sector. Fishing and agriculture (mainly dairy products) employ 6 percent of the people. A little more than half of its import and export deals are with E.U. nations.

Danes have a 99 percent literacy rate and an approximate per capita GDP of $18,000 per year. Their media-related statistics show one television set per 2.7 persons, one radio set per 2.4 persons, one telephone per 1.2 persons and 361 newspaper copies per 1,000 persons.

Finland (admitted in 1995)

Another late entrant (1995), Finland is a constitutional republic of approximately 5 million inhabitants, the vast majority of whom are Finns (94 percent) and Lutherans (97 percent). The largest employment sector (54 percent) is in industry (machinery, shipbuilding, textiles) commerce and finance, while agriculture (grains, potatoes, dairy products, forestry) and fishing employ 9 percent of the population. Forty percent of its exports are related to forestry and approximately half its imports and exports are traded within the European Union.

Finns have a 99 percent literacy rate and a standard of living that falls within the E.U. middle class, with an approximate per capita GDP of $16,000 per year. Their media statistics show that there is one television set per 2.7 persons, one radio set per person, one telephone per 2.1 persons and 521 newspaper copies per 1,000 persons (one of the Union's highest newspaper consumption rates).

France (admitted in 1958)

A member of the six founding partners, France is a republic with a population of 57 million people, most of whom are Roman Catholic (90 percent) but represent a variety of ethnic groups of

European and Mediterranean origin. Almost half of its people work in industry (steel, chemicals, electronics, textiles, wine), and 9 percent work in agriculture (grains, fruits, vegetables) and fishing. France is the European Union's largest food producer and exporter and half of its imports and exports are traded within the Union.

The French have a 99 percent literacy rate and an approximate per capita GDP of $19,000 per year. There is one television set per 2.6 persons, one radio set per 1.1 persons, a telephone set per 1.7 persons and 176 newspaper copies per 1,000 persons.

Germany (admitted in 1958)

Germany, one of the original E.U. members, is a federal republic with a population of just over 81 million (the Union's largest), 93 percent of whom are German; 44 percent are Protestant and 37 percent Roman Catholic. Forty percent of its residents work in industry (vehicles, machinery, electronics) and commerce, 54 percent in services and 5 percent in agriculture (grains, potatoes, livestock) and fishing.

Germany's per capita GDP suffered because of reunification and today stands at approximately $15,000 per year. Its literacy rate is 99 percent. Media statistics show that there is one television set per 2.6 persons, one radio set per 2.3 persons, one telephone per 1.5 persons and 401 newspaper copies per 1,000 persons. More than half of its import/export trade is with other E.U. members.

Greece (admitted in 1981)

Greece is a parliamentary presidential republic of approximately 10 million, most of whom (98.5 percent) are Greek and members of the Greek Orthodox Church (97 percent). Greece has the highest agricultural employment rate in the European Union (28 percent). Its main crops are cotton, grains, corn, wine, tobacco, olives, raisins, fruits and rice. Industry (textiles, chemicals, cement, food processing) occupies 29 percent of Greeks. Forty-two percent of them work in the service sector.

Greece's literacy rate is 93 percent, and its approximate per capita GDP is $8,000 per year, one of the European Union's lowest. There is one television set per 4.5 persons, one radio set per 2.4 persons, one telephone per 2.2 persons and 88 newspaper copies per 1,000 persons. A little less than half of its import/export trade is with other E.U. members.

Ireland (admitted in 1975)

Ireland is a parliamentary republic and has a population of 3.5 million, most of whom are Celtic and Roman Catholic (95 percent). Most of its citizens (51 percent) are employed in the service sector, but 29 percent are employed in industry (textiles, brewing, machinery, food processing) and 15 percent in agriculture (potatoes, sugar beets, fruits, grain, livestock and fishing). Forty percent of its exports and 25 percent of its imports are traded with other E.U. members.

Ireland's literacy rate is 99 percent, and its approximate per capita GDP is $11,000 per year. There is one television set per 3.8 persons, one radio set per 1.7 persons, one telephone per 3.8 persons and 179 newspaper copies per 1,000 persons.

Italy (admitted in 1958)

One of the six founding partners, Italy is a presidential republic of 58 million people, most of whom (98 percent) are ethnic Italians and almost all of whom are Roman Catholic. The services and government sectors are Italy's largest employers (58 percent), while industry (autos, machinery, textiles, shoes, steel) and commerce employ 22 percent and agriculture (grapes, wine, olives, fruits, vegetables, livestock) 10 percent. Almost two-thirds of its importing or exporting is with E.U. partners.

Italy's literacy rate is 98 percent, and its approximate per capita GDP is $17,000 per year. There is one television set per 3.8 persons, one radio set per 3.4 persons, one telephone per 1.8 persons and 142 newspaper copies per 1,000 persons.

Luxembourg (admitted in 1958)

The Grand Duchy of Luxembourg is a constitutional monarchy of 400,000 people, most of whom come from French or German ethnic backgrounds and are Roman Catholic (97 percent). Since there is very little land to cultivate, most of the citizens work in industry (tires, tobacco, steel, beer, metal products), commerce (42 percent) and in the service sector. Its central location and traditionally passive demeanor have earned it a prominent spot in the various structures of the European Union, and much of its economy depends on it.

Luxembourg has a 100 percent literacy rate and an approximate per capita GDP of $20,000 per year. There is one television set per

4 persons, one radio set per 1.6 persons, one telephone set per 2.3 persons and 340 newspaper copies per 1,000 persons.

The Netherlands (admitted in 1958)

One of the founding members of the European Union, The Netherlands is a parliamentary democracy under a constitutional monarchy with 15 million people, most of whom (97 percent) are Dutch; 40 percent are Roman Catholic and 19.3 percent Dutch Reformed. One-third of its population is employed in industry (machinery, metals, chemicals, oil, electronics), 44 percent is employed in the service sector and 1 percent in agriculture (grains, potatoes, flowers, fruits, sugar beets, livestock) and fishing. Almost two-thirds of its export/import trade is with other E.U. partners.

Its literacy rate is 99 percent, and the approximate per capita GDP of the Dutch is $17,000 per year. There is one television set per 3.2 persons, one radio set per 1.2 persons, one telephone set per 1.5 persons and 312 newspaper copies per 1,000 persons.

Portugal (admitted in 1986)

Portugal is a parliamentary democracy of almost 11 million people, most of whom are homogeneous ethnic Portuguese with the exception of a small African minority. Ninety-seven percent are Roman Catholics. Its largest employer is the service sector (46 percent), with industry (textiles, shoes, cork, chemicals, paper) and commerce second (34 percent) and agriculture (grapes, wine, olives, grains, potatoes, forestry and livestock) and fishing third (19 percent). One-third of its imports and almost half of its exports are traded with other E.U. partners.

Portugal's literacy rate is 83 percent, and its per capita GDP is approximately $8,500 per year. There is one television set per 5.8 persons (the highest rate in the Union), one radio set per 4.2 persons, one telephone set per 3.6 persons and 50 newspaper copies per 1,000 (European Union's lowest).

Spain (admitted in 1986)

A constitutional monarchy, Spain has a population of almost 40 million, 90 percent of whom are Roman Catholic, but most of whom come from a variety of related ethnic groups—Spanish (Andalusian, Asturian, Castillian, Valencian), 73 percent; Catalan, 16 percent; Galician, 8 percent; and Basque, 2 percent. Most

Spaniards work in the service sector (52 percent), 24 percent work in industry (machinery, textiles, shoes) and commerce and 19 percent in agriculture (grains, olives, grapes, fruits, vegetables, livestock) and fishing. Fifty-seven percent of Spain's imports and 70 percent of its exports are within the E.U. countries.

Spain has a literacy rate of 97 percent, and its approximate per capita GDP is $12,500 per year. There is one television set per 2.6 persons, one radio set per 3.4 persons, one telephone set per 2.5 persons and 76 newspaper copies per 1,000 persons.

Sweden (admitted in 1995)

One of the newest members of the European Union, Sweden is a constitutional monarchy with a population of almost 9 million people, most of whom (91 percent) are ethnic Swedes, while the rest are Lapps and Finns. Ninety-five percent of Swedes are Lutheran. More than one-third of them work for the country's social services apparatus, while about one-quarter of them work in industry (autos, instruments, shipbuilding, paper) and 5 percent in agriculture (grains, potatoes, livestock) and fishing. A little over half of their import/export trade is with E.U. members.

Sweden's literacy rate is 99 percent, and its approximate per capita GDP is $17,500 per year. There is one television set per 2.4 persons, one radio set per 1.2 persons, one telephone set per 1.1 persons and 572 newspaper copies per 1,000 persons, the European Union's highest.

The United Kingdom (admitted in 1973)

The United Kingdom of Great Britain and Northern Ireland is a constitutional monarchy with a population of 58 million people who are English (81.5 percent), Scottish (9.6 percent), Irish (2.4 percent) and Welsh (1.9 percent). The vast majority belongs to the Church of England and the Roman Catholic Church. The service sector is the largest employer (60 percent), while industry (autos, shipbuilding, textiles, electronics, aircraft, machinery, distilling) employs 26 percent and agriculture (sugar beets, grains, fruits, vegetables, livestock) and fishing employs 2 percent. Approximately half of its import/export trade is with other E.U. nations.

The United Kingdom's literacy rate is 99 percent, and its approximate per capita GDP is $16,000 per year. There is one television set per 3 persons, one radio per person, one telephone set per 1.9 persons and 388 newspaper copies per 1,000 persons.

The E.U. Organization and Procedures

Institutions

The Commission
The most visible and powerful symbol of the European Union is its commission—the central executive administrator of the Union. It is an organization committed to the collective good and, in fact, it personifies the European ideals of the founding fathers as well as the Union's organic and philosophical strengths and weaknesses.

The commission's role, as outlined in Article 155 of the Treaty of Rome, is to initiate legislation, to supervise the correct implementation of E.U. decisions and to implement existing regulations. Furthermore, the commission safeguards the Union's various treaties and administers Union funds (i.e., Regional Fund, Social Fund, etc.). The commission also has several autonomous powers on issues affecting the coal and steel industry, competition policy and the CAP, among others.

Currently the commission has 20 members (two each from France, Germany, Italy, Spain and the United Kingdom and one from each of the rest), who are appointed for a renewable five-year term by the Council of Ministers (see appropriate section) on the recommendation of their national governments. The president of the commission is appointed upon agreement of the member governments for a five-year term. Up to two commissioners may be appointed as vice presidents. Under the Maastricht Treaty, all of these appointments must be approved by the European Parliament (see appropriate section). Each commissioner is in charge of one or more of the commission's jurisdictions and is assisted by a cabinet of aides.

The commission's work is divided among 23 directorates-general (DG):

External Relations
Economic and Financial Affairs
Industry
Competition
Employment, Industrial Relations and Social Affairs
Agriculture
Transport
Development
Personnel and Administration

Information, Communication, Culture and Audiovisual
Environment, Nuclear Safety and Civil Protection
Science, Research and Development
Telecommunication, Information Market and Exploitation of
    Research
Fisheries
Internal Market and Financial Services
Regional Policies and Cohesion
Energy
Credits and Investments
Budgets
Financial Control
Customs Union and Indirect Taxation
Education, Training and Youth
Enterprise Policy, Distributive Trades, Tourism and
    Cooperatives
Consumer Policy

In addition to the above workload divided among jurisdictions, the commission has its own logistical services, such as secretarial, legal, statistical, translation, etc. The commission today employs approximately 13,000 persons, most of whom are based in the commission's headquarters in Brussels, but some of whom work in the commission's offices in other cities and in Luxembourg. Although all member country languages are considered official Union languages, most of the commission's daily deliberations are handled in English or French.

The Council of Ministers

The most powerful of the Union's institutions is arguably the Council of Ministers. It is the Union's main legislative body and acts mainly upon the recommendations of the commission. Its membership changes according to the subject matter, but it consists always of member-country ministers whose portfolio is on the council's agenda. Most frequent participants are the foreign ministers, who also serve as meeting coordinators for their colleagues from other ministries. The foreign ministers also comprise the General Affairs Council and do the groundwork for the semi-annual meeting of the heads of state in the European Council (see appropriate section).

Each government holds a rotating six-month presidency of the council through its foreign minister who sets the council's priorities and agenda for the next six months. In addition to the council's 2,000-member secretariat, the ministers are assisted by their own country's permanent ambassador/delegates to the Union.

The council requires unanimity to alter a commission's legislative proposal and to make a decision on all serious topics (e.g., taxation). The majority of the issues voted on by the council are decided by a "qualified majority" vote, which requires 62 of the current 87 available votes. France, Germany, Italy and the United Kingdom have ten votes each; Spain has eight; Belgium, Greece, The Netherlands and Portugal have five; Sweden and Austria have four; Denmark, Finland and Ireland have three; and Luxembourg has two. A majority vote is sufficient in such areas as research and technology, education, single-market regulation, regional policy, workplace protection, etc.

The European Council

The European Council (not to be confused with the Council of Europe, which is not related to the European Union; see Ch. 2) consists of the heads of state of the Union's members and the commission president. It meets twice annually at the end of each member's tenure as head of the Council of Ministers and is hosted by the outgoing country's officials. Although the council was given legal validity by the Single European Act, it has no defined role other than to afford the opportunity to its members to informally gather and exchange ideas on issues before the Union. Each head of state is assisted only by his or her foreign minister, and the commission president is accompanied only by one vice president.

The European Parliament

What started as a purely advisory body in the ECSC, the European Parliament was given substantial powers through the Maastricht Treaty, and it has become an important player in the Union's life, mainly by providing a political forum for initiatives that may lead to Union policy.

More specifically, the parliament has supervisory powers over the commission and the council (it theoretically has the power to dismiss the commission—something it has never done), and, through the assent procedure, it also has the power to veto new applicants or third-party association agreements and to amend or reject the Union's proposed budget. Furthermore, the parliament has veto power on non-compulsory budgetary items (the council governs on compulsory expenditure issues).

In legislative matters, the parliament through the cooperation procedure has the power to amend proposed laws in many areas and, through the co-decision procedure, it has the power to veto legislation in such areas as the environment, research and development, culture, education, vocational training, etc.

The parliament is organized by political party and not by country. For example, the 1995 membership breakdown of the 626 Members of the European Parliament (MEPs) was as follows:

Socialist Parties, 221 members
Christian Democratic Parties, 173
Liberal and Democratic Reformist Parties, 52
United Left-Nordic Green Parties, 31
Forza Europa, 29
Green Group, 25
Radical Alliance, 19
Europe of Nations, 19
Not attached, 31

The above are divided among member states as follows: Germany has 99 members; France, Italy and the U.K., 87 each; Spain, 64; The Netherlands, 31; Belgium, Greece and Portugal, 25 each; Sweden, 22; Austria, 21; Denmark and Finland, 16 each; Ireland, 15; and Luxembourg, 6.

The work of the parliament is done through its 19 standing committees, which meet regularly in Brussels, and its plenary meetings, which are held at the Palais de l'Europe in Strasbourg.

The Court of Justice

Located in Luxembourg, the Court of Justice is the Union's "Supreme Court," and its task is to ensure that the European treaties are interpreted and implemented according to Union law. The Court's independence is guaranteed, and its decisions are final and binding. The Court accepts cases brought on by another Union institution, a member state, a recognized legal entity or an individual. Cases range from disputes between member states and between member states and the Union, to disputes between individuals and cases that originate in national courts.

The Court consists of one judge from each Union member plus a president. A Court of First Instance (which has a similar composition) was established in 1989 in order to hear mainly cases on steel and coal issues and appeals of commission decisions on competition cases. Its decisions are appealable to the Court of Justice.

The Economic and Social Committee

This is a Brussels-based advisory group that consists of employers and employees, farmers, consumers and others with interest in Union legislation. It assists in the work of the council and the commission. It covers such issues as employment, consumer affairs, energy, environment, etc.

The Committee of the Regions

The statutory responsibility of this committee is to advise the commission and the council on matters concerning culture, economic and social cohesion, public health, etc. Its members are members of regional and local bodies from each member state. The committee deliberates in Brussels.

The Court of Auditors

This Luxembourg-based body is charged with supervising the Union's expenditures by assessing their legality and propriety. It is composed of one person from each member state (appointed by the council in consultation with the parliament) who is appointed to a renewable six-year term.

The European Union's Legal Instruments

The Union's laws generally emanate from its constitutional treaties, its various subsequent conventions and its third-party agreements. Wherever these might conflict, Union law supersedes national law.

The commission and the Council of Ministers exercise their law-making responsibilities in the following five ways:

Regulations are mandatory legal instruments in their entirety and throughout the Union.

Directives set up the mandatory goals that are to be achieved but leave up to the individual member state how to best find the legislative means through which to achieve the intended results.

Decisions have the same power as regulations but narrower applicability; they are fully binding, however, on those to whom they are addressed (be they states, industries, individuals, etc.).

Recommendations and **opinions** are not binding, but they do reflect the Union's prevailing sentiments and are to serve as guidelines for future national laws.

Finally, the **case law**, which is handed down by the Court of Justice, is another way through which national legislation is influenced as the Union continues, slowly but deliberately, on its road to harmonizing the various national laws.

The European Union and the Mass Media

As the Union evolved and various private, national and multinational interests began to massage and exploit its regulatory machinery for their own benefit, the European Union found its regulatory embrace extending to areas of cultural activity that its founding fathers thought should remain the sole purview of national authorities. It seemed as though the complexities of modern economic life and the advancements in technology had made that intrusion unavoidable. It did not take long for the ubiquitous arm of Union regulation to bring many aspects of communication and the mass media under the its authority.

But the centerpiece of the Union's work has always been to create an "economic community" in order to promote "a harmonious development of economic activities, a continuous and balanced expansion, an increase in stability, an accelerated raising of the standard of living and closer relations" among its members.[11] It should not be surprising, therefore, that the mass media, whether print, electronic, cyberspace or celluloid, entered the Union's jurisdiction mainly through their *commercial* dimensions rather than as instruments of *expression*.

Furthermore, although the three major Union institutions (the commission, the council and the parliament) have jointly affirmed their commitment to fundamental human rights, and the last two major Union treaties (the 1985 Single European Act and the 1992 Treaty on European Union) fully endorsed the European Convention on Human Rights (see Ch. 2), nowhere in the Union's treaties or legislation is there an affirmative conferral of a free expression right, a free media prerequisite, to the Union's citizens.

In spite of that, as the following chapters will demonstrate, the Union's decision-making institutions have amassed a respectable record of protection of expression and its various media of communication. More specifically, the media are mentioned in the Union's regulations concerning the free movement of goods, services, persons and establishment (see Chs. 6 and 8). These references address media circulation, ownership, free flow of information and consumer access issues.

Inter-media competition problems are discussed in the competition rules part of the treaty that also addresses monopoly and state licensing issues (see Ch. 8).

Access to classified information of the Union's institutions is prescribed in the Euratom Treaty and the 1990 Directive on Freedom of Information on the Environment (see Ch. 5). The commission also produced a decision in 1993 that dealt with the concept of "transparency" and invited the parliament and the council to come up with a harmonious document that addressed the public demand for more accessibility of the Union.

In another media-related piece of legislation, the Union does create the right of reply in its 1989 Council Directive on television broadcasting activities, the Transfrontier Television Directive (see Chs. 3 and 6).

Finally, the Union has extensive legislation setting parameters on advertising—defining products that cannot be advertised in the media and disallowing advertising that is misleading, dehumanizing, racist or hazardous to human health or the environment (see Ch. 7).

These are the only media-related references in the Union's supranational legal arsenal by which member states must abide. Other regulations that normally affect the media, such as defamation, privacy, obscenity, etc. (see Chs. 3 and 4), clearly fall outside Union jurisdiction, and, therefore, there has not been any centralized official effort to harmonize the national laws that govern them.

NOTES

1. Daniel Pedersen, "A 'Grenade' Aimed at Hollywood," *Newsweek,* October 16, 1989, p. 58.

2. "Rationing 'Dallas' in Europe," editorial, *The New York Times,* October 24, 1989, A 26.

3. "Cultural Protectionism," editorial, *The Boston Globe,* October 24, A 14.

4. Steven Greenhouse, "Europe Reaches TV Compromise; U.S. Officials Fear Protectionism," *The New York Times,* October 4, 1989, A. 1.

5. Daniel Pedersen, "A 'Grenade' Aimed at Hollywood," op. cit.

6. Steven Greenhouse, "The Television Europeans Love, and Love to Hate," *The New York Times,* August 13, 1989, pp. 4, 24.

7. "Europeans Step Up Co-Productions Among Themselves," *Broadcasting,* February 19, 1990, pp. 31.

8. Steven Greenhouse, "The Television Europeans Love, and Love to Hate," *The New York Times,* op. cit.

9. P.S.R.F. Mathijsen, *A Guide to European Community Law* (London, U.K.: Sweet and Maxwell, 1990), pp. 5-6.

10. Dick Leonard, *Pocket Guide to the European Community* (Oxford, U.K.: Basil Blackwell Ltd. and The Economist Publications Ltd., 1988), p. xi.

11. Commission of the European Communities, *Treaty Establishing the European Community,* Article 2 (Luxembourg: Office of Official Publications of the European Communities, 1992), pp. 11-12.

Philosophical and Legal Foundations

Most of the media regulation in the European Union is inspired and guided by the principles expressed in the human rights declarations of covenants of major international assemblies of nations. These declarations explicitly or implicitly view the media of mass communication as natural instruments and extensions of human behavior and expression and therefore make them eligible for both protection and limitation internationally and nationally.

Transnational Freedom of Expression Covenants

The United Nations Provisions

Foremost among the transnational freedom of expression covenants is the Universal Declaration of Human Rights (UDHR) adopted by the United Nations General Assembly, through Resolution 217 A (III), on December 10, 1948. The relevant passages say:

Article 19
Everyone shall have the right to freedom of opinion and expression; this right includes freedom to hold opinions without interference and to seek, receive and impart information and ideas through any media and regardless of frontiers.

Article 20
1. Everyone has the right to freedom of peaceful assembly and association.
2. No one may be compelled to belong to an association.

27

Article 29

1. Everyone has duties to the community in which alone the free and full development of his personality is possible.

2. In the exercise of his rights and freedoms, everyone shall be subject only to such limitations as are determined by law solely for the purpose of securing due recognition and respect for the rights and freedoms of others and of meeting the just requirements of morality, public order and the general welfare in a democratic society.

After the emergence of the Communist bloc and the Third World nations as a power within the international community, Article 19 (the world came to know this as a global "guarantee" of free expression) was revisited and a more detailed and restrictive version appeared as the International Covenant on Civil and Political Rights (ICCPR), which was approved by the United Nations General Assembly, through Resolution 2200 A (XXI), on December 16, 1966. It went into effect on March 23, 1976. The pertinent passages say:

Article 14

1. All persons shall be equal before the courts and tribunals. In the determination of any criminal charge against him, or of his rights and obligations in a suit of law, everyone shall be entitled to a fair and public hearing by a competent, independent and impartial tribunal established by law. The Press and the public may be excluded from all or part of a trial for reasons of morals, public order *(ordre public)* or national security in a democratic society, or when the interest of the private lives of the Parties so requires, or to the extent strictly necessary in the opinion of the court in special circumstances where publicity would prejudice the interests of justice; but any judgment rendered in a criminal case or in a suit at law shall be made public except where the interest of juvenile persons otherwise requires or the proceedings concern matrimonial disputes or the guardianship of children.

Article 17

1. No one shall be subjected to arbitrary and unlawful interference with his privacy, family, home or correspondence, nor to unlawful attacks on his honour and reputation.

Article 19

1. Everyone shall have the right to hold opinions without interference.

2. Everyone shall have the right to freedom of expression; this right shall in-

clude freedom to seek, receive and impart information and ideas of all kinds, regardless of frontiers, either orally, in writing or in print, in the form of art, or through any other media of his choice.

3. The exercise of the rights provided for in paragraph 2 of this article carries with it special duties and responsibilities. It may therefore be subject to certain restrictions, but these shall only be such as are provided by law and are necessary:

a. For respect of the rights or reputations of others;

b. For the protection of national security or of public order *(ordre public)*, or of public health or morals.

Article 20

1. Any propaganda for war shall be prohibited by law.

2. Any advocacy of national, racial or religious hatred that constitutes incitement to discrimination, hostility or violence shall be prohibited by law.

The new additions, especially those contained in Article 19.3, concerning limitations on grounds of national security or public order, and in Article 20, concerning the prohibition of propaganda and the advocacy of hateful thoughts or violence, appeared to Western journalists as thinly veiled threats to freedom of speech and the press; therefore, there was great opposition to the ICCPR. In the United States, in particular, President Carter submitted the covenant to the U.S. Senate for ratification in 1978, but it was tabled until the Bush administration resurrected it and passed it through the Senate in 1992 in spite of protestations by the American Society of Newspaper Editors, Radio and Television News Directors Association and the World Press Freedom Committee. The Bush administration argued that passage would enable the United States to sit on the U.N. Human Rights Committee and better assess press freedom challenges. Some of the administration's important supporters were Amnesty International, Article 19's International Centre Against Censorship and the American Bar Association.[1]

Finally, the United Nations produced a third declaration, the 1965 International Convention on the Elimination of All Forms of Racial Discrimination,[2] which in effect (Art. 4) condemned "all propaganda and all organizations which are based on theories of superiority of one race or group" and prohibited public institutions from promoting or inciting "racial discrimination."[3]

Regional Covenants

In addition to the preceding global covenants, there have been regional or continent-specific declarations that emanate from the same spirit and provide similar protections. The three major declarations have been sponsored by the Council of Europe, the Organization of American States and the Organization of African Unity.

The **Council of Europe,** which on cultural and human rights issues is the equivalent of what the European Union is on economic issues, approved the European Convention of Human Rights and Fundamental Freedoms (ECHRFF) on November 4, 1950, and made it effective on September 3, 1953. The convention was originally accepted by eight members, but today there are 26 signatories and an additional eight (all former members of the Communist bloc) are in various stages of ratification. All of the European Union members have ratified the convention.

ECHRFF's Article 10 is essentially similar to UDHR's Article 19, but there are differences, especially in Section 2.

Article 10

1. Everyone has the right to freedom of expression. This right shall include freedom to hold opinions and to receive and impart information and ideas without interference by public authority and regardless of frontiers. This article shall not prevent States from requiring the licensing of broadcasting, television or cinema enterprises.

2. The exercise of these freedoms, since it carries with it duties and responsibilities, may be subject to such formalities, conditions, restrictions or penalties as are prescribed by law and are necessary in a democratic society, in the interests of national security, territorial integrity or public safety, for the prevention of disorder or crime, for the protection of health or morals, for the protection of the reputation or rights of others, for preventing the disclosure of information received in confidence, or maintaining the authority and impartiality of the judiciary.

The importance of the preservation of order within the member nations, however, seems to be carried to an extreme in Article 16, which contains some apparent contradictions to Article 10. Article 16 says that "nothing" in articles 10 (above), 11 (the article guaranteeing the right to "freedom of peaceful assembly," association, unionization, etc.) and 14 (the article guaranteeing the right to enjoy these "rights and freedoms" "without discrimination" based on gender, race, national origin, ideology, language, religion, property, etc.) "shall be regarded as preventing the High Contracting Parties from imposing restrictions on the political activity of aliens." In a continent that is facing some fundamental challenges on issues related to "aliens," Article 16 takes on a special tint of irony in the context of "human rights."

Regardless of these limitations, ECHRFF and Article 10 seem to have served Europeans well, mainly because of the dual enforcement procedure that employs the services of the European Commission of Human Rights and eventually the European Court of Human Rights. Both of these bodies consist of one representative from each member of the council and are based in Strasbourg. The commission represents the first hearing level after the national judicial system has been exhausted, and if a "friendly settlement" is not reached, the case is referred to the Court.

It should be noted that although the Council of Europe has been eclipsed recently by the notoriety and clout of the European Union and its institutions, it remains the Continent's voice of conscience and carries immense moral authority on matters of its jurisdiction, primarily the monitoring and protection of human rights in member states and even beyond them. The council and its Court of Human Rights are especially important for the press because much of the press-related litigation (defamation, national security, obscenity, etc.) comes through this system and not through the E.U. institutions, which are primarily responsible for adjudicating issues that have commercial and financial implications.

The **Organization of American States** adopted the American Convention on Human Rights (ACHR) on November 22, 1969; it went into effect on July 18, 1978. Article 13 of the ACHR is, in word, spirit, freedoms and limitations, very similar to the ICCPR's Article 19 above. The main exceptions are: Section 2 outlaws "prior censorship" in favor of "subsequent imposition of liability"; Section 4 states that "public entertainment" may be subject to "prior censorship" in order to provide "for the moral protection of childhood and adolescence"; and Article 13.3 bans the "abuse of government or private controls over newsprint, radio broadcasting frequencies, or equipment used in the dissemination of information, or by any other means tending to impede the communication and circulation of ideas and opinions."

The ACHR, however, departs from the other covenants when,

in Article 14, it addresses the issue of the "Right of Reply." "Anyone injured by inaccurate or offensive statements or ideas ... by a legally regulated medium of communication," the article says, "has the right to reply or to make a correction using the same communications outlet. ..." In other sections, the article does not preclude the imposition of "other legal liabilities," and it requests, for "the effective protection of honor and reputation," that each medium "have a person responsible who is not protected by immunities or special privileges."

The **African Charter on Human and People's Rights** (ACHPR) was approved by OAS on June 27, 1981, and went into effect on October 1, 1986. Article 9 guarantees "every individual" the right to "receive information" and to "express and disseminate his opinions within the law." The document also guarantees the rights to free association (Art. 10) and lawful assembly (Art. 11), charges member nations with the "duty to promote and ensure through teaching, education and publication, the respect of the rights and freedoms contained in this Charter" (Art. 25), recognizes that the individual has "duties toward his family, and society, the State and other legally recognized communities and the international community" (Art. 27), and safeguards the entitlement and enjoyment of these rights "without distinction of any kind such as race, ethnic group, colour, sex, language, religion, political or any other opinion, national and social origin, fortune, birth or other status" (Art. 2).

Other related documents expressing similar sentiments and guaranteeing similar rights and responsibilities include the **American Declaration of the Rights and Duties of Man** (Art. 4), approved by the Ninth International Conference of American States on May 2, 1948, as well as three documents drawn under the auspices of the **Conference on Security and Cooperation in Europe** in Vienna (1989) (Art. 24), in Copenhagen (1990) (Art. 9) and in Moscow (1991) (Art. 26).

Human Rights Conventions and the European Union

In at least three instances the European Union, or its predecessors, prominently declared its commitment to human rights and by implication, at least, to freedom of expression and communication. The first was in 1977 when the European parliament, the council and the commission jointly declared that because the Community is based on treaties and legislation emanating from "the general principles of law and in particular the fundamental rights, principles and rights on which the constitutional law of the member States is based," they "stress the prime importance they attach to the protection of fundamental rights, as derived in particular from the constitutions of the Member States and the European Convention for the Protection of Human Rights and Fundamental Freedoms."[4]

The second major reference came in the 1987 Single European Act, which stated in its preamble that member states are "determined to work together to promote democracy on the basis of the fundamental human rights recognized in the constitutions and laws of the member States, in the Convention for the Protection of Human Rights and Fundamental Freedoms and the European Social Charter, notably freedom, equality and social justice. ..." The states further recognized that their ability to speak with "one voice and to act with consistency and solidarity" to protect their common interests, required commitment to the principles of "democracy and compliance with the law and with human rights to which they are attached, so that together they may make their own contribution to the preservation of international peace and security in accordance with the undertaking entered into by them within the framework of the United Nations Charter."[5]

The third reference is in the 1992 Treaty of Maastricht on European Union, in which the Union pledged (Title I, Art. F) to respect "the national identities of its Member States, whose systems of government are founded on the principles of democracy" and the "fundamental rights, as guaranteed by the European Convention for the Protection of Human Rights and Fundamental Freedoms signed in Rome on 4 November 1950 and as they result from the constitutional traditions common to the Member States, as general principles of Community law." Furthermore, the Union asserted that one of its objectives (Title I, Art. B) is to "strengthen the protection of the rights and interests of the nationals of its Member States through the introduction of a citizenship of the Union."

One indirect reference might be made to the Union's founding treaty, the Treaty of Rome in 1957, which said that the Union's intent was to ensure economic and social progress of its members, to improve their standard of living and to assist in the development of their "prosperity, in accordance with the principles of the Charter of the United Nations." This can be accomplished, the treaty said, by members combining their "resources to preserve and strengthen peace and liberty. ..." Furthermore, the treaty outlines in some detail how the freedom of movement of goods, services, capital and people will be enforced, but does, in Article 36, allow members to impose restrictions if they are "justified on grounds of public morality, public policy or public security; the protection of health and life of humans, animals or plants; the protection of national treasures possessing artistic, historic or archaeological value. ..."[6]

Finally, it should be pointed out that as these transnational covenants become ratified by individual nations, the serious problem of their domestic applicability immediately arises. Precedent exists to make the determination that Austria, Belgium, France, Germany, Italy, Luxembourg, The Netherlands and Spain grant such documents, upon ratification, the status of domestic legislation. On the other hand, Denmark, Ireland, Sweden and the United Kingdom require the passage of appropriate national law for the covenant to become effective domestically.

Constitutional Provisions of the E.U. Member Nations

European Constitutionalism

It is interesting to note that despite their rich histories and their immense contributions to political thought, most of the European Union member countries do not have long, uninterrupted traditions in constitutional government. Many of them were monarchies or principalities, and it was not until the French Revolution in 1789 that constitutionalism took root in the continent and inspired many of the peoples of Europe to establish democratic, representative and constitutionally bound forms of government.

France has seen five republics since the revolution, each with its own constitution. Germany was a monarchy until the end of World War I when the Weimar Republic established its first constitution in 1919. That constitution was abolished by Hitler in 1934 and was replaced by the Basic Law after World War II in 1949. Spain, Sweden, Denmark, The Netherlands and Belgium are constitutional monarchies. Finland, Greece, Italy, Austria and Portugal are constitutional presidential republics.

The Constitutions

The constitutional documents themselves are as diverse as their countries of origin and, in many respects, they embody the histories, traditions, fears and aspirations of the peoples they are supposed to govern.

One key characteristic of these documents is that they tend to view press freedom as an extension of the citizen's right to free expression. Another is that their wording, which ranges from the laconic to the Byzantine, divides them into constitutions with brief provisions that positively guarantee a free press; those that prescribe or advocate a free press and generally allude to its limitations "as specified by law" elsewhere in the legal system (such as in the penal and civil codes); and those that prescribe a free press but, within the same constitutional passage, enumerate specific limitations to that freedom.

The most common of the unprotected press activities deal with issues of national security, including public order; morality, which covers the protection of youth and obscenity issues; and personal honor or reputation. It is significant to note that some constitutions specifically exclude the electronic or celluloid media, as well as commercial speech, from the protections afforded the print media. One reason for this may be that it is not entertainment but the circulation of political ideas that European lawmakers wanted to protect and those, until recently, were mainly the purview of the print media. The European tradition of partisan media, in other words, might have dictated the creation of a legal climate that would have guaranteed the functioning of these (print) media only. Another reason might be that until recently the vast majority of European electronic media were in the "safe" hands of democratically elected and generally well-accepted governments, thus making regulation either unnecessary or a moot point.

Finally, the apparent absence of constitutional reference to commercial speech should not be interpreted as a sign of the Union's licentious attitude toward advertising, for example. On the contrary, as Chapter 7 will show, regardless of the huge success of commercial radio and television in Europe in the last decade, commercial speech traditionally has been viewed with suspicion, and a plethora of legal restrictions has been put on advertising, both from national governments and the Union itself. The continental power elite continues to show its discomfort with the institution of commercialism, even after the invasion of MTV, CNN and the many private channels that have sprung up in every country of the Union in the last decade.

Austria's constitutional provisions on expression and the press seem to be some of the Union's briefest. Article 13 of the 1867 Basic Law says that "Everyone has the right to express his opinion freely, within the limits established by law, in speech, in writing, in print or in pictorial form. The press may neither be subject to censorship nor to the license system. Administrative postal prohibitions cannot be extended to apply to printed matter in the country." Furthermore, after Austria incorporated the European Convention on Human Rights (see Transnational Freedom of Expression Covenants at beginning of this chapter) into a domestic constitutional document, it lost several cases before the European Court on Human Rights, and it was forced to review the compatibility of its laws with the convention. Therefore, today's constitutional protection of expression and the press are greater than they were under the Austrian constitution alone: the right to receive information is now recognized, opinions are now better protected, commercial speech has been admitted to the protected areas and, in general, protection can be lifted only in cases of extreme necessity in order to protect a democratic society (as per the parameters set in ECHRFF's Art. 10).[7]

The **Belgian** constitution also is brief and positive in referring to the press. Its Article 25, which dates to 1831 and has not been amended, says, "The press is free; censorship can never be established; security from authors, publishers or printers cannot be demanded. When the author is known and resident in Belgium, neither the publisher, nor printer, nor distributor can be prosecuted." Royal decrees have made it possible for freedom of the press to be suspended in times of war or emergency, and some of the penal code's press violations allow such suspensions to be used as punishment. Of secondary importance to the press has been Article 19, which says, "Freedom of worship, public practice of the latter, as well as freedom to demonstrate one's opinions on all matters, are guaranteed, except for repression of offenses committed when using this freedom."[8]

The shortest of the constitutional press provisions among E.U. members can be found in the 1953 **Danish** constitution's Article 77, which says, "Any person shall be at liberty to publish his ideas in print, in writing and in speech, subject to his being held responsible in a court of law. Censorship and other preventive measures shall never again be introduced."[9] The "censorship" that is never to be introduced "again" is a reference to the Nazi occupation of Denmark.

The 1919 constitution of **Finland** says (Ch. 2, Art. 10), "Finnish citizens shall enjoy freedom of speech as well as the right to publish any written work or pictorial representation in print without prior restraint from anyone. Finnish citizens shall also have the right, without obtaining advance permission, to assemble for the discussion of general issues or for any other lawful purpose as well as to found associations for any purpose not infringing the law or good custom. Provisions on the exercise of these rights shall be prescribed by Act of Parliament." Article 16 of the same section does allow for the parliament to enact restrictive legislation to these rights "in times of war or rebellion, or at other times for persons performing military service."[10] Finland instituted the world's first constitutional press freedom guarantee, approved by King Gustaf III in 1766, when the country was still part of the Kingdom of Sweden. The predecessor to the current passage was composed in 1864 when Finland was part of czarist Russia and its most important accomplishment was the abolition of pre-censorship. The Czar never gave it his imperial assent. Immediately upon its declaration of independence in 1917 the government submitted the Freedom of the Press Bill, which was finally enacted in 1919 after the end of the Finnish civil war.[11]

The Preamble of the 1958 **French** constitution says, "The French people hereby solemnly proclaim its attachment to the Rights of Man and the principles of national sovereignty as defined by the Declaration of 1789, reaffirmed and complemented by the Preamble of the Constitution of 1946." It is Article 11 of the Rights of Man and of the Citizen that is considered the main source of press protection. It says, "Free communication of thought and opinion is one of the most valuable rights of man; thus every citizen may speak, write and print his views freely, provided only that he accepts the bounds of his freedom established by law."[12] Further references to freedom of expression and the press that have constitutional quality are the decisions of the Constitutional Court *(Conseil Constitutionnel),* which in 1984 affirmed the centrality these freedoms hold in French life and expanded them to include the freedom to receive information and the right to a pluralistic marketplace of opinions.[13]

Similar qualifiers to press freedom are also provided by the constitution of **Germany**, which says (Basic Law, Art. 5), "Everyone shall have the right freely to express and disseminate his opinion by speech, writing and pictures and freely to inform himself from generally accessible sources. Freedom of the press and freedom of reporting by means of broadcasts and films are guaranteed. There shall be no censorship." But Section 2 of the same article says, "These rights are limited by the provisions of the general laws, the provisions of law for the protection of youth and by the right to inviolability of personal honor."[14] This article was drafted for the 1949 constitution of the Federal Republic of Germany but remained in effect after the two Germanys re-united in 1990. Each of Germany's 16 states has its own constitution, but freedom of expression and press articles are in full compliance with and very similar to the federal Article 5.

The 1974 **Greek** constitution contains one of the Union's most detailed passages. Article 14, Section 1 guarantees that "Everyone has the right to express and disseminate orally, in writing or through the press his thoughts respecting the laws of the Nation." Section 2 says, "The press is free. Censorship and any other preventive measures are forbidden." Section 3 says, "The confiscation of newspapers or other publications, either before or after their circulation, is forbidden." Court-ordered post-circulation confiscation, however, is allowed in cases involving "offenses against the Christian or any other known religion"; "insult against the person of the President of the Republic"; a publication disclosing national defense information ("composition, equipment and formation of the armed forces," etc.); and in the case of "an obscene publication patently offensive to public decency. ..." The same article says the state has 48 hours within which to make its case or the confiscation order would be lifted. Section 5 says that a law describes how corrective articles are to be treated. Section 6 says that if a publication has been convicted of violating Section 3 three times in five years, the court may approve its permanent or temporary suspension or may prohibit the guilty person from "exercising the journalistic profession."

Article 15 says that these press-protective provisions do not apply to film, radio, television or the recording industry. In fact, the article says, "Radio and television are under the immediate control of the state and shall aim at the objective transmission, on equal terms, of information and news reports as well as works of literature and arts; the quality of programs shall be assured in consideration of their social mission and the cultural development of the country." Under these legal parameters, it has been difficult for Greece to accommodate the status of the many private radio and television stations that have inundated the country since the late 1980s.[15]

The 1937 **Irish** constitution (Art. 40. 6.i) guarantees ("subject to public order and morality") "the right of the citizens to express freely their convictions and opinions."

The education of public opinion being, however, a matter of such grave import to the common good, the State shall endeavor to ensure that organs of public opinion, such as the radio, the press, the cinema, while preserving their rightful liberty of expression, including criticism of government policy, shall not be used to undermine public order or morality or the authority of the state. ... The publication or utterance of blasphemous, seditious, or indecent matter is an offense which shall be punishable in accordance with law.

The Roman Catholic Church had often relied on the section concerning the undermining of "public order or morality" to ensure that no media (domestic or imported) disseminated abortion information (abortion is illegal under the Irish constitution). The European Court of Human Rights, however, in a 1992 decision declared that this information ban was in violation of Article 10 of ECHRFF, which Ireland had ratified. While new legislation is being prepared to accommodate this decision, there has been no medium yet that has taken advantage of the Court's decision.[16]

The **Italian** constitution (Art. 21) guarantees that "All are entitled freely to express their thoughts by word of mouth, in writing, and by all other means of communication. The press shall not be subjected to authorizations or censorship of any kind." But, as is the case with many other constitutions, there are limits. Restrictions may be imposed, the article says, "only by order of the judicial authorities for due and motivated cause, and only in those cases expressly authorized by the laws regulating the press. ..." Only in cases of "absolute urgency ... distraint [sic] may be applied." The authorities have 24 hours to make their case in court,

otherwise, the "distraint is null and void." This provision, however, does seem to allow for preventive censorship, even if it is for
only 24 hours.[17] "Printed publications, entertainment and all
other public demonstration running contrary to public morality
are forbidden," the article concludes.[18] (As in other countries,
"laws regulating the press" refers mainly to the "Press Act" and the
penal code, which forbid dissemination of information concerning state secrets, offenses "against the honor and prestige of the
President of the Republic," "defamation of the Italian Nation," libel and obscenity, etc.[19])

The constitution of the **Grand Duchy of Luxembourg**, including its freedom of speech/press passage, was written in 1868. A year
later, a comprehensive and punitive law (the 1869 *Loi sur la Presse*)
defining the limits of that freedom, including the current "Right of
Reply" provision, was passed. Article 24 of the constitution says,

Freedom of speech in all matters and freedom of the press shall be guaranteed, subject to the repression of offenses committed in the exercise of these freedoms. No
censorship shall ever be introduced. Security shall not be demanded of writers, publishers or printers. Stamp duty on native journals and periodicals is hereby abolished. No publisher, printer or distributor shall be prosecuted if the author is
known, if he is a Luxembourger and a resident of the Grand Duchy.[20]

The constitution of **The Netherlands** has protected the press
since 1815. Article 7 says,

1. No one shall require prior permission to publish thoughts or opinions through
press, without prejudice to the responsibility of every person under the law. 2. Rules
concerning radio and television shall be laid down by Act of Parliament. There shall
be no prior supervision of the content of radio or television broadcast. 3. No one
shall be required to submit thoughts or opinions for prior approval in order to disseminate them by means other than those mentioned in the preceding paragraphs,
without prejudice to the responsibility of every person under the law. The holding
of performances open to person younger than sixteen years of age may be regulated
by Act of Parliament in order to protect good morals. 4. The preceding paragraphs
do not apply to commercial advertising.[21]

It is also interesting to note that Article 110 of the constitution
makes it incumbent upon government to "observe the right of
public access to information," thus giving constitutional validity

to the concept of citizen access to government information.

The constitution of **Portugal** has at least four articles concerning the mass media, the longest such reference in the European Union after Sweden's. Article 37 says,

1. Everyone shall have the right to express and make known his or her thoughts freely by words, images or any other means, and also the right to inform, obtain information and be informed without hindrance or discrimination. 2. The exercise of these rights shall not be prevented or restricted by any type of or form of censorship. 3. Offenses committed in the exercise of these rights shall be punishable under the general principles of criminal law. ... 4. The right of reply and rectification and the right to compensation for losses suffered shall be equally and effectively secured to all natural and artificial persons.

Furthermore, Article 38 guarantees that "Freedom of the press shall be safeguarded" and determines that press freedom means

a) The freedom of expression and creativeness for journalists and literary collaborators as well as a role for the former in giving editorial direction to the concerned mass media. ... b) The journalists' rights of access to the sources of information, protection of their professional independence and secrecy, and election of editorial council, in accordance with the law and c) The right to start newspapers and any other publication regardless of any prior administrative authorization, deposit or qualification.

The same article (Sect. 4) guarantees that the State "shall ensure the freedom and independence of the mass media against political and economic powers," including "multiple and inter-locking financial interests" (a clear reference to Portugal's large and increasing media chain ownership).

Sections 5, 6 and 7 of Article 38 refer to the creation of public radio and television services with ensured "independence against the government." Article 39 creates the High Authority for the Mass Media, a body charged with protecting media independence and pluralism, licensing private television channels and appointing the managers of public television. Finally, Article 40 describes the groups that will be entitled to access public broadcasting ("the political parties, the trade unions, the professional organizations and the organizations representing economic activities") and the method through which they will do it.[22]

Article 20 of the constitution of **Spain** is the main article that addresses freedom of the press and expression. Articles 18, 53 and 55 tend to qualify and limit those freedoms. Article 20, Section 1 guarantees

a) The right to freely express and disseminate thoughts, ideas and opinions by word of mouth, in writing or by any other means of divulgation [sic].

b) The right to literary, artistic, scientific and technical production and creation.

c) The right to professorial freedom.

d) The right to freely communicate or receive truthful information by any means of dissemination whatsoever. The law shall regulate the right to invoke the clause of conscience and that of professional secrecy in the exercise of these freedoms.

Section 2 says that the exercise of these rights "may not be restricted by any kind of prior censorship." Section 3 of the same article defers to other laws the regulation of government-owned media. Section 4 says that these freedoms may be limited "by the right to honour, to privacy, to personal reputation and to the protection of youth and childhood." Section 5 requires that a "legal ruling" is mandatory for the confiscation of "publications and recordings and other information media." Articles 18 and 53 repeat several of the above restrictions, and Article 55 says that these press protections may be suspended in case of "a state of emergency or siege."[23] Spain's Constitutional Court has determined that expression refers to opinions, ideas, etc., while information refers to facts. It has also determined that the requirement of providing (Art. 20, Sect. 1.d) "truthful information" does allow for error, but it "imposes on the journalist the duty to act with due diligence in gathering information. ..."[24]

Sweden's constitutional references to expression and the press are probably the world's most extensive. Two of its three main constitutional documents are the 1949 Freedom of the Press Act (FPA) (the first version of which was written in 1766) and the 1991 Freedom of Speech Act (FSA). The third, the 1974 Instrument of Government, says, in Chapter 2, Article 1,

All citizens shall be guaranteed the following in their relations with the public administration: 1. freedom of expression: the freedom to communicate information and to express ideas, opinions and emotions, whether orally, in writing, in pictorial representations, or in any other way; 2. freedom of information: the freedom to obtain and receive information and otherwise acquaint oneself with the utterances of others.

Sections 3, 4, 5 and 6 guarantee freedom to assemble, demonstrate, associate and worship. Article 12 says that these freedoms may be curtailed "only to achieve a purpose acceptable to a democratic society." Article 13 determines that some of these restrictions may be with regards to "the security of the Realm, the national supply, public safety and order, the integrity of the individual, the sanctity of private life or the prevention and prosecution of crime." FPA's Chapter 1, Article 1 says,

the freedom of the press means the right of every Swedish subject, without prior hindrance by central administrative authority ... to publish ... and not to be prosecuted thereafter on grounds of the content of such matter other than before a court of law, or to be punished therefore in any case other than a case in which the content is in contravention of an express provision of law, enacted to preserve public order without suppressing information to the public.

Article 2 says that "No publication shall be subject to censorship before being printed. ..."

But what gives Sweden the distinction of having the world's most media-friendly legal environment is its public access to government documents: Chapter 2 of the Freedom of the Press Act, Article 1, says that "To further free interchange of opinions and enlightenment of the public, every Swedish national shall have free access to official documents." This access may be restricted *only if* there is a need to protect "the security of the Realm or its relations to a foreign state or to an international organization," the nation's "central financial policy ... ," the nation's investigative activities, the "interest of prevention and prosecution of crime," central and regional economic interests, "the personal integrity or the economic conditions of individuals," and the "interest of preserving animal or plant species." The FSA covers radio, television, film and video, follows the same FPA principles, but protection is not as generous—film censorship, for example, is still permissible.[25]

The **United Kingdom** has no constitution, Bill of Rights or other executive, parliamentary or judicial document that defines freedom of expression or freedom of the press. The implication is that British citizens, as well as journalists, have the freedom to do and say whatever they want as long as that is not expressly forbidden by law. Although the United Kingdom has signed the European Convention of Human Rights and therefore it is obliged to conform to its provisions, the convention is not part of British law and cannot supersede it. For example, when the 1988 British government ban of broadcasting of the voices of Irish Republican Army representatives was challenged as violating ECHRFF's Article 10, Britain's final appeals court, the House of Lords, said the ECHRFF cannot be used as a source for law because it has not been integrated into English law (see Ch. 6). Because there is no legal recognition of the press as a *special* societal institution, as L.C.J. McNae says in his *Essential Law for Journalists,*

The journalist has no *legal right* to go anywhere, do anything, say anything, or publish anything beyond what is the legal right of any private citizen. ... For example, it is accepted as an important part of a journalist's work to report the proceedings in courts of law. In spite of the facilities of the Press box, the journalist is in court in nearly every case merely as a member of the public. Normally he has no right to enter, or to remain, when the public has been legally excluded.[26]

Media and the European Court of Human Rights

One European institution that deals regularly with media issues but is outside the organizational framework of the European Union is the Council of Europe (COE), a pan-European association of nations that aims at safeguarding, among other values, the human rights, including the right to free expression, of those who live in member states. In June 1996, the council, which is headquartered in Strasbourg, France, consists of the following nations: Albania, Andorra, Austria, Belgium, Bulgaria, Cyprus, Czech Republic, Denmark, Estonia, Finland, France, Germany, Greece, Hungary, Iceland, Ireland, Italy, Latvia, Liechtenstein, Lithuania, Luxembourg, Malta, Moldova, The Netherlands, Norway, Poland, Portugal, Romania, Russian Federation, San Marino, Slovakia, Spain, Sweden, Switzerland, the Former Yugoslav Republic of Macedonia, Turkey, Ukraine and the United Kingdom. Croatia was expected to join by the end of 1996.

The council's constitutional document, sometimes referred to as the "jewel in the Council's crown," is the European Convention on Human Rights. Applicant nations must ratify it within one year after joining, and all signatories must ensure that the rights mentioned within it are respected. All member states, except Ireland, Norway and the United Kingdom have incorporated the convention into their own legal systems.

The convention addresses press/media issues primarily via Article 10, the article guaranteeing freedom of expression. Other issues encompassed in the convention are the right to life, liberty and security of a person; freedom of thought, religion and conscience; the right to a fair trial; the prohibition of torture and other cruel punishments, including the death penalty; the outlawing of discrimination; and the collective expulsion of foreigners.

The instruments of the convention's enforcement are the European Commission on Human Rights, the Committee of Ministers and the European Court of Human Rights. Each of these bodies has one representative from each member country, but its final arbiter, the Court, hears cases in smaller groups, usually consisting of nine to 19 members. After a case has exhausted a nation's legal system, it can be appealed to the Court. Before the Court hears it, the case must go through the commission, which will collect and assess the facts and present them to the Council of Ministers or the Court. Of the almost 26,000 cases petitioned to be heard by the Court since its inception in 1955, only approximately 1,900 have been deemed admissible for hearing and fewer than 500 have been heard by the Court.

If an amicable solution can not be found at the initial stages, the commission or the council may refer the case to the Court, whose decisions are final. Member states must abide by the Court's decisions, something often mentioned as the main source for the convention's global respectability over the years—it represents the first international effort to collectively assess and correct human rights abuses via a supranational system with real punitive powers.

The popularity of the Court in the last two decades has increased its work load to impractical limits, and the Commission of Ministers decided in 1993, via Protocol 11, to replace the current system and to adopt a permanent, full-time court structure that will include separate decision-empowered chambers that will hear the cases and, only if necessary, refer them to the Grand Chamber. The new Court scheme will become effective as soon as all member states have signed the protocol.

Since its creation in 1959, the Court has established a strong record on media and freedom of expression issues and has refined many of the gray areas included in Article 10 of the Convention. In every one of its decisions, the Court has tried to address three central issues raised by Article 10—that the prohibition of the expression in question has a "legitimate aim," that it is "prescribed by law" and it is "necessary in democratic society." Practice has shown that the third criterion, the "necessity test is ultimately the relevant and decisive criterion for deciding the legitimacy of restrictions and sanctions on freedom of expression."[27]

Finally, the Court in *Autronic AG v. Switzerland* (Series A, No. 178, Para. 61, May 22, 1990) described its own role regarding the domestic courts this way:

... the Contracting States enjoy a certain margin of appreciation in assessing the need for interference, but this margin goes hand in hand with European supervision, whose extent will vary according to the case. Where there has been an interference with the rights and freedoms guaranteed in paragraph 1 of Article 10, the supervision must be strict, because of the importance of the rights in question; the importance of these rights has been stressed to the Court many times. The necessity for restricting them must be convincingly established.

These words are very similar to those used by the U.S. Supreme Court in the 1971 Pentagon Papers case in which it decided, 6–3, in four sentences, that government interference with the freedom of the press came to the Court

... bearing a heavy presumption against its constitutional validity. The government thus carries a heavy burden of showing justification for the enforcement of such restraint. The District Court ... and the Court of Appeals ... held that the government had not met that burden. We agree.[28]

Through mid-1996, the European Court of Human Rights had decided 39 cases based on Article 10. They included media as well as personal freedom of expression cases. There are two media-related cases of particular importance in which the Court found **no violation** of Article 10. First, in *Engel and others* (Series A, Vol. 22, June 8, 1976), the Court found that disciplinary punishment imposed on Dutch Armed Forces personnel for releasing information that resulted in publication of articles undermining military discipline was not aimed at depriving them of their right to free expression but to punish them for abusing that freedom. Therefore, the government, according to the Court, did not violate Article 10. Second, in *Handyside* (Series A, Vol. 24, December 7, 1976), the

Court decided that the government had a legitimate interest in protecting public morality, as allowed by Article 10, and thus its action in banning the *Little Red School Book,* a book intended for children which contained a graphic section on sex, was within the United Kingdom's "margin of appreciation" of what constitutes appropriate action for achieving its aim. In a 13–1 ruling the Court found that the English court's "fundamental aim" was the "protection of the morals of the young, a legitimate purpose under Article 10 (2)." The Court also noted the government subsequently permitted a revised version of the book to circulate, in an effort to ensure that it restricted its prohibition only "to what was strictly necessary," thus conforming to Article 10's allowed limitations.

In the same decision, however, the Court made clear that it has full respect for freedom of expression as a foundation of a free and democratic society:

Subject to Article 10 (2), it is applicable not only to "information" or "ideas" that are favorably received or regarded as inoffensive or as a matter of indifference, but also to those that offend, shock or disturb the State or any sector of the population. Such are the demands of that pluralism, tolerance and broadmindedness without which there is no "democratic society."

Finally, one of *Handyside's* major contributions was its refinement of the meaning of "necessary in a democratic society":

Whilst the adjective "necessary," within the meaning of Article 10 (2), is not synonymous with "indispensable," neither has it the flexibility of such expressions as "admissible," "ordinary," "useful," "reasonable" or "desirable." Nevertheless, it is for the national authorities to make the initial assessment of the reality of the pressing social need implied by the notion of "necessity" in this context.

In *Barford* (Series A, Vol. 149, February 22, 1989), the Court found that Greenland's penal code was properly enforced when the petitioner was fined after he defamed two lay judges in a newspaper article.

In *Hadjianastasiou* (Series A, Vol. 252, December 16, 1992), the Court reconfirmed its interpretation that a state has a legitimate interest in protecting its military secrets by finding that the petitioner was not improperly convicted by the Greek military courts.

In *Otto-Preminger-Institut* (Series A, Vol. 295, September 20, 1994), the Court said that Austrian authorities acted within their legal rights when they banned the film *Council in Heaven,* which the Innsbruck Roman Catholic diocese had considered blasphemous and in violation of Section 188 of the Penal Code that deals with the "disparagement of religious doctrines." The Court said, in part:

In seizing the film, the Austrian authorities acted to ensure religious peace in that region and to prevent that some people should feel the object of attacks on their religious beliefs in an unwarranted and offensive manner. It is in the first place for the national authorities, who are better placed than the international judge, to assess the need for such measure in the light of the situation obtaining locally at a given time. In all the circumstances of the present case, the Court does not consider that the Austrian authorities can be regarded as having overstepped their margin of appreciation in this respect.[29]

In *Prager and Oberschlick* (Series A, Vol. 313, April 26, 1995), the Court exhibited again its sensitivity to protecting the judiciary, or as Article 10 says, "maintaining the authority and impartiality of the judiciary." It said an article in Vienna's *Forum,* entitled "Danger! Harsh judges!," undermined the judicial system and the local courts properly enforced local laws that deemed to have been "necessary in a democratic society":

Regard must, however, be had to the special role of the judiciary in society. As the guarantor of justice, a fundamental value in a law-governed State, it must enjoy public confidence if it is to be successful in carrying out its duties. It may therefore prove necessary to protect such confidence against destructive attacks that are essentially unfounded, especially in view of the fact that the judges who have been criticized are subject to a duty of discretion that precludes from replying.

The cases in which the Court did find **violation** of Article 10 are as follows: In *The Sunday Times* (No. 1) (Series A, Vol. 30, April 26, 1979), the Court found a U.K. court injunction against *The Sunday Times* inappropriate. The injunction aimed at prohibiting the printing of a story on Distillers, the company that marketed the drug thalidomide, which was associated with birth defects. The British court thought that an article about the company during its litigation would cause a "real and substantial danger of prejudice to the trial. ... Even if the person making the comment honestly believes it to be true, still it is a contempt of court if he prejudges the truth. ..."[30]

The Court, departing from its established protectionist record toward the judiciary, said that the interference of the news story with the administration of justice that the British courts anticipated

... did not correspond to a social need sufficiently pressing to outweigh the public interest in freedom of expression within the meaning of the convention. The Court therefore finds the reasons for the restraint imposed on the applicants not to be sufficient under Article 10 (2). The restraint proves not to be proportionate to the legitimate aim pursued; it was not necessary in a democratic society for maintaining the authority of the judiciary.

The Court continued to promote tolerance toward the press by allowing it unprecedented freedoms to assess with impunity those in power in three key decisions that centered on Austria's defamation statute (see Chapter 3). The Court's rationale on these decisions is reminiscent of the liberal press view expressed by Federal District Court Judge Murray Gurfein, who was the first federal judge to review the government's request in 1971 to restrain *The New York Times* from publishing the Pentagon Papers:

The security of the nation is not at the ramparts alone. ... Security also lies in the value of our free institutions. A cantankerous press, an obstinate press, a ubiquitous press must be suffered by those in authority in order to preserve the even greater values of freedom of expression and the right of the people to know.[31]

In *Lingens* (Series A, Vol. 103, July 8, 1986), a Viennese magazine accused Austrian Chancellor Bruno Kreisky of protecting former Nazi Party members; Kreisky sued for defamation and won. The Austrian court rejected Lingens' contention that the story was based on value judgments protected by the Austrian constitution as well as Article 10. The Austrian court went on to say, in fact, that the role of the press was "to impart information, the interpretation of which had to be left to the reader."

The European Court on Human Rights disagreed, saying that Article 10 applies

... not only to the "information" or "ideas" that are favorably received or regarded as inoffensive or as a matter of indifference, but also to those that offend, shock or disturb. Such are the demands of that pluralism, tolerance and broadmindedness without which there is no "democratic society. ... These principles are of particular importance as far as the press is concerned. Whilst the press must not overstep the bounds set, *inter alia,* for the "protection of the reputation of others," it is nevertheless incumbent upon it to impart information and ideas on political issues just as on those in other areas of public interest. Not only does the press have the task of imparting such information and ideas: the public has a right to receive them. In this connection, the Court cannot accept the opinion, expressed in the judgment of the Vienna Court of Appeal, to the effect that that the task of the press was to impart information, the interpretation of which had to be left primarily to the reader.

For the first time, the Court seemed to expand the limits of controversial political discussion by allowing more freedom for a critical press to perform its function and by recognizing that "the limits of acceptable criticism are accordingly wider as regards to a politician as such than as regards a private individual." It is also significant to note that through this decision the Court ventured into an area that no American court has truly entered: that of guaranteeing a citizen's "right to know"—the people have a "right to receive" whatever the press sees fit to impart.

In *Oberschlick* (Series A, Vol. 204, May 23, 1991), Liberal Party Secretary General Walter-Grabher Meyer won a defamation suit in Austrian courts against a magazine that had accused him of making anti-immigrant statements that violated the National Socialism Prohibition Act. The Austrian court said that Oberschlick had "disregarded the standards of fair journalism by going beyond a comparative and critical analysis. ..."

The Court disagreed, saying that Oberschlick sought to draw the public's attention in a provocative manner to a proposal made by a politician which was likely to shock many people. A politician who expresses himself in such terms exposes himself to a strong reaction on the part of journalists and the public.

In the third related Austrian case, *Schwabe* (Series A, Vol. 242-B, August 28, 1992), the center of controversy was a politician's record of drunk driving and hit and run, offenses for which sentence had already been served and thus legally off limits to journalists in background stories. Schwabe was convicted of using this information and for defamation.

The Court again overruled the Austrian courts and found that mention of past criminal convictions was within the "limits of acceptable criticism in the context of public debate of a political question of general interest." A politician's criminal record, the

Court said, "together with his public conduct in other respects, may be relevant factors in assessing his fitness to exercise political functions."

In *Weber* (Series A, Vol. 177, May 22, 1990), the Court ruled that a Swiss journalist's conviction was in violation of Article 10. Weber had been found in violation of the penal code of the Canton of Vaud for revealing during a press conference information concerning a pending libel suit. The Court concluded that because the revealed information had already been disclosed to the public at another press conference, there was no realistic interest in keeping the information secret and therefore Switzerland's interference with the free flow of information "was not necessary in a democratic society."

The Court in *The Observer and Guardian Newspapers Ltd.* (Series A, Vol. 216, November 26, 1991) and *The Sunday Times and A. Neil* (No. 2) (Series A, Vol. 217, November 26, 1991) had a difficult time balancing the issues of preserving national security and the authority of the judiciary, both worthy of protection under Article 10, against the interests of a free and robust debate on matters of importance to the citizens of a democratic society. When *The Observer, The Guardian* and *The Sunday Times* started printing articles based on *Spycatcher,* the memoirs of former British Security Service officer Peter Wright, the government pursued restraining orders based on national security grounds and on grounds of violation by Wright of his confidentiality contract with his former employer.

Although the majority of the Court's justices wanted to continue stretching the limits of free political debate, it was reluctant to abandon its record of protecting non-political government institutions, such as the courts and the armed services, and sought a safe catalyst upon which to base a judgment of acceptable government interference. The book's publication in the United States gave the Court the opportunity to divide the restraining order time into two segments—the injunctions against *The Observer* and *The Guardian* prior to the book's publication in the United States (June 1986–July 1987) and the injunctions against all three newspapers after the book was published in the United States (July 1987).

Thus, the Court in *Spycatcher* did not break any new ground concerning freedom of expression or of the press, refused to outlaw prior restraint and ruled that the injunctions of the first phase were within the legitimate interference means "necessary in a democratic society," but those following the U.S. publication were not.

Furthermore, the Court's recognition of the delicate nature of prior restraints offered little solace to the media:

The dangers inherent in prior restraints are such that they call for the most careful scrutiny on the part of the Court. This is especially so as far as the press is concerned, for news is a perishable commodity and to delay publication, even for a short period, may well deprive it of all its value and interest.

Little new ground was broken by the Court in *Castells* (Series A, Vol. 236, April 23, 1992), in which it found that the applicant, a Basque militant and member of the Spanish Parliament, was convicted in violation of Article 10 for publishing an article accusing the government of tolerating attacks on Basques:

... Freedom of the press affords the public one of the best means of discovering and forming an opinion on the ideas and attitudes of their political leaders. In particular, it gives politicians the opportunity to reflect and comment on the preoccupations of public opinion; it thus enables everyone to participate in the free political debate which is at the very core of the concept of a democratic society.

Similar was Iceland's *Thorgeir Thorgeirson* (Series A, Vol. 239, June 25, 1992) case, in which the Court ruled that Article 10 had been violated, because information contained in two newspaper articles concerning police brutality, to which Iceland's government had objected, was very much within the public interest and the press had not only the right but also the responsibility to report on this topic.

In 1993 the Court had the opportunity to reiterate its commitment to a pluralistic media system, especially since broadcast deregulation in the late 1980s had enhanced the power of European television, by assessing the meaning of Article 10's provision that states should not be prevented "from requiring the licensing of broadcasting, television or cinema enterprises." In *Informationsverein Lentia and others* (Series A, Vol. 276, November 24, 1993), the Court decided that the rules of the Austrian Broadcasting Corporation, a public monopoly, concerning applicants for new frequencies, were too restrictive on freedom of expression and incompatible with the interests of a democratic society.

Also citing its commitment to pluralism and tolerance of information and ideas that offend, shock or disturb, as per *The Observer* and *The Guardian* principles, the Court ruled in *Vereinigung Demokratischer Soldaten Österreichs and Gubi* (34/1993/429/508) that members of the Armed Forces should enjoy the same Article 10 freedoms as everyone else and that they should have on-base access even to publications that are critical of the military. More specifically, the Court rejected, as violative of Article 10, the defense minister's on-base circulation prohibition of a publication that had negative articles about the armed forces. The Court found that

> None of the issues ... submitted in evidence recommend disobedience or violence, or even question the usefulness of the army. Admittedly, most of the issues set out complaints, put forward proposals for reforms or encourage the readers to institute legal complaints or appeals proceedings. However, despite their often polemical tenor, its does not appear that they overstepped the bounds of what is permissible in the context of a mere discussion of ideas, which must be tolerated in the army of a democratic State just as it must be in the society that such an army serves.

The Court was challenged by the issue of a national security leak in *Vereniging Weekblad Bluf* (44/1993/439/518) but managed to not deviate in principle from its protectionist attitude toward this subject and decided it on narrow circumstantial grounds. It said that the Dutch courts' seizure of the publication was not justified in a democratic society because the information in question (concerning internal security service investigation targets) was six years old, "fairly general in nature," and marked only "Confidential," thus reflecting a "low degree of secrecy" need. Finally, the Court said that the issue became moot when the publishers, after the seizure of their publication, reprinted articles and distributed them in the streets of Amsterdam, thus nullifying any attempt at keeping the information secret. Despite its finding, however, the Court reiterated its view that security services "must enjoy a high degree of protection" from information disclosure and that "National authorities must be able to take measures solely in order to prevent punishable disclosure ..." such as the ones the Dutch law provided.

In an interesting case concerning the unpredictability of damage awards in British libel convictions, the Court ruled in *Tolstoy Miloslavsky* (Series A, Vol. 323, July 13, 1995) that although both the United Kingdom's aim of protecting the "reputation and rights of others" and the "damage award" were "prescribed by law," the size of the award indicated that "the scope of judicial control ... did not offer adequate and effective safeguards against a disproportionately large award" and thus "the jury was free to make any award it saw fit." The Court found that to be in violation of Article 10.

Two significant decisions that go to the heart of the journalistic profession are *Jersild v. Denmark* and *Goodwin v. the United Kingdom*. Both resulted in decisions favorable to the press.

1. The importance of *Jersild* (Series A, Vol. 298, September 23, 1994) lies in the fact that it concerned the dissemination of news items that were **unprotected** by Article 10. In it the Court had to decide if racist remarks made in a television program interview were properly used by Danish courts to convict the journalist interviewer. The theme of the program was racism in Denmark, and some of the interviewees' comments were, "A nigger is not a human being, it's an animal, that goes for all other foreigner workers as well, Turks, Yugoslavs and whatever they are called," "Just take a picture of a gorilla, man, and then look at a nigger, it's the same body structure ...," etc.

The Court, in finding that the rights of the journalist had been violated, ruled that

Taken as a whole, the feature could not objectively have appeared to have as its purpose the propagation of racist views and ideas. On the contrary, it clearly sought— by means of an interview—to expose, analyze and explain this particular group of youths, limited and frustrated by their social situation, with criminal records and violent attitudes, thus dealing with specific aspects of a matter that already then was of great public concern.

Rejecting the government's argument that the journalist made no effort to counterbalance the racist views expressed, the Court assigned significant merit to journalism as a critical societal institution and to the journalistic practice of eliciting information via interviewing.

News reporting based on interviews, whether edited or not, constitutes one of the most important means whereby the press is able to play its vital role of "public watchdog." The punishment of a journalist for assisting in the dissemination of statements made by another person in an interview would seriously hamper the contribution of the press to discussion of matters of public interest. ... There can be no doubt that the remarks in respect of which the Greenjackets were convicted were more than insulting to members of the targeted groups and did not enjoy the protection of Article 10. However, even having regard to the manner in which the applicant prepared the Greenjackets item, it has not been shown that, considered as a whole, the feature was such as to justify also his conviction of, and punishment for, a criminal offense under the Penal Code.

2. Finally, in *Goodwin* (16/1994/463/544, March 26, 1996), the Court had to decide if it were within the "interests of a democratic society" to impose a fine on a journalist for refusing to reveal the source of information that was critical of a company's financial standing. The Court, noting that if journalists were not allowed to keep their sources confidential, the "public-watchdog role" of the press and its "ability to provide accurate and reliable information" will be undermined, ruled:

Having regard to the importance of the protection of journalistic sources for press freedom in a democratic society and the potentially chilling effect an order of source disclosure has on the exercise of that freedom, such a measure cannot be compatible with Article 10 of the Convention unless it is justified by and overriding requirement in the public interest. ... In sum, there was not, in the Court's view, a reasonable relationship of proportionality between the legitimate aim pursued by the disclosure order and the means deployed to achieve that aim. The restriction which the disclosure order entailed on the applicant journalist's exercise of his freedom of expression cannot therefore be regarded as having been necessary in a democratic society. ...

However, the Court continued to show its respect for domestic blasphemy statutes in a 1996 case reminiscent of *Otto Preminger*. It involved Nigel Wingrove's 18-minute film "Visions of Ecstasy," which was alleged to have portrayed Jesus Christ and St. Teresa in a sexual context. The British Board of Film Classification, authorized by the 1984 Video Recordings Act to assess its suitability for distribution, refused to classify the film because it considered it "blasphemous." The law defined blasphemy as "any contemptuous, reviling, scurrilous or ludicrous matter relating to God, Jesus Christ or the Bible...." The board said it did not object to the "sexual imagery" of the film but to the fact that the imagery was "focused on the figure of the crucified Christ." The Court, in *Wingrove v. The United Kingdom* (19/1995/525/611), found no violation of Article 10. It was "not unreasonable for the national authorities," the

Court said, "to consider that the film could have reached a public to whom it would have caused offense." And, "in any event, here too national authorities are in a better position than the European Court to make an assessment as to the likely impact of such a video. ..." Further, the court said:

It is true that the measure taken by the authorities amounted to a complete ban on the film's distribution. However, this was an understandable consequence of the opinion of the competent authorities that the distribution of the video would infringe the criminal law and of the refusal of the applicant to amend or cut out the objectionable sequences. Having reached the conclusion that they did as to the blasphemous content of the film it cannot be said that the authorities overstepped their margin of appreciation.

1. George Garneau, "Reject Rights Treaty, Journalism Groups Urge Senate," *Editor and Publisher,* December 7, 1991, p. 26.

2. General Assembly Resolution 2106 A [XX], December 21, 1965, which became effective January 4, 1969.

3. Coliver, Sandra (Ed.), *Press Law and Practice* (London, U.K.: Article 19, The International Centre Against Censorship, 1993), p. 243.

4. "Joint Declaration," *Official Journal of the European Communities,* No. C 103, April 4, 1977, p. 1.

5. "Single European Act" (1987, June 29), *Official Journal of the European Communities,* No. L/169, June 29, 1987, p. 2.

6. *"The Treaty of Rome"* (London, U.K.: Blackstone Press Limited, 1990), pp. 1, 11, 12.

7. Walter Berka, "Press Law in Austria," in Sandra Coliver (Ed.), *Press Law and Practice,* op. cit., p. 22.

8. *The Belgian Constitution* (Brussels, Belgium: Ministry of Foreign Affairs, 1994), pp. 44-45; and Jean-Marie Van Bol, *The Policy Surrounding Social Communications in Belgium* (Brussels, Belgium: Ministry of Foreign Affairs, 1976), p. 5.

9. *The Constitutional Act* (Copenhagen, Denmark: Press and Cultural Relations Department of the Ministry of Foreign Affairs of Denmark, 1977), p. 3.

10. *The Constitutional Laws of Finland* (Helsinki, Finland: Parliament of Finland, Ministry of Foreign Affairs and Ministry of Justice, 1992), p. 4.

11. *Finnish Press Laws* (Helsinki, Finland: Ministry of Foreign Affairs, Press and Cultural Centre, 1984), pp. 5-6.

12. *The French Constitution* (New York, N.Y.: Ambassade de France, 1987), pp. 1, 35.

13. Roger Errera, "Press Law in France," in Pnina Lahav (Ed.), *Press Law in Modern Democracies* (New York, N.Y.: Longman, 1990), pp. 139-140 and Roger Errera in Sandra Coliver (Ed.), *Press Law and Practice* (London, U.K.: Article 19, 1993), pp. 57-58.

14. *The Basic Law* (Wiesbaden, Germany: The Press and Information Office of the Federal Government, 1979), p. 15.

15. *To Syntagma tis Elladas* (The Constitution of Greece) (Athens, Greece: Pontiki Publications, 1990), pp. 47-49; and Thimios Zaharopoulos and Manny E. Paraschos, *Mass Media in Greece: Power, Politics and Privatization* (Westport, Conn.: Praeger Publishers, 1993), pp. 85-87.

16. *Bunreacht na héireann* [Constitution of Ireland] (Dublin, Ireland: Government Publications Sale Office, 1978), pp. 132-134; and Marcel Berlins, "The Republic of Ireland," in Marcel Berlins, Claude Grellier and

Helle Nissen Kruuse (Eds.), *Les droits et les devoirs des journalistes dans les douze pays de l'Union Européenne* [The rights and responsibilities of journalists in the twelve countries of the European Union] (Paris, France: Centre de Formation et de Perfectionnement des Journalistes, 1994), pp. 129-130.

17. Roberto Petrogani, "Freedom of Information in Italy: Restraints and Problems," in Dan Nimmo and Michael W. Mansfield (Eds.), *Government and the Media* (Waco, Texas: Baylor University Press, 1982), p. 30.

18. *The Constitution of the Republic of Italy* (Rome, Italy: Presidency of the Council of Ministers, Information and Copyright Service, 1990), p. 19.

19. *Occasional Papers: Press Laws* (New York, N.Y.: Instituto Italiano di Cultura, 1990), pp. 2-3.

20. *The Constitution of the Grand Duchy of Luxembourg* (Luxembourg: Ministry of State, Press and Information Service, 1980), p. 67.

21. *Kingdom of The Netherlands: The Constitution* (Rijswijk, The Netherlands: Ministry of Foreign Affairs, 1989), p. 13; and Helle Nissen Kruuse, "The Netherlands," in Marcel Berlins, Claude Grellier and Helle Nissen Kruuse (Eds.), *Les droits et les devoirs des journalistes dans les douze pays de l'Union Européenne* [The rights and responsibilities of journalists in the twelve countries of the European Union] (Paris, France: Centre de Formation et de Perfectionnement des Journalistes, 1994), pp. 176-177.

22. *Constitution of the Portuguese Republic* (Lisbon, Portugal: Directorate-General for Mass Communication, 1989), pp. 29-42.

23. *Spanish Constitution* (Madrid, Spain: Presidencia del Gobierno, Secretaría General Técnica, 1978), pp. 1050-1058.

24. Blanca Rodriguez Ruiz, "Freedom of the Press in Spain," in Sandra Coliver (Ed.), *Press Law and Practice,* op. cit., p. 133.

25. *The Constitution of Sweden* (Stockholm, Sweden: The Swedish Riksdag, 1989), pp. 38-41 and 111; and Robert Picard, *The Ravens of Odin* (Ames, Iowa: Iowa State University Press, 1988), pp. 43-44.

26. L.C.J. McNae, *Essential Law for Journalists* (London, U.K.: Granada Publishing, 1980), p. 1.

27. Dirk Voorhof, *Critical perspectives on the scope and interpretation of Article 10 of the European Convention on Human Rights* (Strasbourg, France: Council of Europe Press, 1995), p. 61.

28. *The New York Times Co. v. U.S.* and *U.S. v. The Washington Post Co., et al.,* 403 U.S. 713 (1971).

29. On very similar grounds concerning blasphemy, the Court, in November 1996, found no violation of Article 10 by the authorities of the United Kingdom in *Wingrove v. U.K.*

30. *Attorney General v. Times Newspapers, Ltd.* (1973), Q.B. 710, D.C.

31. "In the Courts: The Government vs. the Press," *Newsweek,* July 28, 1971, pp. 27-31.

Personal Protections

Defamation

Defamation is the single most important legal issue the press faces anywhere in the world. How often the problem arises and reaches a country's court system depends on the cultural and legal traditions of the country—the public appreciation of self-esteem and honor, the perception of the media's role in society and the importance attached to "injury" correction through litigation. There are two kinds of defamation: libel, defined as printed defamation, and slander, defined as spoken defamation. Most countries, however, assign permanence to mass-communicated statements (print or broadcast) and prefer to use the term *libel* to refer to defamation crimes committed by journalists. *Slander* is mostly reserved for non-mass-communicated messages.

In the **United States**, the concept of defamation and its legal definition, types and remedies, as they have been shaped mainly through Supreme Court decisions, are considered to be some of the most detailed and perhaps *most* media protective in the world. It is perhaps ironic, therefore, that their roots can be traced to none other than early English law, which today stands as one of the world's *least* protective of the press in defamation cases!

Furthermore, a review of the defamation laws of the countries of the European Union clearly shows a considerable commonality with those of the United States. The basic tenets governing those laws can be found within this generally acceptable definition of defamation as outlined in the classic Teeter-Le Duc U.S. media law text *Law of Mass Communications:*

Defamation is communication which exposes persons to hatred, ridicule, or contempt, lowers them in the esteem of others, causes them to be shunned, or injures them in their business or calling. Its categories are libel—broadly, printed, written or broadcast material—and slander—broadly, spoken words of limited reach.[1]

Also utilized to varying degrees in most countries are the five elements of libel—publication, identification, defamation, fault and injury[2]—as well as the differentiation between a public figure or public official and a private person. Nevertheless, in European jurisprudence there is relatively little that resembles the specificity of the requirement of proof of actual malice (knowledge of the story's falsity or reckless disregard of whether it were false or not) as essential for a public person to win or the requirement of proof of negligence (story was published without the care that would have been exercised by the average person) for a private person to prevail in court against the media. However, in the United States new and creative approaches (legal, political, economic, etc.) are continually being invented by those who wish to discourage media from doing controversial stories. The most successful of these efforts was the one involving a supermarket chain that won a multimillion dollar award from a national network on the grounds that the network's reporters used fraudulent means to enter the premises. The accuracy of the story was not part of the plaintiff's case.[3]

All of the E.U. countries are signatories to the European Convention of Human Rights (ECHR) (see Ch. 2), which in Article 10.2 allows members to limit freedom of expression "for the protection of the reputation or rights of others. ..." Protection can be offered through either the criminal or civil codes or both. Many allow the media to use as their defense the argument that the information, if false, was accepted in good faith, a reasonable effort was made to verify it and the item in question was in the public interest. Truth is a defense in most instances, as are opinion statements and communication that is an accurate and fair representation of defamatory information that was obtained as part of official proceedings of governmental bodies (or what is known in the U.S. as *privileged* information).

A good example of a detailed statutory definition of defamation can be found in the **Danish** Criminal Code, Article 267, which says:

Any person who violates the honor of another person through offensive words or conduct or by making or spreading accusations of an act likely to disparage someone in the esteem of his fellow citizens, shall be liable to a fine or simple detention.

Article 268, however, allows for an imprisonment of up to two years and/or a fine, if the "allegation has been maliciously made or disseminated, or if the author had no reasonable ground to regard it as true. ..." Truth and privileged communication on matters of "obvious" public interest are defenses against defamation suits.

In **Austria,** Article 111 of the Criminal Code and Article 1330 of the Civil Code address defamation. The Criminal Code says:

Anyone who in such a way that it may be perceived by a third party accuses another of possessing a contemptible character or attitude or of behavior contrary to honour or morality and of such a nature as to make him contemptible or otherwise lower him in public esteem shall be liable to imprisonment not exceeding six months or a fine. ...

If the above accusation is disseminated "to a broad section of the public" or through the mass media, the penalty doubles. Civil cases may result in recovery of material damages and retractions/corrections. Defenses are the truth of the accusation or the reasonable belief that the accusation was true, that normal journalistic practices were observed and that there was a legitimate public interest in the information. Members of the federal parliament and the national army are specially protected by Article 116 of the Criminal Code and the Austrian nation and its symbols are protected by Article 248.

Similar penalties are provided by the **Finnish** Penal Code, Section 27.1, which says:

Any person who, against his better knowledge and without grounds, states that another person is guilty of a specific offense or a specific kind of crime or of any such deed that could lead to his being in ill-repute and could impede his source of livelihood or his success, or who disseminates lies or unfounded rumors or hearsay about such, shall be sentenced to a term of imprisonment not less than one month and not exceeding one year or to payment of a fine of at least one hundred marks for libel.

If the libel is committed in public or through the printed word or a manuscript or pictorial presentation, which the guilty party circulates or causes to be circulated, the punishment shall be a prison term of not less than two months and not more than two years or else a fine of not less than 200 marks.

The next paragraph says that if the communicator had no knowledge that the information was false, the fines and imprisonment drop to half. Similar provisions are made for insults "by means of a slanderous statement, threat or other derogatory deed" (Sect. 27.3). Truth is a defense except in cases when insult was intended, in which case the person should be penalized for "insulting behavior" (Sect. 27.6). The constitution, Section 6, makes these protections possible by guaranteeing that "every citizen of Finland shall be protected by law in respect of his ... honour ..."

The **Greek** defamation law can be found in three articles of the Penal Code. Article 361 describes as an "insult" whenever a person "insults the honor of another person through words or acts or in whatever other manner." The penalty can be no more than one year in jail or a fine. If the insult was "unprovoked," the guilty party may be punished by a minimum of three months in jail. Article 362 defines *"defamation"* as occurring when "a person by any means disseminates to a third party information that may damage the character or reputation of another person." The penalty is imprisonment of no more than two years or a fine. *"Malicious defamation"* is defined in Article 363 as the same violation as the one described in Article 362, but with the addition that the "information is false and the offender was aware of its falsity." The penalty in this instance is a minimum three-month imprisonment and/or a fine. Truth is a defense. It should be pointed out that the Greek constitution (Art. 14.3) protects from insult the "President of the Republic" and the "Christian or any other known religion. ..."Article 367 decriminalizes "scientific, artistic and professional criticism" and defamatory quotes from government documents or discussions.

The **United Kingdom's** 1952 Defamation Act, which mainly updated the 1843 Libel Act, the 1881 Newspaper and Libel Registration Act and the 1888 Law of Libel Amendment Act, punishes "words calculated to disparage the plaintiff in any office, profession, calling, trade or business." More of the law of defamation, however, can be found in judicial decisions that focus on what tends to bring a person into "hatred," "ridicule" and "contempt" or lowers him in the eyes of his peers. The plaintiff must show injury and identifiability.

But what sets British law drastically apart from that in the U.S., and results in attracting many international cases to be filed in Britain, is that it requires the *defendants* to prove the truthfulness of their statements, something that can be difficult to do when in controversial news stories the sources are protected by confidentiality agreements. Truth, fair comment, privilege and qualified privilege, including allowances for matters of public concern and public benefit, are defenses against libel. British law allows for reporters, editors, owners, sources, printers and distributors to be sued and imposes a three-year statute of limitations.

Less common is litigation on grounds of malicious falsehood and conspiracy to injure, both of which require that the plaintiff prove the falsehood of the publicized statements and presence of malice on the media's part. Criminal libel is used rarely and it is reserved for

a statement so serious in itself, and so greatly affecting a person's character and reputation as to justify invoking criminal punishment instead of, or as well as, the civil law and damages.[4]

In this instance, truth is not a defense "unless the jury is satisfied that publication is for the public benefit."[5] The 1952 Defamation Act, Section 4, provides for "unintentional defamation," when a person published defamatory words "innocently in relation to the other person." The act then specifies a series of corrective measures (such as retractions) that need to be taken until a solution is found that is "accepted by the party aggrieved."

Insulting the government and its officials, or what used to be known as "seditious libel," has not been used against journalists in half a century, and there are no laws in the United Kingdom criminalizing insults to the head of state, the flag, etc.[6]

Some countries consider the protection of a person's honor and/or reputation to be so important that they include protective provisions in their constitutions. For example, the **Irish** constitution serves as the source for that country's individual defamation protection, since defamation is not statutorily defined, even in its 1961 Defamation Act, which deals in procedure.[7]

Article 40.3 of the Irish constitution says:

i. The State guarantees in its laws to respect, and as far as practicable to defend and vindicate, the personal rights of the citizen.

ii. The State shall, in particular, by its laws protect as best it may from unjust attack and, in the case of injustice done, vindicate the life, person, good name, and property rights of every citizen.

A working definition was offered in 1971 by an Irish Supreme Court justice who said that words were defamatory of a person if they attributed to him "conduct which would tend to lower that person in the eyes of a considerable and respectable class of the community. ... The test is whether it will lower him in the eyes of the average right-thinking man. If it does, then it is defamatory if untrue." Truth is a defense, as is fair comment on matters of public interest and fair and accurate reporting of "privileged" information.[8]

Germany's defamation protection emanates from its Basic Law, Article 1.1, which says that "The dignity of man shall be inviolable. To respect and protect it shall be the duty of all state authority." Also Article 2.1 guarantees the citizen the right to the "free development of his personality." The Criminal Code, Articles 186–187, punishes the spreading of information that is "contemptuous" or "degrades a person in public opinion ... if the matter is not true." The penalties are higher if that information was spread via the public media. The crime is especially grave if it is committed with the knowledge that the information was not true. Even if an insult (Art. 185) is truthful, it may still be punishable depending on the circumstances. The Civil Code, Articles 823–826, generally protects the physical person (life, body, health), property and rights (freedom, good credit rating, "or other rights of another person ... ," etc.) and provides for corrective compensation from the person who disseminated the damaging information. Knowledge of the truth or the effort made to discover it play a role in the decision.

Spain's defamation laws also are rooted in that country's constitution, which says, in Article 18.1, "Everyone is entitled to the protection of his honor, his personal and family privacy and his own image." Both the criminal code (Arts. 453, 457, 462 and 463) and the Civil Code (Art. 1.82) protect a person's honor and reputation. However, at times this competes with the freedoms provided by Article 20.1: a. "the right to freely express and disseminate thoughts, ideas and opinions orally, in writing or by any other means of reproduction. ...," and d. "the right to receive and communicate accurate information by any means of dissemination. ..." The Constitutional Court has interpreted the first right as protective of freedom of expression and the second as protective of freedom of information.[9] In spite of some generous interpretations by the Constitutional Court, the latter makes it incumbent upon journalists to exercise extra care in fact checking before facts are disseminated. Because the rules of civil procedure allow more maneuvering room to the plaintiffs and because they have to prove intent (on the part of the media) to defame in criminal procedures, most people prefer civil trials.

Although courts still seek proof of public interest in the information/opinion being challenged, the Constitutional Court has allowed more freedom in the dissemination of both fact and comment concerning politicians. The Spanish Criminal Code offers special protection from defamation to the Heads of State (Art. 147), their agents, the members of the government, the judiciary, the regional governments (Art. 161), the armed forces and public officials in the exercise of their duties (Arts. 240–244). However, in the late 1980s several Constitutional Court decisions weakened these protections in favor of more robust public debate and critical assessment of these functionaries.[10]

Also constitutionally driven is the defamation law of **Sweden.** Its 1949 Freedom of the Press Act, one of that country's constitutional documents, defines as unlawful two kinds of defamatory activities:

Chapter 7, Article 4.14: libel, whereby a person alleges another person is a criminal or is blameworthy in his way of life, or otherwise communicates information liable to expose the other to the contempt of others ... except, however, in cases in which it is justifiable having regard to the circumstances, or in order to provide information in the matter concerned, and proof is presented that the information was correct or that there were reasonable grounds for it;

Article 4.15: insulting words or behaviour, whereby a person insults another by means of offensive invective or allegations or by any other insulting behavior towards him.

But perhaps the major difference between the European and American traditions on defamation is on the issue of protecting those who hold public office. Although it is by no means a universally accepted standard, there are several countries that traditionally have institutionalized respect for those who govern them and criminalized their abuse by the media. The protections afforded by the Austrian, German and Spanish laws (detailed previously) appear to be less stringent than those offered by the laws of France, Italy, Belgium and The Netherlands (to follow). Greece had a strong public-officials protection provision in its criminal code but it was abolished in 1994. In any case, either statutorily or via court interpretation the trend is toward more tolerance of media "abuse" of those in the public arena, especially politicians. The trend seems to be consistent with the mood prevailing in the European Court of Human Rights, which has exhibited a "higher degree of tolerance toward the impugned expressions when the strong wording is aimed at a politician or the Government or public authorities."[11]

The chorus of those seeking more freedom of the press to criticize public officials was joined in October 1996, by the World Press Freedom Committee (WPFC), a group representing 37 news organizations in five continents. Calling "insult laws" a "throwback to the ancient concept of the 'divine right of kings,'" an "insult to democracy" and a "sign of weakness," WPFC called on press organizations to mount a global effort to repeal such laws.[12]

In **France,** Article 29 of the Law of 1881 defines libel as "any allegation or accusation/charge of an act that taints the honor or reputation of the person or the group to whom the act is attributed." Especially protected from defamation, however, are many classes of "public" persons: The President of the Republic (Art. 26), with the understanding that the protection is not aimed at the person who occupies the office but the office itself; chiefs of foreign states and their functionaries (diplomats, representatives, etc.) (Arts. 36–37); and French public servants or public officials, such as court officers, armed forces officials, public administrators (Art. 30), ministry officials, elected representatives and people who, permanently or temporarily, have been given state responsibilities or are paid by the state (Art. 31). *Insult* is defined as any "indecent term or expression of contempt or invective that has no basis in fact."

Truth is a defense except when the allegation "concerns the private life of the individual"; when the act in question occurred more than 10 years before publication; when the allegation refers to an act that has been "amnestied or is past the statute of limitations" or has been dealt with legally through the person's "rehabilitation or review" (Art. 35). Journalists are helped by establishing "good faith," which normally refers to absence of malice on the part of the journalist, the legitimacy of the pursuit of the story (mainly the existence of a serious public interest in the story), that care was taken to establish the facts and that an effort was made to contact all concerned parties.

The **Belgian** defamation law, Penal Code, Article 443, punishes whomever "with malice attributes to a person an act that is capable of bringing dishonor to that person or exposes that person to public scorn" unless the truth of the act can legally be proven. Public officials, including members of the armed forces, are entitled to the same protection of the defamation law as private individuals.

However, Article 275 prohibits acts, words, gestures or threats against members of the legislative chamber, government ministers, members of the judiciary, public administrators, or members of the police forces on account of the performance of their duty. The king is especially protected from attacks on his constitutional authority, "the inviolability of his person, the constitutional rights of his dynasty and the rights and authority of the Chambers [of the people's representatives]." Finally, although private and public individuals are entitled to the same protection under the law, judicial proceedings on press defamation of private individuals can only commence after a complaint has been filed by the offended individual. However, "insult or defamation through the voice of the press of the King, members of his family, military officers, prosecutors or agents of public authority, on matters pertaining to the quality of their work" will be initiated by the public prosecutor. The Law of December 20, 1852, Article 1, restricts offenses (through writings, printing, images, emblems and posters, distributed free or sold) on foreign heads of state.

Although defamation is nowhere defined in detail in the **Italian** Penal Code, Articles 595–597 increase penalties if the defamation was addressed against members of public, administrative or judicial bodies. Especially protected is the honor of the President of the Republic (Art. 278), the honor of the nation and its constitutional institutions and armed forces (Arts. 290–291), the flag and other state emblems (Art. 292), visiting foreign heads of state (Art. 297) and the state religion (Art. 403). A judge decides if the allegations are defamatory of someone's reputation, honor, dignity or propriety. Distinctions are made between alleged fact and a derogatory remark, and between public and private persons. Information about a private person must be justified by serious public interest. In litigation the plaintiff must prove that the offender intended to defame. Negligence, incompetence and typographical errors often prove lack of intent and may help journalists. Fair comment and criticism are allowed (Art. 2 of Law 69 of 1963): "Freedom of information and criticism is a right of journalists that cannot be suppressed. It is limited by observing the rules of law protecting the personality of others." Convictions may result in one of Europe's stiffest defamation penalties—up to three years in prison. In practice, however, the most common penalty is a fine.[13]

Similar protections of public servants are offered by the Criminal Code of **The Netherlands.** Although Dutch law makes a serious effort to distinguish between "opinions and facts," it is not always successful, and the defamation area is problematic.[14] Art. 261 of the Criminal Code defines *defamation* as a "deliberate attack on the honor and good name" of someone that is done through the dissemination of alleged facts. The penalty is a maximum of six months in prison and a fine. "*Insult*" is defined (Art. 266) as information that includes "anything but facts" disseminated on purpose and in public. If the attack is in "writing or with pictures and is distributed publicly," the maximum penalty is one year in prison and a fine. It is a defense for the journalist to have assumed in good faith that what he/she publicized was true and that the issue in question was in the general public interest. However, Article 267 allows for the sentences to be increased by one-third if the insult was aimed at public authorities, officials in the exercise of their duty and heads of friendly states. Especially protected is the royal family—Articles 111–112 provide for a five-year imprisonment or a fine for deliberately insulting the king and a four-year sentence for deliberately insulting the king's spouse, as well as the king's probable successor and his spouse and the regent. Articles 118–119 protect from defamation heads of friendly foreign states and their representatives while on duty in The Netherlands. *Friendly states* are those with whom The Netherlands is not at war. Journalists may also be prosecuted under Articles 6.1–6.2 of the Civil Code, which generally cover "unrightful acts," a term that could be applied to inaccurate reporting.

The **Portuguese** Press Law of 1975, Article 4.e, also specially protects from criticism "organs of the public administration of the state and their agents, as long as they perform within the present law." Article 328 of the Penal Code extends a special protection from defamation to the president of the republic or his substitute. Defamation is more specifically addressed in Article 70 of the Civil Code, which punishes those who cause "physical or moral harm to a person," but mainly in Arts. 180–184 of the Penal Code. Article 180 prohibits the attribution "even if it is only a suspicion, of a fact ... or something offensive to the honor or reputation" of a person. It is a defense to have done so in the pursuit of "a legitimate interest," or if the communicator "proves the imputation to be true or has a serious reason to believe, in good faith, that it is true." Intimate details of one's private or family life are excluded from his defense. Article 182 punishes communications to third parties of "writings, gestures, images and any other form of expression" that injure the honor of a person. Punishment increases, according to Article 183, if the information was known to be false but was still communicated to other people.

Finally, the reputation of the dead is legally safeguarded in Finland, Greece, Portugal and Sweden. The Finnish Penal Code, Article 27.4, says that

A person who defames the memory of a dead man in that he, against his better knowledge, states without foundation that the dead man has been guilty of a specific offense or a specific type of crime or of any other deed that, had the deceased lived, could have led to his being in ill-repute, or who disseminates a lie or unfounded rumor about such, shall be penalized by a prison term of not more than 6 months or a fine. If the person against whom the defamation is committed has been dead 20 years or longer, the right to bring charges of defamation of character shall have lapsed.

Greece's Penal Code Article 365 says that "Anyone who disparages the memory of a decedent by rude or malevolent insult or by malicious defamation shall be punished by imprisonment of no more than six months." The Portuguese Penal Code, Article 185, extends the defamation protection to a deceased person and his/her siblings for up to 50 years past the death of the person.

The Swedish Freedom of the Press Act, Chapter 7, Article 4.14, says that it is unlawful to libel (to allege "criminal" or "blameworthy" behavior or to bring someone to the "contempt of others") the deceased or "to cause offence to his survivors or which might otherwise be considered to violate the sanctity of the grave."

Privacy

Most European Union countries seem to have a view of privacy that is similar to that prevailing in the United States—a legally institutionalized respect for private life and the "right to be let alone," along with a government-aimed set of limits to interference with that right. They also share a widely accepted interpretation that such limits must also apply to the press.

Although the U.S. Constitution does not mention the word *privacy,* the first eight of its amendments aim at limiting the government's powers against unreasonable searches and seizures and in favor of following "due process of law" when dealing with a citizen's private life or space. As government's abilities to intrude into private lives increased, Congress in 1974 passed the Privacy Act, which was "an effort to give citizens some control over the government's enormous system of dossiers, and to let individuals see and correct files about themselves." Courts, however, have applied the act against the media with equal fervor.

Many of the parameters on privacy matters are set by the courts and especially the Supreme Court, which in 1977 unanimously expanded the area of privacy to include not only the avoidance of "disclosure of private matters" but also the "independence in making certain kinds of important decisions."[15]

Much like the United States, E.U. countries have legal instruments (constitutional, statutory and/or common law) that ensure their citizens are not put in a false light by dissemination of facts and are further protected from interference with their

    1. non-public communication media (the mail, the telephone, etc.),

2. physical space (such as protecting their homes from audio/visual surveillance or "intrusion"),

3. personal records/files/matters (which in the 1990s includes electronic data banks) and

4. non-consensual name, image or personality exploitation or appropriation.

Defenses, both in the United States and in the European Union, range from the "public interest" to "newsworthiness" and, of course, consent. Absent any one of these, even truth may not be a defense.

Privacy matters faced a serious challenge with the introduction of the "information society," which made private records and other information easily accessible. The issue was exacerbated by the general E.U. interest in enforcing the 1985 Schengen agreement that aimed at eliminating border checkpoints for E.U. member state citizens. The first enforcement deadline (Jan. 1, 1993) was missed by most of the E.U. members, and even by the "irreversible" deadline of March 26, 1995, seven E.U. members had fully met it. Part of the problem was the slow development and the political implications of the computerized Schengen Information System that was to assist E.U. police and immigration officials in monitoring criminal suspects passing crossing E.U. borders.

In order to safeguard the privacy of E.U. citizens, the commission and the council in February 1995 proposed a directive that would "ensure the balance between the legitimate interests of the controller and the interests of the person concerned." The "person concerned" does have the right to know that his/her records are being processed and the reason why; right to access and correct the data; the right to know the source of the data; and the right to object "on legitimate grounds, to the processing of data" related to him/her. Data processed by the press is covered by the directive, but member states are required to "prescribe the exemptions necessary to reconcile protection of privacy with freedom of expression."[16]

The general spirit of privacy protection for most E.U. countries can be found in the ECHR, Article 8:

1. Everyone has the right to respect for his private and family life, his home and his correspondence.

2. There shall be no interference by a public authority with the exercise of this right except such as is in accordance with the law and is necessary in a democratic society in the interests of national security, public safety or the economic well-being of the country, for the prevention of disorder or crime, for the protection of health and morals or for the protection of the rights and freedoms of others.

A good copy of the ECHR is the **French** Civil Code, Article 9, which simply says that "Each has a right to respect for his private life." Because of cultural reasons and, perhaps, because truth is not a defense in privacy cases, French journalists are very respectful of the private lives of people in the public eye. Furthermore, journalists may take photographs but cannot run them without consent, especially if the photos were taken under questionable circumstances. This triggers Articles 368 and 372 of the Criminal Code that protect the privacy of a person's home, telephone, etc.

The protections provided by the Danish and Finnish criminal codes are more elaborate. Article 263 of the **Danish** code says

Any person who unjustifiably with the aid of equipment, secretly listens to or records statement made in private, telephone conversations or other conversations between others or negotiations in a closed meeting in which he is not himself taking part or to which he has unjustifiably obtained access, shall be liable to a fine, to simple detention or to imprisonment not exceeding 6 months.

A similar spirit and language prevail in Article 264, which defines trespassing as taking someone's picture in a place "not open to the public" and distributing such pictures. The Constitution, Article 72, guarantees the inviolability of a person's home, correspondence and "other papers," and telephone communications unless an exemption is made by a judicial order. Furthermore, the journalists' National Code of Conduct says that information that may violate the sanctity of private life shall be avoided unless an obvious public interest requires press coverage. It also says that special attention should be paid to suicides or attempted suicides and they should not be mentioned unless an obvious pubic interest requires or justifies press coverage and, in such cases, the mention should be made with as much consideration as possible.

The **Finnish** Penal Code, Section 27.3.a, is very similar but does address the key public-interest issue that normally governs the actions of journalists:

A person who without legal justification uses the mass media or some other similar means to spread information, rumors or a picture of another person in such a way as to cause that person damage or distress shall be sentenced to not more than 2 years imprisonment or a fine for violation of privacy. Publication of matters concerning a person's actions in public life or in public office, in economic life, in politics or in any other comparable activity, so long as this publication was necessary for handling a matter of importance to the public, shall not be regarded as a violation of privacy.

Without specific reference to the press, Section 24.1 of the Penal Code says that "Any person who without legal cause and against the will of another forces his way into another's dwelling ... shall be punished for trespassing. ..." Section 24.3.b says that "Any person who without permission and with the aid of technical equipment listens to or records what takes place in a place or area specified in Clause 1 shall be sentenced ... for illicit eavesdropping. Any person ... who takes pictures of a person in an area specified in 1, shall be sentenced ... for illicit surveillance. ..." These provisions emanate from the constitutional guarantees for the protection of one's home and "domestic peace" (Sect. 11) and of the "secrecy of postal, telegraph and telephone communications" (Sect. 12).

Austria's 1981 Media Act, Article 7, requires that negative private information be connected to the "public life" of an individual if it is to be publicized. Furthermore, Article 113 of the Criminal Code prohibits the publication of a past criminal record of an individual if the sentence has been served, but in *Schwabe v. Austria,* the European Court of Human Rights found in 1992 that such publication was permissible if it were in the public interest and overturned the Austrian courts' decisions as violative of Article 10 of the ECHR (see Media and the European Court of Human Rights, Ch. 2).

One of **Germany's** basic rights is the protection of "the dignity of man" (Art. 1.1), the right to "the free development of his personality" (Art. 2.1) and the right to "inviolability of his person" (Art. 2.2). Section 201 of the Criminal Code prohibits telephone tapping and other surveillance devices; Section 202 protects the privacy of the mail; Section 203 defines professional confidences for lawyers, doctors, etc.; and the Federal Law of Data Protection (Dec. 20, 1990) protects personal files. Furthermore, the 1907 Law of Copyrights in Art and Photography requires that pictures may be published only with consent except in cases of public figures and people attending public events. Courts have defined public figures as *absolute* (such as politicians, sports, artists, etc.) and *limited* (defendants in trials or others who are in the public eye because of their involvement in a specific event), in which case their photographs can be printed without their consent only if public interest demands it.[17]

Article 40.3 of the **Irish** Constitution protects the "personal rights" as well as the "person ... of every citizen" from "unjust attack," and the courts have interpreted it as recognizing "the right to privacy, even though that right is not spelled out in the text." They also have held that "it is not an absolute right and can be restricted in the interests of public order, morality and the common good. ..."[18] Additional refinement of the right to privacy has come through the Broadcasting Complaints Commission, which hears complaints about "unreasonable" violations of privacy, and through the National Union of Journalists Code of Conduct, which specifically encourages its members to obtain their information or photographs only by "straightforward means" and to not intrude into private lives, especially in times of "grief or distress."

The Criminal Code of **Italy,** in Articles 615–617, makes it unlawful for anyone using equipment to record private information and/or images in private places. The penalty can be a fine and up to four years in prison. Article 618 protects the privacy of correspondence. Publicizing (without permission) correspondence that was addressed to the recipient is illegal unless "just cause" can be proven. Article 10 of the Civil Code forbids publication of pictures without consent except pictures of people involved in newsworthy events in public places and of people in the public interest. The journalists' Code of Ethics also safeguards the protection of the "privacy of all citizens." Only a "clear and considerable public interest" justifies publication of private information, and the journalist is required to identify himself/herself as a journalist in the pursuit of a story.

Belgium guarantees in its Constitution, Article 15, that "One's domicile is inviolable," and in Article 22, everyone's "right to the respect of his private life, except in cases and under conditions specified by law." Furthermore, Belgium is fully utilizing Article 8 of the ECHR, and judges are free to implement it at their discretion.

Article 8 is also complemented by Articles 1270 and 1306 of the Belgian Criminal Code, which protect the privacy of judicial proceedings in divorce and separation cases, and Article 80 of the Law of April 8, 1965, which protects the secrecy of judicial proceedings involving the identity of minors. Although Belgium is a signatory to the 1991 personal data protection convention of the Council of Europe, it does not provide specific penalties for violations.

In **Luxembourg** privacy is protected by the Law of August 11, 1982, which eventually allows judges to take whatever measures are necessary to guarantee protection through imprisonment and fines. The article outlaws surveillance of private life (audio or visual) and guarantees the protection of correspondence. Consent is required for publication of photographs, and compensation is provided through Articles 1382–1383 of the civil code. The press council also has encouraged the respect of private life.

Article 10 of the Constitution of **The Netherlands** protects privacy, and the Dutch Supreme Court in a 1988 decision ruled that the right to free speech does not override the right to privacy. Privacy also is protected by Article 6.12 of the civil code and by Articles 139 and 426 of the criminal code, which forbid phone tapping and surveillance. The courts, however, have held that persons of "some public fame" must accept some invasion of their privacy. In a controversial position, the Dutch Press Council has recommended that a suspect's privacy needs to be protected. This means that, with some exceptions centering on public figures and public interest, the media may use only the suspect's initials, along with age, residential area and profession. Photographs are not allowed. The ruling has divided the media community. In any case, journalists' actions must be guided by a legitimate public interest.

In **Spain** the right to privacy is guaranteed by Article 20.1 (freedoms of expression "shall be limited by the provisions of implementing laws and in particular by the rights to honor, to privacy, to control the use of one's image ...") and Article 18.1 ("Everyone is entitled to the protection of his honor, his personal and family privacy and his own image"). Also the Criminal Code (Arts. 191, 192, 497, 498) protects the privacy of the mail, telephone and legally confidential/personal information. Similarly, the May 5, 1982, Civil Law, Articles 7–8, forbids listening equipment and revelation of private information that might injure a person's reputation but allows publication or airing of pictures (without consent) in such circumstances as when "broadcasting is expressly authorized by law," when there is a "higher historical, cultural or scientific interest" and when the photographs involve "... persons who are working in a public capacity or well known or public profession and the picture is taken at the time of a public act or in places open to the public."[19]

In the last 40 years, five bills have come before the parliament of the **United Kingdom** attempting to introduce a statutory definition of the right of privacy. All failed. At least three major commissions have studied the issue and all recommended against the adoption of a privacy right definition.[20] Therefore, the safeguarding of privacy has fallen upon the self-policing of the journalistic profession and the Press Complaints Commission, which effectively replaced the British Press Council in 1991. The council oversees accuracy, fairness, privacy protection, source protection, etc. In particular, the council's Code of Practice says,

Article 4. Intrusions and inquiries into an individual's private life without his or her consent, including the use of long-lens photography to take pictures of people on private property without their consent, are not generally acceptable and publication can only be justified when in the public interest.

Article 8.1. Journalists should neither obtain nor seek to obtain information or pictures through intimidation or harassment.

Article 8.2. Unless their inquiries are in the public interest, journalists should not photograph individuals on private property without their consent; should not persist in telephoning or questioning individuals after having been asked to desist; should not remain on the property after being asked to leave and should not follow them.

Furthermore, the BBC Producers' Guidelines limit reporters' imposition on distressed or grieving persons.

Greece's privacy laws consist only of the protection of the mail and the telephone and emanate from the constitution, which says that

Article 9.1. Every person's home is a sanctuary. The personal and family life of the individual is inviolable. No house search shall be made except when and as specified by law and always in the presence of the judicial power.

Article 19. Secrecy of letters and all other forms of free correspondence or communication shall be absolutely inviolable. The guaranties under which the judicial authority shall not be bound by the secrecy for reason of national security or for the purpose of investigating especially serious crimes, shall be specified by law.

Although these provisions obviously aim at limiting government power, recent court decisions have interpreted them as being applicable to individuals who surreptitiously survey other individuals. Articles 57–59 of the Civil Code also have been interpreted to be applicable to privacy through their "protection of the personality" and the "protection of personal life." The courts have said that public figures are entitled to less protection under these statutes.

Swedish law does not explicitly protect privacy. Although by extension the defamation laws try to distinguish between the public interest and public curiosity, the best privacy protection comes from the Code of Conduct for Press, Radio and Television:

Article I. 7. Consider carefully publishing information that can constitute an infringement of privacy. Refrain from such publicity unless an undeniable public interest demands it.

Article I. 8. Observe great caution when publishing about suicide and attempted suicide. Take particularly the relatives and the sacredness of private life into consideration.

Article I. 9. Always show the greatest consideration when dealing with the victims of crimes and accidents. Consider carefully the publishing of names and pictures in such cases.

However, the code provides only few remedies for violations.

In addition to protecting someone's home, correspondence and personal communication means, **Portugal's** privacy protection can be found in the Penal Code, Articles 190–193, which protect the physical, familial and personal privacy of an individual. Illicit surveillance, through any mechanical or personal means, of one's "family or sexual life" is illegal. The only defense is "legitimate public interest and relevance." It is also illegal to create, maintain and utilize computerized information data bases that include a person's "political, religious or philosophical beliefs, party or syndicate affiliation, private life, and ethnic origin." Photographs, video or audio recordings of private matters require consent (Art. 199). Furthermore, the Journalists' Deontological Code, Article 9, says:

The journalist has to respect the private life of the citizens except when the public interest demands the revelation or when the behavior of the person in question is contradictory to the values and principles of the public, which he/she defends.

Right of Reply

Although it exists as a voluntary remedy of press wrongdoing, a government-imposed correction, retraction or right of reply was unanimously rejected in the **United States** by the Supreme Court in *Miami Herald Publishing Co. v. Tornillo* in 1974.[21] In it, the Court said that the First Amendment prohibits interference with the work of editors and, although press responsibility is desirable, it is "not mandated by the Constitution and like many other virtues it cannot be legislated." U.S. broadcasters, however, operate under less freedom because they have to abide by Section 315 of the 1934 Communications Act, which requires licensees to "afford equal opportunities" to all candidates for office if one was permitted "to use the broadcasting station." Although news and documentary programs are excluded, personal attacks and political editorials about candidates require that the station make time available for the candidates concerned to respond (for more details, see Ch. 6).

The European Union has left it up to its member nations to regulate the right of reply, and all of them have chosen to legally provide some form of it for the print media, although some of them make it available to both print and broadcast media. The Union, however, in its 1989 directive on "The Coordination of Certain Provisions Laid Down by Law, Regulation or Administrative Action in Member States Concerning the Pursuit of Television Broadcasting Activities" (89/552/EEC), Article 23, said that "A right of reply or equivalent remedies shall exist in relation to all broadcasters under the jurisdiction of a Member State," if someone's "legitimate interests, in particular reputation and good name, have been damaged by assertion of incorrect facts in a television programme. ..." The directive calls for member states to adopt appropriate means through which to achieve the spirit of the article.

Austria's 1981 Media Act, Article 9, extends the right of reply to all media but grants the media the right to refuse if they think the reply is untrue. If a medium refuses to publish a legitimate reply, the offended person can take it to court, and the medium may be forced to report that a suit has been filed against it or may face daily fines or even confiscation.

In **Belgium** Article 1382 of the Civil Code (applicable to newspapers through decrees of July 20, 1931, and June 23, 1961) says that "Any act of man that causes harm to others obligates him who cause the harm to rectify it." The law also says that a reply must be requested within three months of the publishing of the original article and must be run (free of charge) in the same manner as the original article. The reply may not be longer than 1,000 words or double the length of the offending article. The reply must be used without editing or commentary. A newspaper can refuse to run the article only if it contains material that can cause it legal liability. If a newspaper refuses to run the correction for reasons other than that, it runs the risk of being fined. Opinions and scientific and artistic criticism are excluded from the provisions of the law, and only factual correction within those articles becomes correctable through this law. The Law of March 4, 1972, extends the right of reply to radio and television audiences.

The right of reply is dealt with through the **Finnish** Guidelines of Good Journalistic Practice of the Union of Journalists:

Section 10. Incorrect information must immediately be corrected either on the journalist's own initiative or when requested by the party concerned.

Section 11. Customary political assessment, criticism of the arts or expression of opinion do not ... necessarily carry the right of reply.

Section 12. Corrections and replies are to be published without delay and in such a way that those who have received the original information will be able to notice them easily.

In a very similar manner, **Denmark's** Media Liability Act has authorized the national Press Council to oversee the means of the right of reply. That right is limited to fact correction and to correcting information that has caused financial or other personal damage. The plaintiff must inform the medium of his/her wish to reply within four weeks of publication, and the correction must receive the same treatment as the original story. No editorial commentary is allowed with the correction, but factual information may accompany the reply. Either party can disagree with the process at any point and take the case to the Press Council, which then decides its proper disposition.

The **French** Law of the Press Act of 1881, Article 13, institutionalized the right of reply, and the Act of January 4, 1993, made it available to all those who have been charged and acquitted or whose charges have been dropped. It is a right mainly exercised against newspapers, and only a libelous statement on the broadcast media can result in a request for a correction. The only limitation to the reply is that it cannot include libelous statements either against the author of the original story or against third parties. In addition to the right of reply, Article 13 of the act obligates newspapers to run corrections by public officials who may allege that their performance has been mistakenly reported. In spite of these limitations, these remedies are generally accepted by the media, and there has not been a chilling effect on their work.[22]

All of **Germany's** states have extended the right of reply to anyone who feels unfairly represented in a story. A plaintiff has three months from the time of publication before he/she has to exercise this right. The reply must be no longer than the original article and must address factual information only, not opinions by the writer. The reply must be run without editorial comment except for fact correction and must receive the same treatment as the original—it cannot be run as a "letter to the editor." If a publication refuses to run a reply, it may be ordered by a court to do so.

In **Ireland,** the right of reply or a correction may be found only in the journalists' Code of Ethics:

A journalist shall rectify promptly any harmful inaccuracies, ensure that corrections and apologies receive due prominence and afford the right of reply to persons criticized when the issue is of sufficient importance.

The editor is responsible for deciding if a correction or reply is necessary and what form this might take. In extremely rare broadcasting cases, the Broadcasting Complaints Commission assesses the complaint and decides if a correction or apology is necessary.

A very detailed procedure concerning replies or corrections is stipulated in **Italy's** Law 47 of 1948, Article 8, which forces a publication to run replies when requested by persons who feel that they have been "the object of criticism, of acts damaging to their reputation, or which they consider to be contrary to the truth. ..." A newspaper must run the correction within two days of receipt and place it at the top of the page on the same page where the original article appeared. Non-daily periodicals must run the correction or reply by the second issue after receipt and in the same typeface as the original story. The reply can be no longer than 30 lines. Editors can refuse corrections/replies if they offend their publication or other parties. If the reply or correction has not been run or has not met the guidelines specified, the plaintiff may take his/her case to court. However, the publication is obligated to run the court's decision. Editors prefer to run submitted replies rather than corrections. Broadcast replies are treated in very much the same way by Law 223 of 1990, Article 10. Again, only untrue facts may be challenged. The "Guarantor" judge of the act decides on the suitability of the correction or reply in case of disagreement.[23] Finally, the journalists' Code of Ethics says,

A journalist respects the inviolable people's right to the rectification of incorrect news or news that is wrongly considered prejudicial to people's interests. A journalist makes rectification, therefore, with timeliness and appropriate emphasis, also in case of a lack of specific proof required of all news [items] that, after their wide diffusion, seem to be incorrect or erroneous, especially when the mistakes can damage people, organizations, categories, associations and communities.

In **Luxembourg,** the right of reply is legalized by Article 23 of the Law of 1869, which says that "any person mentioned in a newspaper, whether by name or indirectly, shall have the right to have inserted, free of charge, a reply of double the length of the article. ..." A similar spirit dominates Articles 36–37 of the Law of July 27, 1991, which allows someone a free one-minute reply. Only replies that can cause additional litigation can be refused. Because there is no definition of the type of offense the allegedly offending stories might cause, these laws are considered to be rather oppressive, because theoretically "the right of reply exists even for someone who has been praised."[24]

The Netherlands has no statutorily defined right of reply, but action can be taken against print or broadcast media under Article 6.167 of the Civil Code. This deals with unjust and misleading publications and does provide correction as one of its remedies. Only facts can be corrected, and a court decides the appropriate manner of correction.

Law 2/84 of January 26, 1984, requires all **Spanish** media to run a version of the facts as corrected by a plaintiff, without commentary but with the same prominence as the original story. The publication of a corrected version is not an admission that the original version was incorrect. If a correction is refused, the plaintiff may take his/her case to court.

The **Swedish** right of reply can be found only in the Code of

Conduct for Press, Radio and Television journalists. Article 5 says,

Factual errors are to be corrected when necessary. Anyone with a legitimate reason to reply to a statement has to be given the opportunity to do so. Corrections and replies are to be published in appropriate form without delay in such a way they will be noticed by those who have received the original information.

Much of the Swedish Press ombudsman's work deals with enforcing this code within the larger framework of the Freedom of the Press Act and its provision for defamation and privacy (see previous sections).

In the **United Kingdom**, correction and the right to reply appear only as possible remedies to a defamation action and require the plaintiff's approval. The Journalists' Code of Conduct requires, Article 4, that

A journalist shall rectify promptly any harmful inaccuracies, ensure that correction and apologies receive due prominence and afford the right of reply to persons criticised when the issue is of sufficient importance.

The Press Complaints Commission, through the 1994 Code of Practice, is entrusted with responsibility of enforcing the following:

1. Accuracy
   i) Newspapers and periodicals should take care not to publish inaccurate, misleading or distorted material.
   ii) Whenever it is recognized that a significant inaccuracy, misleading statement or distorted report has been published, it should be corrected promptly and with due prominence.
   iii) An apology should be published whenever appropriate.
2. Opportunity to reply
A fair opportunity for reply to inaccuracies should be given to individuals or organizations when reasonably called for.

The only punitive power of the Press Complaints Commission is that it can publish and disseminate its findings but cannot require the print media to publish them. The Broadcast Complaints Commission, set up by the 1990 Broadcasting Act, on the other hand, does have the power to require broadcasters to publicize its findings, which are mainly about cases that deal with unfair treatment of individuals or invasion of privacy.[25] As is the practice in the United States, letters to the editor are the most common avenue to reply or correction.

The 1995 **Greek** Law on Private Television, Law 2328.12, abiding by the E.U. 1989 directive, guarantees the right of reply to "anyone whose person, personality, honor, dignity, private or family life, professional, social, scientific, artistic, political or other related activity has been insulted" by a radio or television program. The right is also extended to political parties or labor unions "whose views have been amended or silenced in a way that affects negatively the impression of the listener or viewer." The reply can be equal in length to the offending segment, cannot contain legally prohibited material and must be given the same treatment by the station as the offending segment. If the station does not wish to run the reply, it must notify within 24 hours the National Radio-Television Council, which will then decide the case.

The **Portuguese** Press Law, Article 16, guarantees the right of reply by requiring periodicals to "publish any certified letter with a recognizable signature from any one person or entity who feels harmed by the publication." The reply must run free, receive the same treatment as the offending article (placement, typeface, etc.), be no longer than 150 words and appear within the first two issues after the letter has been received or no later than 90 days after receipt, if the publication does not publish daily or weekly. The periodical has a right to comment on the reply but cannot refuse to run it unless it contains illegal material. If the reply is longer than 150 words, then the publication can treat it as an advertisement. The Deontological Code of Journalists, Article 5, says that "The journalist has ... to correct the information proved to be false or inexact." The High Authority of Press and Broadcasting is responsible for enforcing the regulations concerning the right of reply.

Court Coverage

The U.S. Constitution's Sixth Amendment guarantee of a person's right to a speedy and *public* trial, coupled by the media's First Amendment right to report on it, have created a tense relationship between the judiciary and the press. The defendant has a right to a fair trial, the justice system has the responsibility to deliver it and the press has the right and the responsibility to inform its audience about it.

Since there are virtually no restrictions on media in the **United States** about the kind of information they can report about a defendant (his/her history, unconfirmed arrest details, alleged confessions, etc.), the prospects of a fair trial in any community may be jeopardized. The Supreme Court has provided the following guidelines: In the 1966 *Sheppard v. Maxwell*[26] case, the Court said that courts could address sensational media behavior by passing rules ordering trial participants to not talk to the press ("gag" orders), by granting changes of venue or continuances, by either admonishing (instructing it to ignore the publicity) or even sequestering the jury and/or by controlling in-court misconduct of reporters; in the 1976 *Nebraska Press Assn. v. Stuart*[27] case, the Court disallowed all press gag orders except those under "extraordinary circumstances"; in the 1979 case of *Gannett Co., Inc., v. De Pasquale,*[28] the Court allowed under certain circumstances the courtroom closure of pretrial hearings; and in the 1980 case of *Richmond Newspapers v. Virginia,*[29] the Court reaffirmed its commitment (barring extraordinary circumstances) to open courtrooms by declaring that "the right to attend criminal trials is implicit in the guarantees of the First Amendment." Access to trial documents have followed a parallel path to openness, unless there is a "substantial probability" of damaging the defendant's right to a fair trial, and the vast majority of states now allow the unobtrusive presence of cameras in their courtrooms.[30]

In the E.U. countries, court coverage is not so free. In **Austria,** trials and hearings are public except in rare cases when secrecy is essential, especially for the protection of juveniles and public order. No live broadcast transmissions are allowed. Although Article 23 of the 1981 Media Act prohibits the publication of information that might influence a trial's outcome, it allows the publication of confidential information revealed in preliminary hearings, and often excesses occur.

Belgium does not have a specific law protecting the "presumption of innocence," and defamation and privacy laws have traditionally been used to protect the reputation of a defendant who is being "prosecuted but not yet judged."[31] Judicial proceedings are public unless there is good reason to believe that publicity could be detrimental to public order or morality, such as in cases involving minors or marriage dissolutions and children's custodies.

The standards of court reporting are set by the journalists' National Code of Conduct in **Denmark**. Section C of the code says that coverage should present all sides of the case. Stories should not mention "a person's family history, occupation, race, nationality, creed, or membership of organisations ... unless this has something directly to do with the case." During the trial "no information must be published which may obstruct the clearing up of the case, nor must pronouncements to the effect that a suspect or an accused is guilty be published." Only if there is a clear public interest "the names of the persons involved shall be mentioned. A suspect's or an accused's names or other identification should be omitted if no public interest calls for the publication of the name," the code says. "A suspect, accused, or convicted person shall be spared from having attention called to an earlier conviction if it is without importance" to the present case, the code says.

Court reporting in **France** is free, and limitations are imposed only when revelations might injure the rights of the litigants (especially those involving familial issues such as divorce, separation, children's custody, etc., and rape) and in order to protect minors. However, the 1993 Civil Code, Article 9.1, safeguards a person's "presumption of innocence," and if a person "before any sentencing, is presented publicly as being guilty," the court may issue a "rectification or a communiqué in order to put an end to the breach of the presumption."

A continuous free press–fair trial battle is fought in **Germany,** where although video and still cameras are allowed in the courtroom **prior** to the start of the trial, the criminal Code, Article 353.d.3, forbids the verbatim quotation of indictments and other official trial documents.

There is no law in **The Netherlands** controlling what the press may publicize about a trial. Most of the constraints on reporting are either self-imposed or governed by the ECHR's references to protection of family life cases and minors. On rare occasions the police may inform the media but ask them to abide by a *perspauze,* a gag order for a specified period of time. The Press Council suggests that only the initials of an accused, his/her age, hometown and profession may be used. Photos and/or drawings may be used if the person cannot be recognized.

In **Spain** the constitution, Article 120.1, guarantees that judicial proceedings will be public with exceptions provided in instances narrowly defined by the criminal code. Pre-trial motions and evidence are not to be quoted verbatim, but information contained within them may be publicized. Concern about morality and public order are two other reasons that may be used by courts to restrict media access.

In **Sweden** the administration of justice is public, and there are no such legal limitations as gag orders or contempt of court measures. However, the self-restraints of the journalists, as proposed by the Code of Conduct, Article 15, normally call for no identification of the defendants unless an "obvious public interest requires it."

A complicated system of trial reporting exists in the **United Kingdom.** The 1981 Contempt of Court Act, which followed the European Court of Human Rights' decision on the first *Sunday Times* case, says that the overriding principle behind any restriction in court information may be imposed only when publication may create a "substantial risk that the course of justice ... will be seriously impeded or prejudiced." Furthermore, the "strict liability rule" of the act says that "conduct may be treated as contempt of court as tending to interfere with the course of justice in particular legal proceedings regardless of intent to do so." This remains in effect while the case is active in the court system—from the time a suspect has been arrested or charged or a warrant for his/her arrest has been issued to the time the defendant has been sentenced. Controversial cases of high-profile people may be excluded. Trials may be held in secret if they involve national security or if disorder breaks out in the courtroom, if they involve mental patients, family issues and minors. Juvenile hearing may be attended by the press but not the public.[32]

Although public hearings may be reported in the media, there are restrictions on what may be published beyond names, addresses, occupations, ages and charges of the parties involved, unless they agree to more extended coverage.[33] Victims of sexual crimes may not be named, throughout their lifetime, without their consent, unless the court rules that it is in the public interest to divulge the victim's name or unless withholding it will be prejudicial to the defendant. Equally minimal is the coverage allowed on family matters (divorces, custodies, etc.) and crimes by youth (those under 18 years of age). It is an offense to publish information about the evidence and details of jury deliberations. Section 5 of the Contempt of Court Act, however, does allow for a "good-faith" discussion of public issues, thus allowing some legal breathing room for the press to cover serious issues of public importance while the judicial system is assessing the merits of a case. The act is effectively applicable to jury trials where the threat of "prejudice" is more realistic than in cases heard by judges.

Contempt of court legislation, and not the constitution, governs the treatment of the protection of the presumption of innocence in **Ireland,** as well. Lacking contempt specificity, it is the rule of the courts that prevails, and that normally refers to anything that may seriously injure the fairness of a pending trial. For example, the reporting of past criminal records of defendants and information concerning their character or reputation are considered impediments to a fair trial. The 1961 Courts Act allows closed trials to be held in cases involving "a. applications of an urgent nature for relief by way of habeas corpus, bail, prohibition and injunction; b. matrimonial causes and matters; c. lunacy and minor matters; d. proceedings involving the disclosure of a secret manufacturing process."[34]

In **Italy,** the Criminal Code, in Articles 472, 684 and 685, governs what types of information are not suitable to report concerning a trial. Information contained in a preliminary hearing cannot be reported until a trial has been ordered, and then only charges and warrants may be legally reported. The violations of these provisions, apparent in the media daily, are attributed to the pursuit of a "good story" and to the practice that judges themselves pass on the information to journalists.[35]

News Source Protection

Some E.U. countries recognize the legal right of journalists to keep their sources confidential while others rely on the profession's ethical codes to help journalists resist court-imposed questions concerning the origin of their information. But even those countries that do not legally recognize the right to source confidentiality do appreciate the importance of the practice as a valuable news-gathering tool in a democracy. And even those countries that do recognize that legal right also recognize that it has limitations. It is expected that the 1996 European Court of Human

Rights decision of *Goodwin v. the United Kingdom* (see Ch. 2) will help increase the legal weight of that right as well as its popularity among lawmakers so that journalists may be given an even higher degree of freedom to do their work.

In the United States, journalists do not have the right to keep their sources confidential in criminal trials. In the 1972 *Branzburg v. Hayes*[36] case, the Supreme Court said that journalists have the same responsibility as any other citizen to offer evidence to the courts. However, the Court's view was not absolutist, and many states responded by passing "shield" laws that protect journalists' sources. Today two-thirds of the states have such laws, but several journalists annually choose to go to jail rather than reveal their sources.

Robert D. Sack, legal counsel to the Dow Jones Publishing Company, in a brief filed in the Goodwin case on behalf of Dow Jones with the European Commission and the European Court of Human Rights, summarized the status of source confidentiality in the United States and in the United Kingdom this way:

The American system works remarkably well. The privilege to protect a source is seen in most American jurisdictions as qualified, i.e., when a litigant can prove that source disclosure is necessary—'really needed'—a reporter may be required to disclose the source. Yet this exception is almost entirely theoretical. Civil cases in which source disclosure has been required are all but non-existent. Perhaps this is not surprising. Reporters typically know not what they observe but what is told to them. The information they have is almost always not theirs but obtainable elsewhere. The privilege merely requires the litigant to obtain it from elsewhere and not from the reporter, thereby protecting simultaneously the reporter's ability to make and keep his or her pledge and the ability of litigants to obtain justice.

Guarantees of fundamental individual rights, on the other hand, are hollow, indeed, if they consist of no more than judges deciding what, in a particular instance, is 'good,' 'right,' or, in Mr. Goodwin's case, 'in the interests of justice.' That course leaves too much to the subjective judgment of men and too little to predictable rules assuring individual freedom. It gives too much power to the government and too little force to the guarantees of the Convention.[37]

In general, however, journalists in the E.U. countries have more legal protection in keeping their sources confidential, because most countries explicitly recognize that as a journalist's right.

The 1993 **French** Code of Criminal Procedure, Article 109.2, for example, allows journalists to be "free not to disclose" their news sources. Article 56.2 allows for media offices to be searched only if they "do not endanger the free exercise of the profession of journalism and do not obstruct or cause an unjustified delay to the distribution of information."

Austria's Media Act, Article 31, recognizes the right of journalists to keep their sources confidential. The act also prohibits the electronic surveillance of media unless a court orders it as part of the investigation of a crime that carries a minimum imprisonment of 10 years.

In **Germany** the Länder press laws, Sections 13–20 and 24; the Civil Code, Section 383; and the Criminal Code, Section 53, all recognize the right of journalists to refuse to divulge their sources. However, there have been instances when that right was considered by a judge to be subservient to the right of the state to know; for example, that its law enforcement agents were bribed.[38] Furthermore, Section 53 does not protect journalists from having to turn over photographs or film (video, although not specifically mentioned, in practice is also unprotected). Section 97 of the Criminal Code prohibits searches of media offices and shields material that is by law authorized to be kept secret, unless the person who holds it is a suspect in the crime being investigated. In the famous 1962 Spiegel case, the German Federal Constitutional Court in a split 4–4 decision declared the search of the magazine's offices legal because the magazine was suspected of divulging military secrets, which was a violation of the federal treason law. Although in 1965 the court held that the rights of the magazine had not been violated, it said that the charges against the editor, who had remained in prison for more than three months, had to be dropped. Following the public's outrage, the Penal Code was revised in 1968 and allowed more protection for journalists who cover national security issues.

One of the strongest protections of news sources is found in **Sweden**. According to the Freedom of the Press Act, journalists not only have the right to keep their sources confidential, but they may be sued by the news source himself/herself if they reveal his/her name without consent. "In legal proceedings concerning offences against the freedom of the press, the question of the identity of the author or of a person who has communicated information ... may not be raised ...," says the act, Chapter 3.2. Exceptions are the presence of a clear danger to national security (espionage, treason, incitement to crime, etc.) or an overriding private or public interest, such as access to information that would prove the innocence of a defendant or access to evidence police need in their investigation. Although the latter may appear to offer wide latitude to judges, reality has shown that judges exercise that right extremely rarely and only as a last resort when all other sources of the information have been exhausted.

Italian Law 69 of 1963, Article 2, says that "Journalists and publishers must respect professional secrecy pertaining to their sources of information, as required by their confidential character." The idea is also supported by the Journalists' Charter that defines the rights and responsibilities of the profession. The Criminal Code allows some protection to registered journalists to keep sources confidential, but if the judge decides that the information a journalist possesses is instrumental to a case and the journalist is the only person with the ability to shed light, he/she may be forced to reveal the name of his/her source.

According to the Contempt of Court Act of 1981, Section 10, in the **United Kingdom**, a judge may compel a journalist to reveal his/her source only if it is "necessary in the interests of justice or national security or for the prevention of disorder or crime." However, all these grounds can be very nebulous, and journalists have been forced to reveal sources according to judges' interpretations. Furthermore, the 1984 Police and Criminal Evidence Act allows judges to issue search warrants for reporters' property if "there are reasonable grounds for believing ... that a serious arrestable offense has been committed" and that there is material in the premises that would be of "substantial value" to the investigators. However, "journalistic material" acquired for reporting purposes and "held under an 'undertaking, restriction or obligation' of confidence" is excluded. The Goodwin case, which was decided by the European Court of Human Rights in April 1996 (see Media and the European Court of Human Rights, Ch. 2) in favor of a right of source confidentiality, could give British journalists more legal room to resist requests for names of news sources. It is doubtful, however, that Goodwin will have any direct effect on the temporary 1989 Prevention of Terrorism Act, which forces journalists to give the police any information they have if it is to help prevent terrorism or bring a terrorist to justice. The act also provides police with wide powers to question journalists and search their offices.

Denmark's Administration of Justice Act, Article 172, recognizes the right of the journalists to keep their sources confidential but allows the courts to ask journalists to reveal their sources if the issue involves a "serious offense" that may result in a minimum of four years imprisonment. The "seriousness of the crime or ... other special public or private interests" may outweigh "the regard for the protection of the source. ..." A Danish Supreme Court 1993 decision also determined that source protection does not extend to reporters' notes and office files.

Although Article 20.1.d of the **Spanish** constitution makes a clear reference to the need for a statute to govern the issue of source confidentiality, there is no legal defense for journalists who, if required by court, must name their sources. The Statute of the Journalists' Profession, Decree 477 of April 13, 1967, which carries mainly moral weight, says that journalists have a "duty to maintain their professional secrecy" unless the "administration of justice" or the "common good" dictate otherwise.[39]

In **The Netherlands** there is no law that protects journalists from having to divulge their sources if a court so demands, but the Dutch Press Council has added its weight to the argument of those journalists who seek to obtain a legal right to confidentiality. The journalistic community, however, is by no means united on this subject because of its long tradition of independence from any government-sponsored measure concerning the press. The lack of clear guidelines, however, often leads to acrimony, especially when the police ask television reporters for video of situations that might lead to criminal prosecutions, such as hooligans in soccer matches. The journalists union, NVJ, has criticized the police and advised its members to "hand over the material to NVJ instead," which might "perhaps take it out of the country," a test that has never been faced.[40]

Portuguese journalists, as well as their editors, under the 1975 Press Law, Article 5.4, "do not have to reveal their sources of information and they cannot be forced directly or indirectly to break their silence by sanctions." The 1988 Administration of Justice Act, Article 135, also recognizes the right to not reveal sources, but it does allow the Supreme Court to override it if the case involves an insult to the memory of someone who has been dead fewer than 50 years. However, the journalists' Code of Ethics says, in Article 6, that "The journalist must not reveal, not even in the court, his/her confidential sources. ..."

Greek journalists have no legal right to keep their sources confidential, but they rely on the Code of Ethics, Section i, which says that "The observance of professional secrecy and confidentiality of sources of information is considered as the main duty and also a right" of journalists. Similarly, **Irish** journalists rely on the National Union of Journalists' Code of Conduct, Section 7, that says, "A journalist shall protect confidential sources of information." **Luxembourg's** journalists rely on their code that calls on them "to keep secret their sources of information."

1. Dwight L. Teeter, Jr., and Don R. Le Duc, *Law of Mass Communications* (Westbury, N.Y.: The Foundation Press, Inc., 1995), p. 103.

2. Ibid., pp. 108-115.

3. An interesting twist in U.S. media litigation occurred in December 1996, when a Greensboro, N.C., federal jury found in favor of a grocery store chain that had sued ABC's "Prime Time Live" *not* under libel law but under fraud and trespassing law. The Food Lion grocery store chain, a unit of the Belgian Ets Delhaize Freres et Cie "Le Lion" SA, had accused some of the show's reporters and producers of going to work undercover as Food Lion employees and then using hidden cameras to document alleged unsanitary practices at the supermarket for a story broadcast in 1995. [Estes Thompson, "Jury Finds ABC Guilty of Fraud," *The Boston Globe*, Dec. 12, 1996, Section D, p. 1.] The jury awarded the company $1,402 in compensatory damages for wages paid the ABC employees and $5.5 million in punitive damages. [Peter S. Canellos, "ABC Ordered to Pay $5.5 m to Food Lion," *The Boston Globe*, Jan. 23, 1997, Section A, p. 1.] The supermarket company, which did not challenge the veracity of the broadcast, had sought $1.7 billion in damages. [Reuters News Service, "Food Lion Awarded $1,402 in ABC Case," Dec. 30, 1996.] The case was appealed.

4. Tom Crone, *Law and the Media* (Oxford, U.K.: Focal Press, 1995), p. 58.

5. Article XIX, *Press Law and Practice* (London, U.K.: Article XIX, 1993), p. 176.

6. Ibid., p. 177.

7. Marie McGonagle, *A Textbook on Media Law* (Dublin, Ireland: Gill and Macmillan Ltd., 1996), p. 63.

8. Marcel Berlins, "The Republic of Ireland," in Marcel Berlins, Claude Grellier and Helle Nissen Kruuse (Eds.), *Les droits et les devoirs des journalistes dans les douze pays de l'Union Européenne* [The rights and responsibilities of journalists in the twelve countries of the European Union] (Paris, France: Centre de Formation et de Perfectionnement des Journalistes, 1994), p. 135.

9. Article XIX, op. cit., p. 113.

10. Ibid. p. 142.

11. Dirk Voorhoof, "Defamation and Libel Laws in Europe—the Framework of Article 10 of the European Convention of Human Rights," in *Journal of Media Law and Practice*, Vol. 13, No. 4, 1992, p. 260.

12. James H. Ottaway, Jr., and Leonard H. Marks, *Insult Laws: An Insult to Press Freedom* (Reston, Va.: World Press Freedom Committee, 1996), pp. 13-15.

13. Marcel Berlins, "Italy," in Marcel Berlins, Claude Grellier and Helle Nissen Kruuse (Eds.), *Les droits et les devoirs des journalistes dans les douze pays de l'Union Européenne* [The rights and responsibilities of journalists in the twelve countries of the European Union] (Paris, France: Centre de Formation et de Perfectionnement des Journalistes, 1994), p. 151.

14. Evert A. Alkema, "The Protection of the Freedom of Expression in the Constitution and in Civil Law—Netherlands," in *Netherlands Reports to the Thirteenth International Congress of Comparative Law* (The Hague: T.M.C. Asser Instituut, 1990), p. 386.

15. *Whalen v. Roe,* 429 U.S. 589 (1977).

16. Commission of the European Communities, *Europe Without Frontiers,* OJC, 288, 1995.

17. Article XIX, op. cit., p. 87.

18. McGonagle, op. cit., p. 124-5.

19. Claude Grellier, "Spain," in Marcel Berlins, Claude Grellier and Helle Nissen Kruuse (Eds.), *Les droits et les devoirs des journalistes dans les douze pays de l'Union Européenne* [The rights and responsibilities of journalists in the twelve countries of the European Union] (Paris, France: Centre de Formation et de Perfectionnement des Journalistes, 1994), p. 225.

20. Crone, op. cit., p. 209.

21. *Miami Herald Publ. Co. v. Tornillo,* 418 U.S. 241, 94 S. Ct. 2831 (1994).

21. 418 U.S. 241 (1974).

22. Article XIX, op. cit., p. 68.

23. Berlins, "Italy," op. cit., p.156-7.

24. Berlins, "Luxembourg," op. cit., p. 167.

25. XIX, op. cit., p. 177.

26. *Sheppard v. Maxwell,* 384 U.S. 333, 86 S. Ct. 1507 (1996).

27. *Nebraska Press Assn. v. Stuart,* 427 U.S. 539, 96 S. Ct. 2791 (1976).

28. *Gannett Co., Inc. v. De Pasqualle,* 443 U.S. 368, 99 S. Ct. 2898 (1979).

29. *Richmond Newspapers v. Virginia,* 448 U.S. 555, 100 S. Ct. 2814 (1980).

30. Wayne Overbeck and Rick D. Pullen, *Major Principles of Media Law* (Ft. Worth, Texas: Harcourt Brace College Publishers, 1994), pp. 231-236.

31. Claude Grellier, "Belgium," in Marcel Berlins, Claude Grellier and Helle Nissen Kruuse (Eds.), *Les droits and les devoirs des journalistes dans les douze pays de l'Union Européenne* (Paris, France: Centre de Formation et de Perfectionnement des Journalistes, 1994), p. 13.

32. Article XIX, *Press Law and Practice,* op. cit., p.181.

33. Tom Crone, *Law and the Media* (Oxford, England: Focal Press, 1995), pp. 119-126.

34. Marie McGonagle, *A Textbook on Media Law* (Dublin, Ireland: Gill and Macmillan, 1996), p. 183.

35. Berlins, "Italy," op. cit., p. 156.

36. *Brausburg v. Hayes,* 408 U.S. 665, 92 S. Ct. 2646 (1972).

37. Robert D. Sack, *"Goodwin v. United Kingdom*: An American view of protection for journalists' confidential sources under UK and European law," in *Journal of Media Law and Practice,* Vol. 16, No. 3, 1995, p. 93.

38. Article XIX, op. cit., p. 93.

39. Article XIX, ibid., p. 147.

40. Helle Nissen Kruuse, "The Netherlands," in Marcel Berlins, Claude Grellier and Helle Nissen Kruuse (Eds.), *Les droits and les devoirs des journalistes dans les douze pays de l'Union Européenne,* [The rights and responsibilities of journalists in the twelve countries of the European Union] (Paris, France: Centre de Formation et de Perfectionnement des Journalistes, 1994), p. 183.

CHAPTER 4

National Security, Public Order and Morality-Oriented Limitations

National Security and Order

Despite the significant progress made toward a more united or a war-free Europe since World War II and the economic euphoria that the European Union has yielded, European nations still cling very strongly to their national identity, their cultural independence and their national security. The preservation of the latter, in fact, has been used by lawmakers as a justification for the establishment of a series of laws that curb expression and affect the work of the news media.

Normally known as laws of sedition or seditious libel, these laws have a "long and bloody history"[1] and aim at protecting the preservation of the system of government by controlling criticism of the system's authorities, institutions and laws. (The previous chapter discussed the special protections afforded public servants by the various countries' defamation laws.) Much like the practice in the United States, E.U. nations infrequently use these laws and have confined their application to well-prescribed communication acts that advocate the violent overthrow of the government or constitute treason or espionage. Although there are few European examples of the kind of tolerance prevalent and legally available in the United States (from defamation of public officials to tolerance of flag or cross burning and "hate speech" as acts of symbolic expression of intolerance[2]), nations of the European Union, with the concurrence of the European Court of Human Rights, have shown

considerable accommodation toward communication that is critical of the system or the state, and there are clear signs in most
countries that the trend will continue in that direction.

Even **Sweden,** one of the countries most sensitive to press and
expression, through its Constitutional Freedom of the Press Act,
Chapter 7.4, punishes expression deliberately aiming at bringing
Sweden "under the subjection of a foreign power by violent or
other unlawful means. ...."; "instigation of war. ...."; "dissemination
of rumours endangering the security of the Realm, ... when the
country is at war. ... "

In **France,** in addition to protecting the reputation of public
servants mentioned in the previous chapter, the 1881 Act, Article
30, criminalizes libel against the judicial system, the armed forces
and the public administration of the State. Law of July 28, 1894,
forbids the publication of information concerning "anarchist
plots" that may endanger public order. Much of the communica-
tion-related provisions are found in the treason and espionage
statutes, which are rarely applied to the press. Article 74–76 prohibit secret defense information from being disseminated to those
unauthorized to receive it. These are similar to the protections provided by the **Spanish** Penal Code, Articles 147 (on the "Head of
State"), 242 (on the "Armed Forces") and 161 (on the royal, judicial
and legislative organs of the State). However, a Constitutional
Court in 1989 reversed a previous decision and ruled that "national security" is not necessarily threatened by criticism of state
institutions and that the "reputation of public institutions constituted a weaker limitation on freedom of speech or information
than the honor or privacy of individuals."[3]

Several sections of **Germany's** Criminal Code, as empowered
by the constitution, Article 18, which punishes those who would
use freedom of the press "to combat the free democratic basic order," penalize insults against the constitution and agencies of the
State, Section 84; the Republic, its legislative and judicial organs
and its symbols, Section 90; and those advocating disturbance of
"public order," Section 123. Related Article 21.2 of the constitution
declares as "unconstitutional" those political parties whose behavior and goals are to "impair or abolish the free democratic basic order or to endanger the existence of the Republic of Germany." Finally, Article 5.3 of the constitution, which guarantees freedom of

"art, science, research and teaching" does not recognize the teachers' right to be disloyal to the constitution. The constitution requires that all these *content-based limitations* be enforced only "with the approval of the Federal Constitutional Court."[4]

In the **United Kingdom,** the law of seditious libel is still in effect, although it has not been used against the media for many years. The law basically aims at preventing expression that could endanger the government and those in authority by bringing them into disrepute and causing a subversion of the existing order. National security information is governed by the 1911 Official Secrets Act, Section 1, which safeguards the "safety or interests of the State." The act, and its 1989 amended version (Sect. 2 of the original act), mainly deal with state documents and secrets and will be discussed in Chapter 5.

The **Irish** Constitution, Article 40.6.1, says that "the State shall endeavour to ensure ... " the protection of press freedom as long as it is not used in order to "undermine public order, or morality or the authority of the State." The most relevant statutory extensions of the constitution are the "Offenses Against the State Act 1939," which specifically prohibits expression that undermines state authority and questions the legitimacy of the government or the armed forces, and the "Broadcasting Authority (Amendment) Act 1976," which allows government to prohibit the dissemination of anything that "would be likely to promote, or incite to, crime or would tend to undermine the authority of the State. ... " It is generally accepted that this act was devised primarily in order to control reporting on "the troubles" in Northern Ireland.

The **Italian** Penal Code, through Articles 290–292, forbids defamatory statements against "the Republic," the "Constitutional Institutions," the "Armed Forces," the "Italian Nation" and the "National Flag and any other State Emblem." Similarly, in addition to its treason and espionage articles, the **Austrian** Penal Code, Article 248, specifically punishes insults against the Austrian state and its symbols.

Belgium's Penal Code, Article 123, forbids acts that threaten to violate the country's "external security." The Law of July 20, 1831, punishes anyone who "maliciously and publicly attacks the obligatory force of the law or directly incites to its violation," and the Law of March 25, 1891, Article 1, prohibits the "public incitement to criminal acts through writings, printings, images, emblems and posters distributed free or for sale." Finally, in war time, it is prohibited to disseminate information concerning the morale and condition of the armed forces.

Similarly, **Greece's** Constitution, Article 14.3.c, forbids dissemination of information concerning the

> ... composition, equipment and set-up of the armed forces or the fortifications of the country, or [that] which aims at the violent overthrow of the regime or is directed against the territorial integrity of the state.

In addition to the Espionage Act of 1936, which forbids the "publication of any military information without prior written approval of the appropriate military authority," the Penal Code, Articles 184 and 186, punish "the public incitement to the commission of crime," and Article 185 forbids the "public praise of a crime." Furthermore, Article 181 of the Penal Code forbids the public show of "insult, hate or contempt through removal, damage or defacement" of the "official national flag or symbol of the sovereignty of the state," and Article 183 forbids the public incitement to violation of "statutes or ordinances or other lawful orders of authorities." The notorious anti-terrorism law 1916/1990, facetiously known as "tromonomos," or terror law, which (Art. 6) prohibited media from publicizing "any kind of statements" of a terrorist group, was so badly received nationally and internationally that it was eventually withdrawn in 1993.

More troublesome and controversial, however, are the Greek Penal Code's Articles 191–192, which criminalize the dissemination of "false information or rumors which may cause uneasiness or fear in the citizens or undermine public confidence in the state authority. ... , in the armed forces, ... the national monetary system, ... or international relations" (Art. 191). Article 192 punishes anyone who incites "citizens to commit acts of violence ... or to disturb the peace through disharmony among them. ... " Although these articles are rarely applied to the press, their presence is a cause for continuous concern among Greek journalists.

The **Portuguese** Penal Code, Article 316, punishes anyone who might "endanger the interests of the Portuguese State relative to its national independence and unity, the State integrity and internal and external security" by transmitting information to another person not authorized to receive it. Article 326 also makes it illegal to incite Portuguese citizens or the military or security forces to civil war or violent acts. Article 330 goes even further by criminalizing the "revelation of false news or news with the intent to provoke alarm or disquiet among the populace," the provocation of division among the members of the armed and security forces or the "incitement to violent political confrontation." Article 332 prohibits the insult, through words, gestures, writings and any other forms of expression, of the Portuguese State, flag, national emblems and national anthem.

Obscenity and Insult to Public Morals

In spite of their reputation as morally "liberal," the nations of the European Union have faced problems similar to those of the United States when it comes to defining and controlling sexually explicit material. Litigation has shown that, with the concurrence of the European Court of Human Rights, the major divergence from the United States is that the European trend toward increased tolerance of sexually explicit expression is accompanied by considerably less tolerance toward violence. Furthermore, it is important to note that although these subjects are dealt with by E.U. nations individually, there are some Europe-wide statements that specifically address pornography and violence. The European Union's 1989 directive on "The Coordination of Certain Provisions. ... Concerning the Pursuit of Television Broadcasting Activities" says, Article 22, that member states should take appropriate regulatory steps to prohibit programs that "might seriously impair the physical, mental or moral development of minors, in particular those that involve pornography and violence." Furthermore, Article 7 of the Council of Europe's Convention on Transfrontier Broadcasting says,

All items of programming services, as concerns their presentation and content, shall respect the dignity of the human being and the fundamental rights of others. In particular, they shall not: (a) be indecent and in particular contain pornography; (b) give undue prominence to violence or be likely to incite racial hatred.

There is considerable discussion on pornography as a violator of the human rights and dignity of women and children as evidenced by the positions taken by two pan-European conferences: the 1993 Third European Ministerial Conference on Equality Between Women and Men, which criticized the emergence of European networks of "traffic in women" and the production and distribution of "violent, brutal or pornographic products" exploiting women, and the 1993 Vienna Conference on Human Rights, which condemned "gender violence" and the sexual exploitation of children.

A significant consensus on child pornography was reached on Nov. 28, 1996, in Brussels by the E.U. member states' Justice Ministers, who agreed on a definition of sexual exploitation of children, austere punishment for convicted pedophiles and criminalization of production and distribution of child pornography (mere possession of it failed to become a crime because of objections by the Dutch). The issue was placed on the commission's agenda by Commissioner Christos Papoutsis, responsible for tourism, who was motivated by the transportation of children and women across borders to be sexually exploited.[5] In a little-noticed recommendation a month earlier, the commission had produced a communication addressed to the council, the parliament, the Economic and Social Committee and the Committee of the Regions, which addressed "illegal and harmful content" on the Internet. In its recommendation, the commission described potential and present "illegal" and "harmful" messages on the Internet and took the clear position that "all these activities fall under the existing legal framework." Thus, cybercommunications, the commission said, do not

exist in a legal vacuum, since all those involved (authors, content providers, host service providers who actually store the documents and make them available, network operators, access providers and end users) are subject to the respective laws of the Member States.[6]

The commission's communication was careful to differentiate between categories of recipients (adults vs. children) and between "illegal" and "harmful" content accessible to those receiving publics. The commission, however, did not elaborate on how to keep the balance between its commitment to free expression and the prohibition of a "harmful" expression, which, it said, may be a "content expressing political opinions, religious beliefs or views on racial matters," and, the communication admitted, "depends on cultural differences." Thus the definition of harmfulness was left up to the member states.[7]

However, a considerable amount of public impatience and ire were raised in 1996 when a Belgian pedophile ring was believed to be implicated in the murders of at least four girls. Those wishing serious action both at the national and Union levels took to the streets and lobbied their representatives for some controls over the freedom to communicate "harmful" material. The argument was not new, but it had gained momentum. A good summary of its key sentiments is given by Catherine Itzin, an inspector of the British Department of Health and researcher in the Violence Abuse and Gender Relations Research Unit of the University of Bradford:

There are certain freedoms that people have agreed to forgo because of the damage and harm they do to other people. These include the freedom to steal, to assault, to rape, to murder, and in the U.K. to incite to racial hatred and race discrimination and to discriminate in employment on the grounds of race or sex. The freedom to incite sexual hatred, sexual violence and sex discrimination through pornography is another freedom people should arguably agree to forgo in order to ensure and safeguard the civil liberties and human rights of women. Adoption of a civil approach to pornography would enhance women's chances for greater freedom and safety from personal harm. The rights of women to be free of the mistreatment of pornography is arguably a fundamental human right with the potential for being addressed as such in European law.[8]

Since these arguments have not gained enough recognition to be formally "addressed as such in European law," the prevailing methods of dealing with pornography are not unlike those used in the United States. The concept of the "average person applying contemporary community standards," for example, and the assessment of the work's "literary, artistic, political, or scientific value" used in the United States since *Miller v. California* in 1973, are very similar to the measurements used by Europeans to evaluate the merits of contested messages, with the results being similar to those obtained in the United States—uncertain. On the other hand, restrictions in Europe on material that depicts sexual violence and on the sale of pornographic material to minors are common.

The law closest to the American practice is that of the **United**

Kingdom's Obscene Publications Act 1959, amended in 1964. It defines as obscene an article (in written, visual or audio form)

if its effect or (where the article comprises two or more distinct items) the effect of any of its items, if taken as a whole, such as to tend to deprave and corrupt persons who are likely, having regard to all relevant circumstances, to read, see or hear the matter contained or embodied in it.

The act allows as defense proof that the distributor of the contested communication "had not examined the article ... and had no reasonable cause to suspect" that it would be obscene and a communication that is "for the public good, on the ground that it is in the interests of science, literature, art, or learning, or other objects of general concern." The 1978 Protection of Children Act forbids the taking, showing, publishing or distribution of "indecent photographs of children" under the age of 16.

The **Irish** Censorship of Publications Act 1929 (amended in 1946), Section 2, defines as "indecent" anything that may be "suggestive of or inciting to sexual immorality or unnatural vice or likely in any other similar way to corrupt or deprave." Also in effect in Ireland are the Censorship of Films Act 1923; the Defamation Act 1961, which forbids defamation that attributes obscene acts to an individual; the Radio and Television Act 1988, which safeguards "good taste or decency"; and the Video Recordings Act 1989, which allows the censorship of videos that contain "obscene or indecent matter" or "acts of gross violence or cruelty ... toward humans or animals."

Austria's Criminal Code, Articles 218–220, outlaws the publication of certain kinds of pornography and other materials that offend public morality. In **The Netherlands,** Article 240 of the Criminal Code outlaws "pictures or items that offend public morality." Article 240.A forbids publication of material that "can be considered damaging to persons younger than 16." Article 240.B forbids the manufacturing and distribution of material "containing sexual activities by someone younger than 16."

In **France,** the interior minister, through the Act of 1949, Article 2, may restrict sale to minors of publications that include

... any illustration, account, chronicle, rubrique or insertion showing gangsterism, lying, rape, laziness, cowardice, hatred, debauchery in a positive light; nor any criminal acts or offensive acts; nor any acts conceivable as detrimental to children's or youth's morals or as inspiring or perpetuating ethnic prejudices.

Furthermore, obscenity, although not defined, can be prosecuted under Article 283 of the Penal Code.

In **Germany,** Article 5 of the Basic Law recognizes that freedom of expression may be limited by "the provisions of laws for the protection of youth," and Article 184 of the Criminal Code forbids the dissemination of material that depicts "violence, abuse of children, or sexual activity with children." Stores accessible to minors cannot sell such material, and the post office will not deliver it. Material of a nature different from the above may be distributed but not to those younger than 18. Each German state is responsible for determining "whether a particular publication would be banned under either the law to protect youth or the law to protect public decency."[9]

The **Spanish** Constitution, Article 20.4, recognizes press freedom limitations if they are intended to "protect youth and children." As a result, the Criminal Code, Article 432, forbids the distribution of "pornographic material to people under 16 or mentally handicapped."

The **Swedish** Freedom of the Press Act, Chapter 7.4, punishes

12. criminal acts of child pornography, whereby a person portrays a child in a pornographic picture with the intent that the picture be disseminated. ... ;

13. unlawful representations of violence, whereby a person depicts sexual violence pictorial with the intent that the pictures be disseminated. ...

The **Belgian** Penal Code, Articles 383–386, addresses indecent behavior, offenses against public morality and the restriction of obscene publications.

Greece's obscenity laws are confined to Legislative Order 5060/1931, which forbids anything that "according to public sentiment insults decency." Another law that has been applied to mass media is Article 353 of the Penal Code, which punishes anyone "who knowingly insults the morals of another by performing an obscene act in his presence." Along with the provisions of the 1989 E.U. law on broadcasting, the 1995 Law on Private Television, Article 14, prohibits programs that "may seriously harm the physical, mental or moral growth of adolescents, and especially programs that contain pornographic images or acts of needless violence or depict in their news programs unnecessary physical violence. ... " Programs that may cause "... less than serious harm" may start being presented after 9:30 p.m.

In **Italy** obscene publications are dealt with in Articles 528–529 of the Penal Code and in Article 725 that controls the sale of materials "contrary to public decency."

In **Portugal,** the 1990 Complementary Law on Television, Article 17, forbids the showing of programs that are pornographic or likely to incite "violence, criminal behavior, or generally cause behavior that may violate the rights, liberties and fundamental guarantees" or may "have a negative influence on the formation of the personality of children or adolescents or other vulnerable members of the audience. ... "

Blasphemy and Racism

Another significant difference between the historical, cultural and legal traditions of the E.U. countries and the United States is evidenced by the legal treatment afforded religion and race or ethnicity. In the United States even "hateful speech" has been ruled protected by the First Amendment and only in very special circumstances (especially when it involves "substantial privacy interests" or "imminent incitement" to unlawful conduct) may it be controlled.[10] The role of *religion* in the civic life of most European nations, however, is considerably larger, and most nations have either a formally declared state religion or one that clearly predominates. In either case, religion is a concept that has attracted legal attention through control of blasphemy.

On the issue of *racism*, the most pertinent international statement on discrimination is found in the United Nations 1965 International Convention on the Elimination of All Forms of Racial Discrimination, which has been ratified by almost all the E.U. member states. It requires, in Article 4, that signatories

... condemn all propaganda and all organizations which are based on ideas or theories of superiority of one race or group of persons of one colour or ethnic origin, or which attempt to justify or promote racial hatred and discrimination in any form, and undertake to adopt immediate and positive measures designed to eradicate all incitement to, or acts of, such discrimination. ...

The article also asks that signatories take legal measures to punish discrimination, dissemination of racially hateful ideas and acts of violence against racially identifiable or ethnic groups. The 1989 E.U. directive on "The Coordination on Certain Provisions. ... Concerning the Pursuit of Television Broadcasting Activities" asks member nations to "ensure that broadcasts do not contain any incitement to hatred on grounds of race, sex, religion or nationality."

Furthermore, the outbursts of racism in several parts of Europe in the early 1990s and the press's failure to play a catalytic role in this dilemma[11] prompted the 1993 Council of Europe Summit in its Vienna Declaration to recommend that the media help create a "cohesive but yet diverse Europe" by respecting the rights and cultural heritage of "national minorities" and by fighting against "all ideologies, policies and practices constituting an incitement to racial hatred, violence and discrimination. ... " Similarly, the 1994 European Ministerial Conference on Mass Media Policy in Prague approved a Declaration on Media in Democratic Society, which called on the media and the Council of Europe member governments to find ways through which to combat "all forms of expression which incite to racial hatred, xenophobia, antisemitism and all forms of intolerance, since they undermine democratic security, cultural cohesion and pluralism."[12]

Article 188 of the **Austrian** Penal Code is typical of a blasphemy law:

Whoever, in circumstances where his behaviour is likely to arouse justified indignation, disparages or insults a person who, or an object which, is an object of veneration of a church or religious community established within the country, or a dogma, a lawful custom or a lawful institution of such a church or religious community, shall be liable to a prison sentence of up to six months or a fine of up to 360 daily rates.

Articles 218–220 and 283 prohibit hostile acts against any ethnic group as well as the dissemination of Nazi propaganda.

Germany protects the religious and racial sensitivities of its citizens through Article 3 of the Basic Law, which guarantees that "No one may be prejudiced or favoured because of his sex, his parentage, his race, his language, his homeland and origin, his faith, or his religious or political opinions"; Article 33, which guarantees the "enjoyment of civil and political rights" to all Germans "independent of religious denomination ... or ideology"; Article 166 of the Criminal Code, which prohibits the public dissemination of messages insulting people's beliefs; and Articles 130–131 of the Penal Code, which protect racial groups against violence, discrimination and defamation. Article 139 protects the prohibition of apology or praise of Nazism, which was enacted as the law for the Liberation of the German People from National Socialism and Militarism after World War II. Furthermore, Article 12 of the Press Council's Publicity Principles says that

> There must be no discrimination against anyone on grounds of sex, race, ethnic background, religion, social group or nationality. In crime reports, the fact that a suspect or offender belongs to a particular religious, ethnic or other minority should only be mentioned if the information is important for understanding the reported events.

Although there is no blasphemy law in **France**, the anti-discrimination statutes are encompassing enough to punish acts of racism. The Act of July 1, 1972, outlaws publications that "provoke discrimination, hate and violence against persons or groups because of their origin, race, ethnic group or nationality." Penal Code Articles 187 and 416 punish discriminatory acts against a religious, racial or "ethnic group or nation," and the Law of July 13, 1990, forbids the public questioning of the Nazi crimes against humanity and the public praise of fascism.

The Criminal Code of **Denmark**, Article 140, punishes anyone who "exposes to ridicule or insults the dogmas or worship of any lawfully existing religious community. ... " On racist communications, Article 266.b of the Code says:

> Any person who, publicly or with the intention of disseminating it to a wider circle of people, makes a statement, or other communication, threatening, insulting or degrading a group of persons on account of their race, colour, national or ethnic origin or belief shall be liable to a fine or to a simple detention or to imprisonment for a term not exceeding two years.

In **The Netherlands**, Article 1 of the constitution outlaws discrimination based on "religion, belief, political opinion, race or sex or on any other grounds." Article 137 of the Penal Code prohibits "public insults" and the "incitement to hatred" based on "racial, religious, gender and sexual preference discrimination," although it makes allowances for "factual information," as seen in the case of defamation. Article 147 prohibits public blasphemy against any religion.

Sweden's Freedom of the Press Act, Chapter 7.4.11, outlaws

Persecution of a population group, whereby a person threatens or expresses contempt for a population group or other such group with allusion to its race, skin colour, national or ethnic origin, or religious faith.

The journalists' code of conduct also advises its members to "not emphasize the race, sex, nationality, profession, political affiliation or religious views if it is irrelevant to the story or causes disrespect to some groups of people."

In the **United Kingdom**, the 1976 Race Relations Act amended the 1936 Public Order Act by defining "racial hatred" as "hatred against a group of persons in Great Britain defined by reference to colour, race, nationality (including citizenship) or ethnic or national origin." It also added Section 5A, which says that a person commits an offense if he publishes and distributes, displays or uses in a public performance, in a recording, in a broadcast program, in a public meeting or in a procession, material that is "threatening, abusive or insulting" and through which

(a) he intends thereby to stir up racial hatred or
(b) having regard to all the circumstances racial hatred is likely to be stirred up thereby.

In the United Kingdom, blasphemy, although originally aimed at protecting Christianity and the Bible, today is interpreted to provide protection from insult to the Anglican Church. Specifically, a publication is considered blasphemous (Art. 214 of Stephen's Digest of the Criminal Law) if it "contains any contemptuous, reviling, scurrilous or ludicrous matter relating to God, Jesus Christ or the bible, or the formularies of the Church of England as established by law. It is not blasphemous to speak or publish opinions hostile to the Christian religion, or to deny the existence of God, if the publication is couched in decent and temperate language." The law is considered so anachronistic, however, that "the Law Commission and high ranking members of the Anglican

Church have recommended the abolition of the offense."[13]

Similarly protective of the Christian religion is **Irish** law, which does not statutorily define "blasphemy," but does control offensive language through the 1994 Criminal Justice (Public Order) Act. Other references to blasphemy can be found in the Censorship of Films Act of 1923 and the Defamation Act of 1961. Just as in the United Kingdom, the Irish Law Reform Commission has said that "blasphemous libel" is incompatible with a nation that respects freedom of speech, although the Irish Constitution, Article 40.6. 1, clearly considers "the publication or utterance of blasphemous, seditious, or indecent matter" punishable offenses.

The constitution of **Greece**, in Article 14.2.a, prohibits the "insult of Christian and any other known religion." The Penal Code, in Arts. 198–200, punishes those who "publicly and maliciously and by any means blaspheme God," those who "publicly manifest a lack of respect for the divinity," those who "publicly and maliciously and by any means blaspheme the Greek Orthodox Church or any other religion permitted in Greece ... ," those who "maliciously attempt to obstruct or intentionally disrupt a religious assembly or service or ceremony permitted under the Constitution ... ," and those who "commit blasphemous, improper acts in a church or in a place devoted to a religious assembly permitted under the Constitution. ... " The only legal measure that might be applicable to addressing racism is Article 192 of the Penal Code, which punishes those who "publicly and by any means cause or incite citizens to commit acts of violence upon each other or to disturb the peace through disharmony among them. ... " The 1995 Law on Private Television, Article 14, outlaws programs that might "encourage hatred based on race, gender, religion or nationality."

The **Spanish** Constitution, Article 16, guarantees freedom of "ideology, religion and worship" without any limits other than those "necessary in order to maintain the public order protected by law." A Spaniard "may not be compelled to make declarations regarding his religion, beliefs or ideologies." "There shall be no state religion," but the authorities shall take into consideration the religious feelings of the Spanish people and "maintain the consequent relations of cooperation with the Catholic Church and the other faiths."

Italy's Penal Code, Article 402, punishes "defamation of the State religion" and Article 406 punishes insults against other religions that are "recognized by the State." Also Italy's Charter of Journalists' Duties says that "A journalist has to respect people ... and never discriminate against anyone because of his race, his religion, his sex, his mental and physical condition, his political views."

In **Finland,** the Penal Code, Section 13.5, punishes by up to two years in prison anyone who "spreads among the public statements or other information in which a population group of defined race, colour, nationality, ethnic origin or religious affiliation is threatened, abused or affronted. ... "

In **Belgium,** a country deeply divided along ethnic, cultural and linguistic lines, the Constitution, Article 11, says that

Enjoyment of the rights and freedoms recognized for Belgians should be ensured without discrimination. To this end, laws and decrees guarantee notably the rights and freedoms of ideological and philosophical minorities.

The Law of July 30, 1981, as amended in 1993, punishes those who, in a public way, disseminate information that may "incite to discrimination, hate or violence against a person because of the person's race, color, ancestry, national origin or ethnicity." Furthermore, the Law of March 23, 1995, Article 1, punishes anyone who "denies, minimizes, offers justification to or approves of the genocide committed by the nationalist-socialist regime of Germany during the second world war."

1. Dwight L. Teeter, Jr., and Don R. Le Duc, *Law of Mass Communications* (Westbury, N.Y.: The Foundation Press, Inc., 1995), p. 22.

2. See *R.A.V. v. City of St. Paul,* 112 S. Ct. 2593 and discussion on this and other cases in Wayne Overbeck and Rick D. Pullen, *Major Principles of Media Law* (Fort Worth, Tex.: Harcourt Brace College Publishers, 1994), pp. 63-68.

3. Article XIX, *Press Law and Practice* (London, U.K.: Article XIX, 1993), p. 142.

4. Donald P. Kommers, *The Constitutional Jurisprudence of the Federal Republic of Germany* (Durham, N.C.: Duke University Press, 1989), pp. 375-377.

5. Commission of the European Communities, "Proposals for Action Against Sex Tourism," Ref. IP/96/1093, Nov. 27, 1996, p. 1.

6. Commission of the European Communities, *Communication to the Council, the European Parliament, the Economic and Social Committee and the Committee of the Regions,* COM(96) 487, Oct. 16, 1996, pp. 10-12.

7. Ibid, p. 11.

8. Catherine Itzin, "Pornography, harm and human rights—the European context," *Journal of Media Law and Practice,* Vol. 16, No. 3, 1995, p. 113.

9. Article XIX, op. cit., p. 95.

10. See *Cohen v. California,* 403 U. S. 15, 21 (1971), *Brandenburg v. Ohio,* 395 U. S. 444, 447 (1969), *R.A.V. v. City of St. Paul,* 112 S. Ct. 2538 (1992).

11. Teun A. van Dijk, *Racism and the Press* (London, U.K.: Routledge, 1991), pp. 244-245. Although van Dijk found the coverage of minorities and race issues to be "less blatantly racist," he still considered the press's role in this crucial social issue to be highly inappropriate and unhelpful.

12. Council of Europe, *European Ministerial Conferences on mass media policy: Texts adopted* (Strasbourg, France: Directorate of Human Rights, 1995), p. 43.

13. Article XIX, op.cit., p. 191.

Secrecy and Access to Information

The E.U. nations have different historical, cultural and legal traditions from the United States, as described in the last chapter's discussion on the special protections afforded public authorities and national leaders. Through a completely different interpretation of the worth and role of government and those who run it (from heads of state to simple bureaucrats or public servants), European law systems extend their considerable individual protections more generously to those who govern them. In fact, unlike the U.S. constitutional tradition, which aims primarily at limiting the power of government, the European view seems to be that the government is more than the guarantor and protector of the citizens' rights enumerated in each country's legal documents; it is a partner in the citizens' pursuit of happiness. In other words, government, as a representative of the public at large, is seen as a benign vehicle through which citizens get things accomplished, progress and receive life-long protection from life's hazards.

Protecting government information, therefore, is a natural outgrowth of that philosophy, and Europeans, including journalists, do not seem to have the same kind of mistrust of government that is prevalent among journalists in the United States. With notable exceptions, mainly among journalists in the United Kingdom, instead of doubting the word of government as American journalists instinctively do, European journalists are much slower to question government officials. The appreciation and culture of government allow it a considerable amount of *legal* freedom to control its activities and protect its information. As many European reporters were saying in the 1970s, the journalistic feats of the Pentagon Papers and Watergate could not have happened in any of the European democracies.

Another reason that contributes to the preservation of a high degree of government secretiveness is the attitude of egalitarianism that dominates most European governments; this requires the appearance of consent, and that is better manufactured under tight information controls.

In the United States, on the other hand, there are several well-defined areas of legally allowed governmental sources, but even those can be trespassed, with the blessing of the courts, if the press can prove that its motives were noble, as it did in the cases of the Pentagon Papers and Watergate. In fact, instead of a dreaded sign of systemic weakness, media coverage of embarrassing, incompetent or illegal activities by those in power are considered a sign of strength for American democracy as it manages time and again to accommodate these press-government adversarial relationships, withstand the resultant civic anomalies and benefit from them.

Prior restraint was outlawed by the U.S. Supreme Court in *Near v. Minnesota* in 1931,[1] and the only remedy for those the media offend, including the government, remains punishment after publication. Usually, because of the press's function as the servant of a general public interest, government in the United States has a much harder time winning a case against the press than do individuals, especially individuals who are not in the public eye.

The U.S. Freedom of Information Act and the Government in the Sunshine Act provide a detailed system of access to government documents and meetings respectively. The burden is on government to make a legally defensible case when it refuses to comply with a citizen's request for access. Exceptions generally fall into the following categories: information that is specifically authorized to be kept secret, especially on matters of national defense and foreign policy; internal personnel matters; matters specifically authorized by law to be kept confidential; trade secrets, financial and commercial information; inter-agency and intra-agency memoranda on policy issues; personnel records, such as medical files; law enforcement files; matters of financial institutions; and geological and geophysical information.

The idea of more openness and more government accessibility

is a relative recent phenomenon in Europe. Sweden, Austria and The Netherlands were among the few European nations that had a constitutionally or statutorily mandated government obligation to openness prior to the ratification problems faced by the 1991 Treaty of Maastricht. Its initial defeat in Denmark and the narrow approval in France pointed out the large gap that existed between European citizens and those who govern them, especially the Eurocrats in Brussels. The difficulty the treaty encountered in getting public approval was directly attributed to the lack of information citizens had about the treaty in particular and the proposed European Union in general.[2] It was then that the concept of *transparency,* the European Union's Freedom of Information Act equivalent, took hold in the Brussels Commission and the governments of the member states.

E.U. Regulations on Access

The first attempt by the European Union, originally the European Economic Community, to codify its methods of releasing information was made in the Treaty Establishing the European Atomic Energy Community (Euratom), which decreed, Article 24, that because disclosure of the information "the Community acquires as a result of carrying out its research programme ... is liable to harm the defence interests of one or more Member States," a time- and-grade-based information classification system had to be devised to protect the individual and collective interests of all concerned. Article 25 required that all communications be "subject to the consent of the State of origin," and that consent may be withheld "only for defence reasons."

In 1958 Euratom came up with a system very reminiscent of that prevailing in the United States. It instituted the following classifications: Eura-Top Secret, Eura-Secret, Eura-Confidential and Eura-Restricted. There are specific time intervals and authorization checkpoints attached to each but no penalties for unauthorized disclosures.

The second major E.U. attempt to deal systematically with information dissemination came in the 1990 Council Directive on the Freedom of Access to Information on the Environment, which aimed at ensuring access to information "held by public authorities and to set out the basic terms and conditions on which such information should be made available." At the heart of that directive was the idea that authorities should make environmental information available to anyone without inquiring about that person's reasons to know. The directive also requires a public agency to respond within 30 days and to make a legally acceptable case if it refuses to give the information. The legally acceptable justifications for secrecy are the security of the public, national defense and foreign relations, legal or disciplinary investigations, expected increased environmental damage and volunteer testimony by a third party.

The Union, however, did not start to focus on its information policies until the Treaty of Maastricht began to face serious questions both before and after its signing in December 1991 and February 1992. Criticism came from within and outside the Union. Commissioner João de Deus Pinheiro, in a stinging review of the commission's performance on communication issues, said that the "importance of information and communication is not generally appreciated within the Commission," which "lacks a coordinated overall strategy to communicate its political objectives ... " and allows its policies to create "a quantitative surfeit of information but often of insufficient quality." More typical, however, was the sentiment expressed by Veerle Deckmyn, publications director of the European Institute for Public Administration:

It is no longer possible for European unification to be a matter for a small political elite as was formerly the case; from now on it has also to be a matter for the European citizens.[3]

Indeed, the 1991 Maastricht Summit yielded a declaration, which was not part of the treaty but did recognize the need for a change:

The Conference considers that transparency of the decision-making process strengthens the democratic nature of the institutions and the public's confidence in the administration. The Conference accordingly recommends that the Commission submit to the Council no later than 1993 a report on measures designed to improve public access to the information available to the institutions.[4]

In May and June 1993, the commission submitted recommendations that included the following:

1. the recognition that "improved access to information will be a means of bringing the public closer to the Community institutions";

2. the recognition that, in addition to the authorities making information available to the citizens, there had to be a method through which citizens may request information from the authorities;

3. a plan through which more "papers" become more widely distributed to assess reaction from concerned groups and individuals;

4. a plan through which the working documents of the commission and the secretariat-general will become more available;

5. a plan through which refusal to give a document to a member of the public is based on grounds of "personal privacy," "industrial or financial confidentiality," "public security including international relations and monetary stability" and "information passed to the institutions in confidence."[5]

In February 1994, the commission approved the proposals with minor modifications and gave the European Union its first comprehensive system of access to its records. The decision provides, among other measures:

Article 1, that applicants must submit their requests "in writing to the relevant Commission department at its headquarters, Commission Offices in the Member States or Commission Delegations in non-member countries";

Article 2, that an officer specially appointed by the department to handle such requests "shall inform the applicant in writing, within one month" of the status of his/her application. If it is refused, the applicant has a month in which to appeal to the commission's secretary-general;

Article 3, that the commission president, the secretary-general and other "relevant" commissioners may review and assess the application.

Other articles describe the fees involved and the facilities and methods where such access could be physically handled.[6]

An annex to the decision defined *document* as any "written text, whatever its medium, which contains existing data and is held by the Commission or the Council." Accessed documents may be required not to be reproduced or circulated for profit without prior authorization. As feared, however, the exceptions to openness multiplied:

The Institutions will refuse access to any document where disclosure would undermine:
—the protection of the public interest (public security, international relations, monetary stability, court proceedings, inspections and investigations),
—the protection of the individual and of privacy,
—the protection of commercial and industrial secrecy,
—the protection of the Community's financial interests,
—the protection of confidentiality as requested by the natural or legal persons that supplied the information or as required by the legislation of the member state that supplied the information. They may also refuse access in order to protect the institution's interest in the confidentiality of its proceedings.

The last sentence, of course, may take away all that has been gained, but so far the policy has not caused any major controversies.

Finally, it should be noted that more than a decade before the European Union began showing interest in the subject, the Committee of Ministers of the Council of Europe had recommended to member states that they adopt "effective and appropriate means" through which their citizens could have access to government information. The recommended limitations were to be guided only by "what is necessary in a democratic society for the protection of legitimate public interests (national security, public safety, crime prevention, individual privacy, etc.)."[7]

National Frameworks

The Scandinavian countries have the most comprehensive and most media/citizen-sensitive government information access laws, which are reinforced by the presence of an administrative "ombudsman," the office or person whose job is to assess complaints about administrative performance.

Sweden, for example, the country with probably the world's oldest government openness statute, offers its citizens and its press more access than any other European country. Its Freedom of the Press Act, Article 1, not only guarantees the *right* of access to official documents, it also specifies in Article 2 that "any restriction ... shall be scrupulously specified in the provisions of a special act of law. ... " Documents are "any written matter, picture, or record which can be read, listened to, or otherwise comprehended only by mechanical means." Any documents in the custody of the authorities are considered official. Public authorities are considered to be the local, regional and national governmental agencies as well as the General Assembly of the Church of Sweden (Art. 5).

But what is considered to be the most notorious part of the act is its provision in Article 4 that says:

A letter or other communication which is addressed in person to the holder of an office in a public authority shall be deemed to be an official document if it refers to a case or other matter which falls within the purview of that authority, and if it is not intended for the addressee solely in his capacity as incumbent of another post.

This has caused plenty of embarrassment to many Swedish politicians and bureaucrats. One of the most interesting cases involved John Stonehouse, a former British cabinet minister and member of the parliament, who had fled to Australia in 1974 following allegations of corruption connected to his business activities. A few months later he wrote a letter to then-Swedish Prime Minister Olof Palme in which he said that he would renounce his British citizenship if Palme would issue him a Swedish passport. Stonehouse explained in his letter that he was the victim of "the most vicious campaign of prosecution by the British press of any figure in British public life." Palme, who had not seen the letter until he read about it in the newspapers, was considerably embarrassed.[8]

In Sweden, access can be restricted because the following concerns are at stake, as stated in Article 2:

1. the security of the Realm or its relations with a foreign state or an international organization;

2. the central finance policy, monetary policy, or foreign exchange policy of the Realm;

3. the inspection, control or other supervisory activities of a public authority;

4. the interest of preventing or prosecuting crime;

5. the public economic interest;

6. the protection of the personal integrity or economic circumstances of private subjects; or

7. the preservation of animal or plant species.

The Act also provides details on the physical access of the documents as well as an appeals procedure in case an application for a document is rejected.

The policy on government document accessibility is similar in **Finland,** where the 1951 Act on Publicity of Official Documents (9.2.1951/83 and 22.12.1951/650) defines *public documents* as "any document prepared and/or issued by a public authority as well as all documents sent or given to a public authority and in its possession." Public authorities are considered all local, regional and national agencies as well as the "ecclesiastical authorities of the Evangelical Lutheran Church." Police documents are not public until a "case has been brought to court or dropped." Citizens are entitled to have access to all public documents. If an official rejects a request for the delivery of an official, but not necessarily public, document, the applicant may appeal to the official's supervisor and eventually all the way to the Supreme Administrative Court.

Documents that are legally allowed to be kept secret are those relating to the security of the state (mainly national defense, nuclear energy, and foreign relations on political and economic issues); the prevention of crimes or the bringing of charges; the "administration of the State or of a self-governing entity"; the management of a private company; commercial competition; active legal proceedings; and an "individual's significant private interests from the viewpoint of spiritual care, care of prisoners, taxation or official inspection. ... " Unless otherwise specified by act of parliament, most of these documents can be made public 25 years after their classification. Documents about the "spiritual care" of an individual can be declassified 20 years after the death of the individual or by his/her consent.

The 1970 **Danish** Act on Access to Public Administration Files (amended in 1985 and 1991) offers similar definitions of public authorities and documents as well as exceptions to openness. Particular attention is paid to the restriction of information relating to the financial status of a person (Arts. 12.1 and 12.2, "information on the private circumstances of individual persons, including their finances" and "information ... of material importance to the economy of the person") as well as the State (Arts. 13.2, 13.4 and 13.5, information concerning "Danish external economic interests," "measures planned under taxation law" and "protection of public financial interests"). Of all European bureaucrats, Danish administrators are allowed the shortest time period—10 days—within which they must respond to a release request.

France is the only E.U. country that has a special agency dedicated to systematically assessing administrative openness. The 1978 Act on Freedom of Access to Administrative Documents, complemented by the 1979 Act on the Motivation of the Administrative Acts and the Improvement of the Relations Between the Administration and the Public, set up the Commission of Access to Administrative Documents (CADA), whose job is to evaluate a public authority's refusal to release a document or help a public authority decide if a document should be released. CADA is composed of judges, National Assembly members, senators and representatives from the prime minister's office, the French Documentation Department, the State Archives, municipalities and universities. Figures show that CADA's advice is followed by the administration in 80–90 percent of the cases.[9]

The 1978 act provides eight exceptions to openness: executive branch deliberations, public safety issues, national security/defense/foreign policy matters, personnel and medical files, commercial/industrial competition information, information about the operation of the courts and pre-trial proceedings, tax and customs investigations and information about monetary policy. National security is also protected by the Penal Code's Articles 74–78, which generally prohibit the dissemination of defense and security information to anyone not authorized to receive it. Civil servants are bound by professional secrecy requirements not to disclose information acquired during the course of their work unless the information points to an illegality.

In **The Netherlands,** Article 110 of the Constitution guarantees the right of "public access to information in accordance with rules to be prescribed by Act of Parliament." The Act of 31 October 1991, on Public Access to Information, Article 10, applies to government-held information of all means (written, digital, film, etc.) and provides both for *absolute* and *relative* exceptions. *Absolute* exceptions, where there is no weighing of conflicting rights, concern the "unity of the Crown," national security and the secrecy of information given confidentially to the government by third parties. *Relative* exceptions are meant to safeguard information on foreign relations, the financial interests of the State, active investigations and the protection of individual privacy. Article 11 exempts from openness internal executive branch memoranda. Authorities must decide on the request within 15 days. One unique aspect of the act is that it tends to be based on specific information rather than a specific document release. This means that "the information requested has to be transmitted to the requester, but it is up to the administration to decide *how* they answer the request."[10] Finally, civil service regulations demand professional secrecy, and the Penal Code's Article 98 prohibits the revelation of information labeled "secret" by the State. Appeals of openness rejections are heard by the Council of State.

The **Austrian** Constitution, Article 20.4, says that all local, state and national government institutions and "all corporations under public law" must provide the public with information on issues "within their responsibility unless laws protecting confidentiality provide for non-disclosure. ... " Article 20.3, however, requires that public employees "are pledged to secrecy about all facts of which they have obtained knowledge exclusively from their official activity and whose concealment is enjoined by the public interest or that of the parties concerned." However, recent practice has shown that journalists can publicize information received from a public servant with impunity, while the public servant may still be liable for the breach of professional secrecy. State Freedom of Information Acts provide definitions and details. The Penal Code, Article 255, prohibits revelations that may harm Austria's national security and international relations.

Germany's Basic Law, Article 5.1, guarantees a citizen the right to "inform himself from generally accessible sources." The Federal Constitutional Court has interpreted that to mean that the citizen has a legitimate right to access to government information. Government, according to Section 4 of the state and federal press laws, can refuse to release secrets, which are normally understood to be facts about national security, public safety, judicial proceedings, police investigations and significant private interests. Authorities can refuse to release information relating to these issues or if the requested "volume of facts exceeds acceptable limits." The law covers all information and data in the custody of the government regardless of the means of storage or accessibility. Section 93 of the Penal Code prohibits the revelation of state secrets, and Section 203 prohibits the dissemination of secrets about private persons. Section 93, however, adds that facts that are "in contradiction to the free democratic order or that are kept from treaty partners in violation of arms limitation agreements are not state secrets" and it is not a crime to reveal them. The administrative courts are responsible for hearing appeals.

The **Spanish** Constitution, Article 105.b, says that the "Law shall regulate ... access by citizens to the administrative files and records, except as they may concern the security and defence of the State, the investigation of crimes and the privacy of individuals." Exceptions to openness are regulated by Law 9/68 and Law 48/78, which define state secrets but leave up to the executive branch (the government or the military authorities) the method of their classification as *secret* or *reserved* or their release. The types of secrets mentioned follow the same pattern as those of the other E.U. countries. The Penal Code, Article 135, details the penalties for violations. The Constitutional Court is responsible for hearing appeals.

Although the **Portuguese** Constitution, Article 48, provides citizens with the "right to be informed by the Government and other authorities about the management of public affairs," parliament in 1993 passed the Act About State Secrets, which is viewed by local journalists as being too general and therefore subject to restrictive interpretation. But the act's major weakness may be its long list of agents authorized to classify documents—the president of the country, every government minister and the prime minister, the president of the parliament, the president of the regional government and the governor of Macau. The Press Law, Article 5.2, forbids access to information that concerns "legal proceedings and military or state secrets." The Supreme Administrative Court is responsible for hearing cases of the act's violations and refusals of appeals to openness.

Similarly, **Italy's** most important law on journalism, Law 69 of 1963, Article 2, guarantees "freedom of information," but there is very limited access-to-government-information legislation. The 1990 Access to Administrative Documents Act allows only those with a legal interest to apply; the 1990 Local Autonomy Act allows, in Articles 22–28, access to some official documents in the possession of the localities, and the 1989 Ministry of the Environment Act allows some access to the documents of that ministry. The Penal Code treason statutes, Articles 272 and 279, may be used against journalists who print information deemed unsuitable for public release by the State.

In **Greece**, the 1986 Act on the Relationship Between State and Citizen, the Establishment of a New Type of Identification Cards and Other Provisions, Law 1599/1986, Article 16, says that citizens have a "right to access to administrative documents, with the exception of documents that refer to private or family life of third parties." Administrative documents are those that are "drafted by organs of the state." Computerized documents are not mentioned in the act. Grounds for refusal of access are "the violation of the confidentiality of meetings of the cabinet and other government organizations, [violation of] the confidentiality of national defense and foreign policy, public confidence and monetary policy, national security and public order, [violation of] the medical, mercantile, banking and industrial confidentiality, and [violation of] any other confidentiality provided for in other laws." Release of documents that "may impede judicial, police, military or administrative investigations" may also be denied. Those who request information do not have to give a reason for their request, but an administrative refusal of the request must be justified in writing within a month of the request's submission. The act's major weakness seems to be its provision, in Section 4, that cabinet ministers "in a common decision with the Press Minister" are allowed to introduce new access restrictions by simply publishing their decision in the official journal, the *Newspaper of the Government.*

Belgium addresses government openness in a general way through its Constitution, Article 32, which says that "Everyone has the right to consult any administrative document and to have a copy made, except in cases and under conditions stipulated by law, decrees or rulings referred to in Article 134." Article 134 grants determining power to local authorities.

Luxembourg, Ireland and the United Kingdom do not have specific laws granting general access to information. In fact, what has prevailed in the **United Kingdom** is a tradition almost exactly the opposite of that of the United States—British citizens and media may have access to government information only if a law specifies it or if the government wishes it. The infamous but rarely used Official Secrets Act, first approved in 1911 and most recently amended in 1989, penalizes any public employee who "without legal authority" discloses "any information, document or other article ... which is or has been in his possession by virtue of his position" on national security and intelligence matters, national defense, international relations, information useful to a criminal or resulting in the "commission of a crime," wire-tapping and information entrusted in confidence to other States or international organizations. Proof of damage is required in the first three types of disclosure. The act, in Article 2, defines as *damaging,* anything that

damages the capability of, or any part of, the armed forces of the Crown to carry out their tasks or leads to loss of life or injury to members of those forces or serious damage to the equipment or installations of those forces; or

... endangers the interests of the United Kingdom abroad, seriously obstructs the promotion or protection by the United Kingdom of those interests or endangers the safety of British citizens abroad. ...

There is no "public interest" provision for any access to government information, and no protection is offered "whistleblowers," except if they can prove that "they did not know, and had no reasonable cause to believe" that the information they released was related to the above categories or that it would be damaging to the interests of the state. Government records are normally kept secret for 30 years.

In the 1960s and 1970s several efforts were made in the United Kingdom to introduce some sort of access legislation with no success. In the 1980s, however, the Local Government (Access to Information) Act 1985 was passed, and it allowed disclosure (of minutes of meetings, information used in government decision making, etc.) on public interest grounds. It was followed by a 1987 bill that allowed individual access to personal files and a 1988 bill that allowed access to personal medical records.

The best that civil libertarians were able to achieve was the approval in 1994 of a Code of Practice document, in which the government pledged to increase its accessibility in order to make "information about the policies, actions and decisions of Government departments, agencies and public bodies more widely available."[11] The government promised that the "presumption is in favor of the release of information," but that it would "honour personal privacy and commercial confidences," "good management and internal decision making," or "such functions as law enforcement and defence."[12] The code also described the application method and an appeals process, listed the fees involved and promised to respond to each application in 20 days. The code has been criticized for providing information and not documents, for including exceptions too vague to favor openness, for an expensive price structure, for lack of punitive provisions for erring public servants and for lack of direct appeal to the parliamentary ombudsman (citizens have to first go to their representative member of parliament).

Complementing the Official Secrets Act is the *D-notice* system, which is a voluntary way through which the government and the media have "an alternative and more civilized form of coexistence" on the treatment of sensitive national security issues.[13] A *D-notice* is normally a letter sent by the Defence, Press and Broadcasting Committee to news media asking them not to publish information on a specific subject unless they clear it with the defense ministry first. The committee, which consists of members of the press, the armed forces and the civil service, meets twice a year to review the validity of existing *D-notices*. Between 1962 and 1995 there have been approximately nine such notices, mainly affecting information about defense installations, intelligence gathering and armed services equipment and plans.

The legal structure on access in **Ireland** is very similar to the British example, and equally rarely used. The Irish Official Secrets Act 1963 follows closely the spirit and word of the U.K. Act. Section 2 protects any "secret official code word or password, and any sketch, plan model, article, note, document or information which is secret or confidential or is expressed to be either. ... " Public employees are restricted in the same way as in the British Act.

1. *Near v. Minnesota,* 283 U.S. 697, 51 S. Ct. 625 (1931).

2. Finn Laursen, "Denmark's 'Yes, But,'" *EIPASCOPE,* No. 1993/3 (Institut Européen d'Administration Publique), p. 12.

3. Veerle Deckmyn, "La transparence et l'information européenne," *EIPASCOPE,* No. 1994/2 (Institut Européen d'Administration Publique), p. 6.

4. Council of the European Communities, *Treaty on the European Union* (Brussels, Belgium: Office of Official Publications of the European Communities, 1992), p. 229.

5. Commission of the European Communities, "Openness in the Community," *Communication to the Council, the Parliament and the Economic and Social Committee,* COM (93) 258; Commission of the European Communities, "Public Access to the Institutions' Documents," *Communication to the Council, the Parliament and the Economic and Social Committee,* COM (93) 191.

6. European Commission, *Access to Commission Documents: User's Guide* (Luxembourg: Office for Official Publications of the European Communities, 1994), pp. 19-23.

7. Council of Europe, Committee of Ministers, Recommendation No. R(80)2 and No. R(81)19.

8. Roger Choate, "The Public's Right to Know: Access to Public Documents," *Current Sweden* (Stockholm, Sweden: Svenska Institutet, 1975), No. 93, p. 1.

9. Herbert Burkert, "An overview on access to government information legislation in Europe," *Journal of Media Law and Practice,* Vol. 11, No. 1, 1990, p. 12.

10. Ibid., p. 10.

11. *Open Government* (London, U.K.: Office of Public Service and Science, 1994), p. 2.

12. Ibid.

13. Tom Crone, *Law and the Media* (Oxford, U.K.: Focal Press, 1995), p. 185.

CHAPTER 6

Broadcasting Content/ Program Regulation

In the 1980s technological innovations, especially in television, outgrew the national and international assumptions that had governed the medium's regulation until then. Cable television, direct broadcast satellites, digitization, etc., eliminated borders, expanded markets and, in general, made life more exciting for consumers but more difficult for governments. The old state monopolies of the audiovisual media became increasingly anachronistic as private radio and television, now commercially funded, began challenging the legal and market status quo by stretching the perimeter of what was permissible as they searched for new or larger audiences. Soon their strategy started to pay off, and they began to attract audiences away from the established public channels by providing market-driven, albeit not necessarily high-quality, programming.

Soon the excitement of the televised message, along with the medium's ubiquity and global appeal, pointed toward a huge potential for power, including economic and political power. This unchecked potential, however, along with television's preoccupation with high ratings, questionable program quality and domination by American themes and production values, began undermining the medium's support among the various power elite. The first issue to enter the arena of public debate was television's influence on national culture. It was followed by issues of political and partisan utilization of the medium and how best to solve its access problems. It did not take long for both national and international institutions to be involved in the fray. Their aim was to find a formula that would fairly balance the communicators' rights to free expression with the rights of citizens and the state's legitimate interests in protecting the national language, value systems and traditions.

The European Union, entrusted with creating an environment that secures the free movement of services, people, goods and capital, looked upon television regulation more from a consumer, competition and investment/protection perspective, while the Council of Europe looked at it from a cultural and political perspective. By 1990 both organizations had approved a set of minimum "transfrontier television" guidelines addressing the medium's importance and impact on existing exportable commodities and services, as well as on culture, including taste and language. It is significant to note that for both the Union and the council, the starting point of any debate about television and its political and economic potential is that television is a public trust first and then a money-making or influence-peddling enterprise. It is this philosophy that guided the "transfrontier television" regulations through these two organizations. It is also the yardstick used to measure fairness, egalitarianism, moderation, quality, diversity and accessibility in television programming available in member states.

The guiding principles of broadcast activities in the **United States** are guided by the capitalist ideals and by laws and regulations concerning content (defamation, obscenity, etc.), ownership (as an anti-monopoly factor), advertising (especially children's) and technical matters. The latter will not be addressed by this study. Advertising is discussed in Chapter 7.

The prevailing U.S. Federal Communication Commission (FCC) rules on ownership, adopted in 1992, allow one individual or company to own up to 18 AM and 18 FM stations. Television station ownership is limited to 12, but no one company may own stations that reach more than 25 percent of the nation's households, which, in effect, precludes ownership by the same person or company of stations in the top 12 largest markets of the United States. Furthermore, although the FCC grandfathered all existing print-broadcast cross-ownerships in existence in the mid-1970s and gave some waivers, no new ones are to be allowed, thus respecting the rule that forbids one person or company from owning the main print and broadcast media in one market. In 1992 the FCC allowed cable television networks to own cable systems that reach up to 10 percent of the nation's households. Newspaper and television stations cannot own a cable system in their own market.

Broadcast content regulation in the United States centers around political candidacies and indecency. As discussed earlier, the 1934 Communications Act provided, in Section 315:

If any licensee shall permit any person who is a legally qualified candidate for any public office to use a broadcasting station, he shall afford equal opportunities to all other such candidates for that office in the use of such broadcasting station ... and ... afford reasonable opportunity for the discussion of conflicting views on issues of public importance. ...

Newscasts, news documentaries and news events are excluded from this provision, which in 1984 was extended to include public affairs programs and most talk shows. In 1991 the FCC refined its rule to specify that the section applied only to content controlled (prepared, approved, sponsored) by the candidate. Section 315 is complemented by Section 312.a.7, which requires licensees to provide "reasonable access" of their facilities to candidates in federal elections. Section 315 survived the Supreme Court's constitutionality check in the 1981 case of *CBS, Inc., v. FCC*,[1] in which the Court ruled that under the circumstances the First Amendment rights of the broadcasters were outweighed by those of the candidates and the public. "Reasonable access" or "reasonable opportunities" does not imply free access, although the "lowest unit charge" of Section 315 does require that during campaign periods the stations charge candidates the lowest rate available to commercial advertisers.

The most Draconian of content regulations in the United States, however, the Fairness Doctrine, was abolished in 1987. It required fairness and balance in public affairs programming. Its vagueness had contributed to its inapplicability—few disciplinary actions and no license denials. The only elements of the doctrine still in effect are the Personal Attack Rule, which requires notification of a victim of such an attack and often donation of a free air time to reply, and the Political Editorializing Rules, which require the donation of reply time to candidates whose opponents have been endorsed by the station.

Federal law prohibits the broadcasting of indecent material

(words or visual images), even though it may not be legally obscene and, therefore, publishable in other media forms. The first test involved comedian George Carlin's 1978 monologue, "Filthy Words," which aired at 2 p.m. on WBAI in New York. The FCC found the language "patently offensive," but not obscene, and put a warning notice in the station's license application file. Importing language and rationale from its obscenity decisions, the Supreme Court, in *FCC v. Pacifica*,[2] agreed as it interpreted "indecency" to be "language or material that depicts or describes ... sexual or excretory activities or organs," in a manner that is "patently offensive" according to "contemporary community standards for the broadcast medium."

Carlin's seven "filthy words," however, were not for long an accurate yardstick of words to avoid. In 1987 the FCC began cracking down on several stations that thought adult programming was safe after 10 p.m., and in 1992 it imposed on Infinity Broadcasting the largest fine in the history of American broadcasting, $600,000, for airing risqué language and innuendoes. Sexual or scatological language on radio and nudity on television continued to be the FCC's main indecency targets and were used in station fines. Since 1991, and with the encouragement of a federal court decision, the FCC has adopted a relaxed enforcement procedure of indecent but not obscene material between 8 p.m. and 6 a.m., when adult themes and language are allowed.[3]

Finally, another sensitive issue in American broadcasting has been children's programming. Advocates of the spirit of the 1990 Children's Television Act have long and loudly complained that manufacturers of children's products (from toys to foods) have been exploiting children by the amount and type of advertising and by creating programs around products. Although some tightening of the advertising time and type has taken place, nothing significant had been done to address the act's requirement that broadcasters offer educational and informational programs until 1996. In July of that year President Clinton and the National Association of Broadcasters reached an agreement that committed the networks to reserve, starting in September 1997, an average of three hours a week for educational and informational programs for children age 16 and younger. In August 1996, despite some commissioner fears about creating a precedent for other "First Amendment incursions," the FCC unanimously approved the agreement, and

President Clinton hailed it as the fulfillment of the promise of the CTA.[4]

The E.U. Directive (89/552/EEC)

The main developments that propelled the European Union (then still the European Community) to enter the area of broadcasting regulation were the introduction in the early 1980s of satellite television transmission, which revolutionized the way Europeans used television, and the launching of Rupert Murdoch's Europe-wide, *commercial* Sky Channel in 1982. Alarmed by the speed of the medium's commercialization and fearful of its possible domination by American-style, bourgeois programming, the European Parliament passed a resolution recommended by its Committee on Youth, Culture, Education, Information and Sport that called for a common European resistance against the invading and invasive American products. The resolution specifically called for the development of "community level" broadcasting rules that would ensure the protection of youth and honesty and fairness in advertising.[5] The issue presented an immense challenge to European leaders as they tried to assess the impact privatized television might have on the potential 350 million viewers whom advertisers inevitably would try to reach by spending from $4.3 billion in 1983 to an estimated $20 billion in the year 2000.

The commission responded a year later with its own report, "Realities and Tendencies in European Television: Perspectives and Options," which discussed the cultural implications of transborder television and reviewed the status of member nations' television systems and the laws governing them.[6] The parliament continued to put pressure on the commission and in 1984 passed another resolution calling for community-wide regulation and attached a report that warned about over-commercialization and eventual ownership concentration.[7] In the same year, the commission published its Green Paper, "On the establishment of the common market for broadcasting, especially by cable and satellite," in which it outlined its arguments for establishing jurisdiction over a seemingly cultural issue like broadcasting.[8] The commission said that broadcasting was a transborder *service* within the common market and therefore came under commission authority.

The parliament responded by passing several resolutions and

reports by cultural, economic and consumer committees, expressing its strong desire for regulation on cultural and commercial
grounds and adding a new item to the list of ills the regulation
should address: the potential for ownership concentration, a trend
that was beginning to be a global media malaise.[9] The commission
prepared a directive, and the parliament approved it with some
amendments in 1987. After two years of often petty negotiations in
the Council of Ministers, the directive was finally approved in the
Rhodes summit on Oct. 3, 1989, without reference to media concentration.

The Community Directive is very similar to that approved by
the Council of Europe a few months earlier, although it attempts to
draw the distinction that the community's regulation was primarily "prompted by economic considerations."[10] It saw television service as a popular commodity that should be entitled to freely cross
borders and be consumed, with a minimum of *common* limitations, in all 15 E.U. member states. As the guarantor of the establishment of "closer relations between the States belonging to the
Community," ensurer of the "economic and social progress of its
countries" and remover of the barriers to freedom of movement in
Europe, the Union mainly set out to accomplish the following objectives:

1. to propose a set of measures that would "permit and ensure
the transition from national markets to a common programme
production and distribution market and to establish conditions of
fair competition without prejudice to the public interest role to be
discharged by the television broadcasting services";
2. to encourage the freedom of transmission of television services, taking into consideration the needs and rights of freedom of
expression, national cultures and independent producers and investors; and
3. to protect the consumers (especially minors) from harmful
programs and advertisements and guarantee the fair representation of news and the right of reply to those who feel wronged by a
program.

Chapter I of the directive defines "television broadcasting,"
"television advertising," "surreptitious advertising" (subliminal or
misleading advertising) and "sponsorship." Chapter II requires

that the member state from which transmission originates ensure broadcaster compliance with its laws and not "restrict transmission on their territory of broadcasts from other member States" unless the broadcasts are harmful to the "physical, mental or moral development of minors." (The European Court of Justice has been asked several times to assess how fairly national authorities comply with this part of the directive, which demands, barring serious reasons, the same treatment of national and international transmissions from sister member states. In perhaps the most controversial of its rulings, the Court found that the United Kingdom was imposing different standards of treatment to a controversial Dutch company's transmissions to the United Kingdom, and therefore it "failed to fulfill its obligations" under the directive.[11]

Probably the most controversial of all chapters, however, is Chapter III, Article 4, which asks that member states

reserve for European works ... a majority proportion of their transmission time, excluding the time appointed for news, sports events, games, advertising and teletext services.

Article 5 requires that at least 10 percent of the transmission time or 10 percent of a broadcaster's budget be reserved for works by European producers "who are independent of broadcasters." European works are defined, Article 6, as "works originating from Member States," works from "European third States party to the European Convention on Transfrontier Television of the Council of Europe" and others that are dominated by artists and producers residing in member states. Article 7 prohibits the televising of a film until "two years have elapsed since the work was first shown in cinemas" in an E.U. member country.

Chapter IV of the directive deals with advertising. Article 10 requires the clear separation between a program and an advertisement, and Article 11 requires that advertisements be placed between programs and within programs only if the programs are longer than 45 minutes and "the integrity and value of the program" are not violated. News, public affairs programs, documentaries, religious programs and children's programs are not to be interrupted commercially if they last less than 30 minutes. Religious services should never be interrupted for advertising purposes (Art. 11.5). Article 12 requests that all advertisements should refrain

from harming "respect for human dignity"; encouraging discrimination on "grounds of race, sex or nationality"; offending "religious or political beliefs"; and promoting "behavior prejudicial to
health or to safety" or "... to the protection of the environment."

Articles 13 and 14 prohibit advertising of tobacco products and
prescription drugs and treatments. Alcoholic beverage advertising
is allowable, in Article 15, only if it is not aiming "specifically at minors" or depicting "minors consuming these beverages"; not link-
ing alcohol consumption with driving, enhanced physical performance or "social or sexual success"; not promoting alcohol as a
therapeutic, stimulant, sedative or "a means of resolving personal
conflicts"; not discouraging abstinence or moderation; or empha-
sizing high alcoholic content as a "positive quality of the beverages."

Article 16 prohibits advertising that may cause "moral or physical detriment to minors" by asking them to buy a product or a service, thus "exploiting their inexperience or credulity"; by encouraging them to "persuade their parents or others to purchase the
goods or services being advertised"; by exploiting "the special trust
minors place in parents, teachers and other persons;" or by unreasonably showing them in "dangerous situations."

Article 17 requires that program sponsors not have any influence on the content or scheduling of their programs, be clearly
identified, not encourage the purchase of their products and not
be in the manufacture or sale of tobacco or prescription drug products or treatments. News and current affairs programs cannot be
sponsored. Advertising cannot occupy more than 15 percent of the
daily transmission time or 20 percent of any one transmission
hour (Art. 18).

Minors are more specifically protected in Chapter V, which requires member states to enact legislation to prohibit programs that
"might seriously impair the physical, mental or moral development of minors, in particular those that involve pornography or
gratuitous violence." Programs promoting "hatred on grounds of
race, sex, religion or nationality" should be prohibited. Any such
programs might be allowed if they are presented at times when minors are not likely to view them or if they can be technologically
screened from minors.

Finally, Chapter VI legitimizes the "right of reply" for any natural or legal person whose "legitimate interests, in particular reputation and good name, have been damaged" by a television pro-

gram. Member states are to prescribe the details of the exercise of this right.

As expected, the most controversial of the directive's provisions were those that dealt with advertising and the European works quotas. The debate on the merits of advertising regulation was led by the United Kingdom, whose representatives felt that the proposals were too restrictive and would impair their nation's broadcasting industry that heavily relied on advertising money. The European works quotas discussion was led by the French, who felt that more time should have been reserved for European works (they proposed a settlement at 60 percent) and restrictions ought to have been imposed at the time of showing of non-European works. In the end, the directive was approved in its present form by a 10–2 vote, with Belgium and Denmark opposing it.[12]

One of the first obstacles these directives encountered was their applicability to the private-sector broadcasters. Tradition dictated that the public channels were to provide a nationally accessible non-commercial service that offered a comprehensive variety but impartial programming that promoted mainstream cultural and educational programming and advanced national goals. The introduction of private broadcasters gave birth to new philosophies concerning the symbiosis of the two systems and called for a complementary co-existence of the private and public channels, with the former being left free to focus more than the latter on entertainment programming. As the University College London media law professor Eric Barendt writes in comparing the new European broadcasting systems:

Public broadcasters are required to provide the basic broadcasting service. ... They must show a comprehensive range of programmes, presenting the views of all important political and social groups. In contrast private broadcasters are free to offer specialist channels, while the degree of fairness required of each station may be lower than that expected of public broadcasters.[13]

Furthermore, the same attitude is prevalent among E.U. member countries when it comes to program standards, in general: public broadcasters operate under more restrictions and standards of higher quality than their private counterparts, and their news departments are under considerable public scrutiny to ensure sobriety, middle-of-the-roadness and impartiality.

For example, when the public British Broadcasting Corporation

(BBC) began its ascendancy just after World War II to one of the world's best broadcast organizations, it followed a formula of "a somewhat stuffy set of ideas about good taste and rather middle-class values," writes Philip Schlesinger, Thames Polytechnic senior sociology lecturer. Its news programming in particular, he says, thrived on being "an 'objective', 'impartial', 'neutral' product," that was not "legitimized as an *interpretation* of reality, but rather as a straightforwardly factual presentation of it."[14] "There was," he says, "a tendency to eschew the reporting of crimes and accidents, a lack of humorous or 'light' stories, and an absence of colourful adjectives." The emphasis was on accuracy and not on scoops.[15] BBC chronicler Burton Paulu concurs: "There is no hurry to be first. ... When the facts are indisputable they are broadcast, not before."[16]

The logical extension of the issue of fairness, however, eventually spills into the issue of *access* to the broadcast media, and although there are E.U. countries, such as The Netherlands, that provide proportional access to political, religious and labor organizations through a detailed formula, most of them do not recognize a constitutional *right* of access by either individuals or groups. The most used access methods are through the "right of reply" rules provided by every E.U. member country, the enforcement of impartiality rules applicable during campaign and election periods, including time allocation to political parties, and through the representation of diverse societal groups in the various national or regional broadcasting councils, which oversee the licensing and performance of television stations and networks.

The success of the directive's implementation is unclear. Countries that have quotas stricter than those called for in the directive, such as the United Kingdom, which allows no more that 14 percent of foreign programming and France, which allows no more than 40 percent, regularly levy fines on violators; France, for example, in the first years of the its domestic quota law, levied fines of approximately $10 million on violators.

Two issues have emerged as critical to the directive's enforcement: monitoring methods and replacement programming. Neither can be easily addressed.[17] The latter, in fact, despite the clear aim of the directive to promote domestic production, has failed to produce the desired results because most of the E.U. artistic and telecommunication endeavors traditionally have been dependent on heavy government subsidies, and their economies were in financial strains because of huge welfare commitments and competitive pressures from the United States and the Far East. Secondarily, the envisioned pan-European market for either E.U. programs or products simply has not materialized, and therefore neither capital nor incentive has been forthcoming to compensate for the lack of subsidies.

Finally, exacerbating the directive's problem is its "non-binding" status, which confuses those on both sides of the argument and disorients domestic regulators. Perhaps the only constructive way to assess the directive's success is through the eyes of then Commission Vice Chairman Martin Bangeman, who, in a classic Eurocratic style, sought to appease both proponents and opponents of the directive by telling the press conference following the directive's passage: "It's not a legal obligation. It's a political commitment."[18]

The haziness of this very issue, however, proved to be the directive's Achilles' heel, and by 1995, the commission was ready to amend it. On March 23, 1995, the commission proposed a series of amendments that aimed at improving the directive's effectiveness, enforceability and fairness. The main recommendations were that

1. the non-binding nature of the "European works" provision become mandatory;
2. the "European works" quotas be abolished in ten years;
3. new broadcasters will have three years in which to meet the quota requirement;
4. specialized home shopping channels will not have to abide by the directive's advertising limits;
5. advertising intervals will become more flexible.[19]

In June 1996 the council recommended their approval to the parliament, but in November 1996 the parliament failed to gather enough of a majority to approve them, thus handing a serious defeat to supporters of a tighter directive who had worked for more than a year to devise appropriate language to amend it. The parliament's failure to approve the amendment was surprising because, despite the directive's requirements, the E.U. nations in 1995 had a $6.2 billion deficit in audiovisual product trade with the United States and American films represented 80 percent of the films shown in the E.U. countries and 60 percent of the drama and comedy programming shown in the television screens of the E.U. member nations.[20]

The commission and the council had taken their action after reviewing data and hearing arguments from each nation member's relevant constituencies. The data showed that only Denmark, Ireland, The Netherlands, Portugal and the United Kingdom were in full compliance with the directive's European works majority requirement.[21] In fact, a commission-requested Green Paper on European Audiovisual Policy criticized the audiovisual sector of the member nations for failing to overcome nationalist tendencies, to promote "intra-European distribution of programs" and to raise enough capital to "get out of its chronic loss-making situation."[22] Furthermore, the paper said, the commission must seek "a change of attitude" in Europe if the Union was to "invest in the future of the programme industry," and that would require the integration of "the cultural and the economic, the product and the audience, the small business structure and the industrial constraints. ..."[23]

National Frameworks

In addition to the E.U. television directive's prescription of program standards calling for the avoidance of "pornography or gratuitous violence" as well as of "hatred on grounds of race, sex, religion or nationality," the most generally accepted program requirements are those of impartiality or objectivity in the treatment of public affairs programs and the fair treatment of candidates during campaign periods.

The multi-party political systems of the E.U. countries necessitate a rather complex set of rules providing access to and coverage by their countries' electronic media. It has become tradition that the political parties be given free air time on the public airwaves and often the private airwaves as well. Each country's legislative body has jurisdiction over its own rules, the most common of which involve proportional but not equal time for all parties. Two key indicators normally used in deciding time allocation are vote strength in last election and relative strength in various parts of the country. Each country has its minimum requirements that parties must meet before they are given broadcast time.

Other program requirements may include rules seeking to generate programs that protect and/or teach the national language, promote domestic arts (music, drama, opera), support national health initiatives and provide a diverse set of services for children, sports fans, scientists and consumers, including news consumers.

In the **United Kingdom,** the 1990 Broadcasting Act prohibits public broadcasters from expressing any opinion on issues of "political or industrial controversy or relating to current public policy." However, all broadcasters are to abide by the rule of "due impartiality," which does not necessarily have to be achieved in one program but in a series "considered as a whole." The Independent Television Commission's Programme Code says that "due impartiality" should be "adequate and appropriate to the nature of the program" and not pursued only "in a mathematical sense" or be interpreted to mean that "equal time must be given to each opposing view." However, before this provision was adopted, the Thatcher government bitterly fought public broadcasting programs thought to be critical of it and in 1990 it made the corrective proposal that

programmes on current controversies "lacking in impartiality" should be "balanced" by means of a concluding studio discussion, fifteen minutes in length, in which alternative viewpoints could be put.[24]

Program requirement enforcement is overseen by the Independent Television Commission and the Radio Authority, which also assess if an applicant is "fit and proper" to hold a license. Political parties and their affiliates, advertising agencies, churches and other religious groups, tax-supported organizations, local authorities and individuals or organizations not residing or incorporated in an E.U. country are not eligible for broadcast licenses. The rules concerning cable television and restricted radio services are more relaxed.

News program requirements differ from other program requirements in that parties or governments are not supposed to have control over their content. The Broadcasting Complaints Commission reviews private and public broadcasters' performance by using the measures of "accuracy" and "impartiality" in assessing "unjust or unfair treatment" of people or parties. "Fair" coverage of candidates, however, does not mean "equal" coverage.

German requirements are very similar to the British, with the exception that they demand that the licensee company be head-quartered in Germany, which may contradict at least the spirit of the Union's goal for the free movement of goods, people, services and capital, if not the letter of Article 52 of the Treaty of Rome, which guarantees "freedom of establishment" of a citizen of one member state in another member state or

the right to take up and pursue activities as self-employed persons and to set up and manage undertakings, in particular companies or firms within the meaning of the second paragraph of Article 58, under the conditions laid down for its own nationals by the law of the country where such establishment is effected. ...

Furthermore, the Constitutional Court has said that in terms of the private broadcaster, impartiality may be measured not necessarily in each program but over time. It also has said that Saxony's law, which disqualified "political parties, public employees, and public law organizations" from licensing eligibility, is constitutional.[25]

In **Greece,** where the constitution itself demands that broadcasters transmit "objective ... information and news reports as well as works of literature and the arts" of high enough quality to match the "social mission and the cultural development of the state," the 1995 Private Television Act meets all the requirements of the E.U. "transfrontier television" directive but exceeds them when it comes to the use, protection and teaching of the Greek language. Chapter A, Article 3.18, provides that stations

have the obligation to take all the necessary measures (by hiring expert scientists and proof readers and organizing seminars) to promote the correct use of the Greek language by the journalists and producers of informational and educational programs, and for the scripting of language that is orally used in the presentation of entertainment programs as well as in dubbing and subtitling of foreign programs.

All Greek stations are required to spend at least 25 percent of their air time (excluding news, sports, game shows and advertising) on works originally composed in Greek and to air at least 30 30-minute programs per year on the promotion of the Greek language and its teaching to foreigners and illiterates. At least five minutes daily are to be spent on news presentations using sign language and subtitles and two minutes a day on free airing of public service announcements, addressing especially health issues and the needs of the handicapped.

Election coverage is always a controversial topic of discussion, and parliament traditionally approves campaign coverage recommendations proposed by the National Radiotelevision Council (NRC). In the Fall 1996 campaign, for example, the NRC rules were that every station was to have conducted a 60-minute interview with the head of each political party; organized at least four debates among party representatives; offered a free ten-minute period weekly to each party; and run no political opinion polls in the last ten days of the campaign. All regulation enforcement as well as licensing are handled by the NRC, as discussed in Chapter 9.

Portugal, on the other hand, although in compliance with the E.U. directive, has been accused of having loose programming regulations, of attempting to appease "powerful political and economic lobbies" and of being "insensitive to the cultural dimension of media, as demonstrated by the almost non-existent cultural requisites imposed on public service broadcasting."[26] The 1990 Television Law requires that broadcasters promote and defend "cultural values that express national identity," assist in the development of a national critical conscience, creativity and free expression and contribute to the "entertainment and education" of the Portuguese people. Forty percent of air time must be devoted to Portuguese origination programs (in the Portuguese language), only one-quarter of which may be produced by the station itself. The 1990 law also established the High Authority for Social Communication, the agency that monitors and licenses Portuguese broadcasters and whose membership is dominated by the country's political parties, which appoint, through parliament and the government, eight of the body's 13 members. The country's Supreme Council of Judges appoints the authority's president, and these members select the remaining four.[27]

The **Irish** Broadcasting Acts of 1960 (amended in 1976) and 1993, the Radio and Television Act of 1988 and the Wireless Telegraphy Act of 1926 still govern broadcast programming. Twenty percent of daily airtime is to be devoted to news and public affairs programs. The Irish language, culture, talent and minorities are to be promoted through appropriate programs. Section 9 of the 1988 act prohibits the airing of material that might undermine the authority of the state or incite to or promote criminal activity. Impartial-

ity, fairness and the promotion of balance on controversial subjects are advanced by the Act as is the fair, but not necessarily
equal, treatment of candidates. Broadcast regulations, following
the E.U. directive, are monitored, licenses are issued by the Independent Radio and Television Commission and complaints are
heard by the Broadcasting Complaints Commission, whose only
punitive power is to publicize its decisions.

Finland's program regulations call on broadcasters to "support
democracy by providing a wide variety of information, opinions
and debates on social issues, also for minorities and special
groups," "support, produce and develop Finnish culture," promote
educational and religious programs and provide programming
that satisfies the language needs of the country's Finnish-,
Swedish- and Lappish-speaking citizens. Operations are based on
the commitment to human rights and values, "peace and understanding between nations," equality, tolerance of others and "responsibility for the environment and the natural world." Information must be "truthful, important and varied," facts thoroughly
checked and distinctions between fact and opinion clear. The
monitoring authority is the Administrative Council, established
by the 1993 Act on Yleisradio. The council also appoints the five-
member program review committee (consisting of media ethics experts, a journalists' union representative and a representative of
the Finnish radio-television), which assesses program complaints.

Italy's broadcasting regulation started in 1947 when the initial
charter of Radio Audizioni Italia (RAI), the public radio and television network, offered to "gratuitously put at the disposition of the
government," two to three hours daily for "government communications."[28] Today, the Italian broadcasting law requires that programming, in both the public and private sectors, be comprehensive, pluralistic and impartial. License candidates must be
dedicated to broadcasting, entertainment or publishing and must
possess a minimum of $2 million for a television station and
$500,000 for a radio station. Program requirements, including
those concerning campaign coverage and political broadcasts, are
made and enforced by the Parliamentary Commission on the General Direction and Supervision of the Radiotelevision Services,
which also appoints the services directors. Italian courts have refused to interfere with the Commission's work when smaller parties have complained about inadequate coverage.

The corporate model of public broadcasting, so competently practiced by the BBC, has been imitated by the Swedish authorities, except that the private owners of the service are representatives of a variety of societal groups.[29] The seven-member **Swedish Broadcasting Commission (SBC)**, which consists of representatives from a variety of political, religious, labor, media and arts groups, is responsible for overseeing that Swedish broadcasters present programs that are "without bias and prejudice and based on fact" without interfering with their "freedom of expression and freedom of information."[30] As dictated by the E.U. directive, care must be exercised in cases of content that contains violence, sex or drugs, and no program should discriminate against anyone on the basis of gender and ethnicity or should violate an individual's privacy, unless compelling public interest demands it. Licensing agreements with the state demand correction of "factual inaccuracies" and adherence to the "right of reply" rules. The SBC may decide in three ways: *exoneration*, indicating the broadcaster was not at fault; *criticism*, indicating the broadcaster's program was lacking but not in any major way; and *censure*, indicating a serious violation on the part of the broadcaster. Censures may be followed by *injunction*, which may imply the imposition of a fine. The decisions are publicized.

The **Austrian** Radio and Television Corporation (ORTF), demands impartiality, objectivity, balance and pluralism of its programs, while it guarantees its personnel independence from governmental and other political pressures and autonomy in carrying out their duties. Supervision of programming is exercised by a commission consisting of 17 members, nine of whom must be judges, and whose responsibility is to enforce the rules of the Radio and Television Act.

The 1969 **Dutch** Broadcasting Act is probably the most complex but most egalitarian of the world's broadcasting regulations. It allows a great variety of political, religious and other groups to use the state broadcast facilities based on a formula that allots time according to the *size* of the group. The groups' aims must be to satisfy "cultural, religious or spiritual needs felt among the population." Programs must be informative, educational, cultural and entertaining and must not contain anything that threatens the "security of the State, public order and morality." Expectations are that each group will provide programming that approximately is divided into *at least* 25 percent informative, 25 percent entertainment, 20 percent cultural, and 5 percent educational. Supervision is exercised by the government commissioner "who may not censor the programmes but who can sanction irregularities afterwards by imposing fines or reducing broadcasting time."[31] Licensing and time allocation is done by the Media Board.

Much like the Dutch system, the **Belgian** broadcasting system allots time to various non-commercial groups of society, including political parties, as dictated by the Decrees of December 12 and December 28, 1979. The broadcasting service, much like almost every other service in Belgium, is divided into French and Flemish components. Belgium is "the world's most densely cabled nation,"[32] and the non-Belgian programming carried by the cable companies dominates the broadcasting environment, especially in the entertainment sector.

The Radio Council is responsible for assessing radio and television programming in **Denmark.** Its 27 members are appointed by the Ministers for Cultural Affairs and for Public Works, the Parliament, political parties and Danish Radio. Impartiality and pluralism are the main values sought in programming.

Spain's broadcasting regulation has been almost totally absorbed by ownership and regional autonomy issues. The democratization that followed Franco's death in 1975 soon gave way to regional chauvinism until finally in the mid-1980s, the Socialist government emerged as Europe's most capitalist by allowing foreign ownership of Spain's broadcast media and forbidding any one person or institution from owning more than 25 percent of any one broadcasting company. The result was that today more than one-quarter of private broadcasting ownership in Spain belongs to banks and approximately 38 percent to foreign investors, including Italian media king and former prime minister Silvio Berlusconi. The pursuit of ratings has turned programmers to "audience merchants," away from "news, investigative reports and talk shows" and more toward game shows, foreign films and variety shows.[33] Public broadcasters succeed less as centrally located programmers and more as regional, ethnic culture purveyors. Quality standards are non-existent, and thematic controls emanate almost exclusively from the E.U. directive.

It took approximately 30 years of organizational difficulties and "often heavy handed political interference" by the de Gaulle, Pompidou and Giscard regimes before **French** broadcasting began to move forward.[34] In fact, it was not until television journalists in 1968 went on strike to protest their politicization that the French establishment was shaken into realizing what was at stake. As television was treated like "a political football kicked around by governments of different political persuasions," it became obvious that partisan news programs were incompatible with a contemporary, open, democratic society such as France.[35] Not surprisingly, therefore, its programming requirements, set by the 1987 and 1989 Broadcasting Acts and applicable mainly to public broadcasting, are based on "rigorous impartiality and strict objectivity" with further regulations applying to matters of individual rights, pluralism and the protection of public interests.[36] Companies are allowed to apply for both television (cable, broadcast or satellite) and radio licenses, but foundations and associations (profit and non-profit) can apply only for radio licenses. The charge of each licensee is different—public broadcasters, for example, are required to give comprehensive coverage to campaigns and elections as well as to parliamentary deliberations.

Licensing and regulation enforcement are supervised by the High Audiovisual Commission (HAC), whose nine members are appointed, in equal numbers, by the president of the republic, the president of the assembly and the president of the senate. HAC is largely responsible for modernizing the administration and elevating the standards of French broadcasting. This is possible because the HAC took over from the government the power of directors-general appointments and the supervision of the day-to-day operations of the broadcasting industry, thus largely insulating broadcasters from political pressure. HAC is also responsible for overseeing that broadcasters adhere to "the public service norms contained in their operating conditions, for example with regard to news coverage."[37] If this sounds reminiscent of the principles that govern American television, it might be because, regardless of their vehement protestations, the French in the post–World War II period have been following American media models to revive their own uninspiring and commercially weak print and broadcast media.[38]

However, although the E.U. member countries offer several remedies to those who feel they have been treated "unfairly" in a broadcast news or public affairs program, judicial interference in the pursuit of "impartiality" or "fairness" is extremely rare because it runs squarely against the well-established and respected right of free expression and/or journalistic independence that are guaranteed to all broadcasters by all E.U. countries.

Judicial interference, however, was what was sought by *both* the government and the media in Europe's most controversial broadcast content regulation—the imposition by the governments of the United Kingdom and Ireland of a ban on material that was representative or supportive of the viewpoint of a terrorist organization, which mainly referred to Northern Ireland's Sinn Fein.

The **Irish** ban was instituted in 1971 under the auspices of the 1960 Broadcasting Authority Act, Section 31, which allowed the prohibition of transmission of material that might promote "aims or activities of any organization which engages in, promotes, encourages or advocates the attaining of any particular objective by violent means." Section 31 was amended in 1976 to include the prohibition of transmission of material that might "promote, or incite to crime, or would tend to undermine the authority of the State. ... " More specifically, the government disallowed the broadcasting of any matter that is

a. a broadcast, whether purporting to be a political party broadcast or not, made by, or on behalf of, or advocating, offering or inviting support for, the organization styling itself Provisional Sinn Fein.

b. a broadcast by any person or persons representing, or purporting to represent, the said organization.

The **British** ban was imposed in 1988 and, under authority of the 1981 Broadcasting Act, Section 29.3, allowed the secretary of state to prohibit

the broadcasting of any matter which consists of or includes any words spoken, whether in the course of an interview or discussion or otherwise, by a person who appears or is heard on the programme in which the matter is broadcast where, a. the person speaking the words represents or purports to represent an organization specified in paragraph 2 below, or b. the words support or solicit or invite support for such an organization.

The organizations mentioned in paragraph 2 were those listed in the 1984 Prevention of Terrorism Act, Sinn Fein, Republican

Sinn Fein and the Ulster Defence Association. Parliamentary discussion reports and election campaign coverage were excluded from the ban.

The Irish ban was more encompassing than the British one in that it applied even to material that was not necessarily supportive of the target organization; it was aimed at journalistic coverage of information, and not just direct statements by supporters of the target organization, and it did not exempt coverage of campaign information. Nevertheless, Irish courts and the European Commission on Human Rights, in *Purcell v. Ireland,* allowed the ban to stand. The commission in 1991 found that the Irish government had "convincing reasons" to assume that there was indeed a "pressing social need for imposing the impugned restrictions on the applicants" and considered the difficulties journalists faced in covering Northern Ireland merely an "inconvenience in the exercise of their professional duties." The British ban had the same treatment by British Courts and the European Commission of Human Rights in 1994 in *Brind and others v. U.K.* The rationale in letting both bans stand was that the limitation imposed was "reasonable" for a democratic society and "proportional" to the legitimate interests that state is entitled to protect. In short, the interference with freedom of expression was judged to be minimal, appropriate and within the allowable limits of Article 10 of the ECHR.

However, the continued expansion of satellite transmissions and the large presence of Cable News Network (CNN) in Europe made the bans less effective and more difficult to enforce, and by 1995 both had been lifted. The legacy they left behind, however, seemed to be inconsistent with such Western values as freedom of expression, pluralism and tolerance. As legal scholar Caroline Banwell wrote,

It has been demonstrated all too apparently in the UK courts that the broadcasting ban is both futile and pointless. If anything it gives greater publicity to those it seeks to affect because of the advantage broadcasters have taken of the "lip-synching technique" ... As a result of [Gerry] Adams appearance on the CNN programme *Larry King Live,* which is usually broadcast around the world, the whole of Europe was subjected to the UK's requirements to comply with the ban so that Europe received a dubbed version. This had the effect of making the UK appear bigoted and tyrannical.[39]

NOTES

1. *CBS, Inc., v. FCC,* 453 U.S. 367, 101 S.Ct. 2813 (1981).

2. *FCC v. Pacifica,* 438 U.S. 726, 98 S.Ct. 3026 (1978).

3. *Action for Children's Television v. FCC,* 932 F.2d 1504, cert. den. 112 S. Ct. 1281.

4. Chris McConnell, "Kids' TV Accord Reached," *Broadcasting and Cable,* August 5, 1996, pp. 5-12; and Chris McConnell, "Three Hours of Kids' TV," *Broadcasting and Cable,* August 12, 1996, pp. 11-13.

5. EC, European Parliament, Working Document 1-1030/81.

6. COM 229/83 Final.

7. OJ 1984 C 117/201.

8. COM 300/84 Final.

9. Rebecca Wallace and David Goldberg, "The EEC Directive on Television Broadcasting," in A. Barav and D.A. Wyatt (Eds.), *Yearbook of European Law* (Oxford, U.K.: Clarendon Press, 1990), p. 194.

10. Rebecca Wallace and David Goldberg, "Television Broadcasting: The Community's Response," in *Common Market Law Review,* 26:717-728 (1989), p. 717.

11. Court of Justice of the European Communities, "Judgment of the Court," Case C-222/94, Sept. 10, 1996, p. 17.

12. Maria K. Nelson in "'Television Without Frontiers': The EC Broadcasting Directive," in Ralph H. Folsom, Ralph B. Lake and Ved P. Nanda (Eds.), *European Community Law After 1992* (Deventer, The Netherlands: Kluwer Law and Taxation Publishers, 1993), pp. 629-630.

13. Eric Barendt, *Broadcasting Law—A Comparative Study* (Oxford, U.K.: Clarendon Press, 1993), p. 76.

14. Philip Schlesinger, *Putting "Reality" Together: BBC News* (London, U.K.: Constable and Company Ltd., 1978), p. 46.

15. Ibid., p. 38

16. Burton Paulu, *British Broadcasting: Radio and television in the United Kingdom* (Minneapolis, Minn.: University of Minnesota Press, 1956), p. 159.

17. Nelson, "'Television Without Frontiers': The EC Broadcasting Directive," op. cit., p. 647.

18. Steven Greenhouse, "Europe Reaches TV Compromise; U.S. Officials Fear Protectionism," *The New York Times,* Oct. 4, 1989, p. A1.

19. Commission of the European Communities, *Television Without Frontiers: New Rules and Legal Framework for the Internal Market Information Society Services,* Ref. ip/95/287, March 22, 1995, pp. 1-2.

20. Tom Buerkle, "Parliament Calls Truce in Fight with Hollywood," *International Herald Tribune,* Nov. 13, 1996, p. 1.

21. Commission of the European Communities, *Communication from the Commission to the Council and the European Parliament on the Application of Articles 4 and 5 of the Directive 89/552/EEC, Television Without Frontiers,* COM(94) 57 Final, p. 17.

22. European Commission, *Audiovisual Policy of the European Union* (Brussels: Directorate-General for Information, 1994), p. 43.

23. Ibid., p. 42.

24. Brian McNair, *News and Journalism in the UK* (London, U.K.: Routledge, 1994), p. 79.

25. Ibid., pp. 86-87.

26. Nelson Traquina, "Portuguese television: the politics of savage deregulation," in *Media Culture and Society* (London, U.K.: Sage, 1995), p. 237.

27. Ibid., p. 228.

28. Roberto Petrogani, "Freedom of Information in Italy: Restraints and Problems," in Dan Nimmo and Michael W. Mansfield (Eds.), *Government and the News Media: Comparative Dimensions* (Waco, Tex.: Baylor University Press, 1982), p. 35.

29. Sydney W. Head, *World Broadcasting Systems* (Belmont, Calif.: Wadsworth Publishing Company, 1985), p. 84.

30. Swedish Radio Act, Paragraph 6.

31. Evert A. Alkema, "The Protection of the Freedom of Expression in the Constitution and in Civil Law," in *Netherlands Reports to the Thirteenth International Congress of Comparative Law* (The Hague, The Netherlands: T.M.C. Aser Instituut, 1990), pp. 376-377.

32. G. Fauconnier and Dirk De Grooff, "Belgium," in Philip T. Rosen (Ed.), *International Handbook of Broadcasting Systems* (New York, N.Y.: Greenwood Press, 1988), p. 31.

33. Richard Maxwell, *The Spectacle of Democracy* (Minneapolis, Minn.: University of Minnesota Press, 1995), pp. 141-142.

34. Donald R. Browne, *Comparing Broadcast Systems* (Ames, Iowa: Iowa State Univerity Press, 1989), p. 61.

35. Barendt, op. cit., p. 18.

36. Barendt, ibid., pp. 101-102.

37. Raymond Kuhn, *The Media in France* (London, U.K.: Routledge, 1995), p. 175.

38. Jeremy Tunstall, *The Media are American,* (New York, N.Y.: Columbia University Press, 1977), pp. 253-257.

39. Caroline Banwell, "The courts' treatment of the broadcasting bans in Britain and the Republic of Ireland," in *Media Law and Practice,* Vol. 16, No. 1, 1995, p. 29.

Advertising

The deregulation, privatization and commercialization that overtook the electronic media in the E.U. countries in the 1980s revolutionized the advertising business, enriched most of those media, baffled and excited the consumers and presented a huge dilemma for the E.U. member governments. It brought into direct conflict four tenets upon which their democracies were founded: their commitment to free speech, their trust in capitalism, their commitment to civic egalitarianism and fairness and their belief in the duty to protect citizens from, among other things, exploitation, commercial or otherwise.

Advertising came of age in the 1970s when advertising proliferation caused various nations to examine the aims and methods of the advertising industry. As J.J. Boddewyn, international business professor at Baruch College, City College of New York, put it,

Advertisers used to be able to take their chances: "Raise the flag and see who salutes," was Madison Avenue's motto. If a complaint ensued, one only had to gather evidence to prove, if possible, that the claim was truthful or not misleading. This little game is increasingly difficult to play. The new rule is: "Get your facts straight *before* you run the ad."[1]

It did not take long for the battlelines to be drawn and the antagonists to identify themselves. After several years of often acrimonious public debate, consumer groups, politicians, private companies and government agencies began to synthesize the principles that were to guide public policy on advertising. Paul P. deWin, director general of the World Federation of Advertisers and a consultant to the European Union and the United Nations Educational, Scientific, and Cultural Organization (UNESCO) on matters concerning advertising, attributes part of the reason for the ten-year-long discussion of the policy before it was adopted partly to the advertising industry itself, advertisers and advertising agencies and the media, which "although in favor of a directive could not accept the first proposals.

These were drafted in such a way that no advertisement whatsoever could pass the non-misleading test. After consultations and discussion at community level as well as at national level, we came finally to an agreement on a framework law which was deemed to be useful, sufficient and applicable. This Directive also mentioned self-regulation, in that the preamble includes the statement that "the voluntary control exercised by self-regulatory bodies to eliminate misleading advertising may avoid recourse to administrative or judicial action and ought therefore to be encouraged."[2]

The debate finally culminated in the 1984 E.U. Misleading Advertising Directive and was revisited in the 1989 Transfrontier Television Directive. As technology, media consumption and consumer behavior changed, advertising regulation entered center stage again in the 1990s, and the Union is in the final phase of approval of a "comparative advertising addendum" to its 1984 directive.

In assessing the advertising regulation evolution in the E.U. member countries, it becomes obvious that their views have much in common with the views held in United States. Some of these common views are that advertising is speech worthy of at least some constitutionally empowered protection; commercial advertising is different from political advertising; political advertising especially should be regulated to ensure fairness during pre-election periods; commercial advertising should not be deceitful; and some products (such as tobacco and alcohol) present such a danger to the public that they should be seriously restricted in their advertising.

In spite of significant changes in many E.U. governments' attitudes about the role of government vis-a-vis its citizens (mainly emanating from financial weaknesses due to global competition), the traditional European government inclination toward citizen partnership or even paternalism has yielded a significantly more detailed and regulatory attitude toward advertising than that prevailing in the United States.

In the **United States,** for example, it was advertiser abuse that invited the intervention of government, which mainly through its Federal Trade Commission (FTC) has criminalized false advertising since 1938 and deceptive advertising since 1985. The FTC Act, Section 15a, defines *false advertising* as advertising that is "misleading in a material respect." *Deceptive advertising,* by omission or commission, is defined as a claim or a practice that "is likely to mislead" a reasonable consumer.[3] *Comparative advertising,* which is prohibited in several E.U. countries and frowned upon in the rest, is widespread in the United States and, in fact, as long as claims can be substantiated, has been encouraged by the FTC "in the belief that this will assist consumers in getting more needed information about products." Substantiation requires, at a minimum, that the advertiser has "a reasonable basis" for the claims.[4] Another valuable but relatively unused weapon in the FTC's arsenal is that of "corrective advertising," or the legal imposition on a company to run advertisements "especially designed to correct previous claims made by the advertiser."[5]

Although the print media have the right to refuse any advertising, the broadcast media cannot refuse advertisements by candidates for federal office during a campaign period (see also the introduction to Ch. 6, preceding). Furthermore, since 1972, with the blessing of the Supreme Court, Congress has banned tobacco advertising on radio and television. Alcohol can be advertised in both the print and broadcast media, but the liquor industry since 1934 had voluntarily limited its advertising to the print media, billboards and sports-events sponsorship. In June 1996, however, the Canadian distiller Seagram tested whiskey radio commercials in Corpus Christi, Texas, and in September 1996 it expanded its advertisements to several New England states.[6] The success of these advertisements encouraged the industry to officially and fully end its ban, and two days after the November 1996 election victory of President Clinton, who had campaigned on restricting cigarette marketing, it announced that

the absence of spirits from television and radio has contributed to the mistaken perception that spirits are somehow "harder" or worse than beer or wine and thus deserving of harsher social, political and legal treatment.[7]

Broadcast advertising in the United States is further restricted when it is aimed at children. The 1990 Children's Television Act limits the advertising time allowed in children's programs to 10.5 minutes per hour on weekdays and 12 minutes per hour on weekends.

The First Amendment extends its protective coverage with more certainty to commercial speech that is less about advertising products or services and more about issues of public concern, debate and controversy, including political advertisements and political speech by corporations. In general, the Supreme Court has said that government may restrict a non-misleading advertisement of a legal product or activity only if the government has a good reason (a "substantial interest") for the restriction, if the restriction advances the government's cause and if the restriction is appropriate for that cause.

The E.U. Framework

The most important measures the European Union has taken on the advertising issue are the 1984 **Misleading Advertising Directive,** which bears many similarities to the U.S. Deceptive Advertising Act and addresses all types of advertising in considerable detail, and the 1989 **Transfrontier Television Directive** which, in part, describes forbidden types of advertisements and specifically addresses the issue of advertising placement on television. These directives are now the legal foundation upon which the domestic legislation of the E.U. member nations is based.

The aim of the **Misleading Advertising Directive**, Article 1, is to

protect consumers, persons carrying on a trade or business or practising a craft or a profession and the interests of the public in general against misleading advertising and the unfair consequences thereof.[8]

Misleading advertising is defined in Article 2.2 as

any advertising which in a way, including its presentation, deceives or is likely to deceive the persons to whom it is addressed or whom it reaches and which, by reason of its deceptive nature, is likely to affect their economic behavior or which, for those reasons, injures or is likely to injure a competitor.

In assessing whether or not an advertisement is misleading, the directive says in Article 3 that "all its features" must be taken into consideration, especially the "characteristics of goods and services," "the price or the manner in which price is calculated," and the "nature, attributes and rights of the advertiser, such as his identity and assets, his qualifications and ownership of industrial, commercial or intellectual property rights or his awards and distinctions." The directive, in Article 4, requires member states to police its provisions by providing "adequate and effective means," either through the courts or through administrative means.

In 1994, however, the commission decided to focus on comparative advertising itself, in order to "harmonise legislation," to "ensure consumers' rights" and because,

The current situation in which comparative advertising is authorized in certain Member States and banned in others puts consumers, advertisers and publicity workers in certain Member States at a disadvantage, and the medium used (press, radio or television) leads to substantial distortions in competition. ...

After positions were expressed by the commission, council, and parliament, a draft emerged that said that "comparative advertising shall be allowed only provided that it objectively compares the material, relevant, always verifiable, fairly chosen and representative features of competing goods and services."[9]

The final version of the draft was eventually approved in March 1996 and made the following main additions to the Misleading Advertising Directive:

1. It defined "comparative advertising" as "any advertising which explicitly or by implication identifies a competitor or goods or services offered by a competitor";

2. It required the specification of dates when an offer for a product starts and ends and if the "special offer is subject to the availability of the goods and services";

3. It asked member states "to ensure that adequate and effective means exist for the control of misleading advertising and for the compliance with the provisions of comparative advertising," including cease-and-desist punitive measures;

4. It allowed voluntary controls by self-regulatory bodies to exercise parallel policing authority over comparative advertising;

5. It gave member states a maximum of 30 months to comply with the directive; and, most important,

6. In an addition to Article 3 of the Misleading Advertising Directive, it specified the conditions under which comparative advertising will be permitted:

Article 3a

a. it is not misleading according to Art. 2(2), 3 and 7(1);

b. it compares goods or services meeting the same needs or intended for the same purpose;

c. it objectively compares one or more material, relevant, verifiable and representative features of those goods and services, which may include price;

d. it does not create confusion in the market place between the advertiser and a competitor or between the advertiser's trade marks, trade names, other distinguishing marks, goods or services and those of a competitor;

e. it does not discredit or denigrate the trade marks, trade names, other distinguishing marks, goods, services or activities of a competitor;

f. for products with designation of origin, it relates in each case to products with the same designation;

g. it does not take unfair advantage of the reputation of a trade mark, trade name or other distinguishing marks of a competitor or of the designation or origin of competing products.[10]

Through these austere provisions, the Union continued to express its determination to keep advertising within the bounds of civility and fairness, while keeping the avenues of competition open and the spirit of free movement of goods and services intact.

The guarantor of assessing compliance with the spirit of free movement of goods and services, the **European Court of Justice,** had also assisted in policing advertising regulation enforcement, by holding consistently that E.C. treaty articles had priority over domestic regulation. Some of the most relevant articles that concern the free movement of advertising and products are Article 30, which prohibits national "quantitative restrictions of imports," and Articles 59 and 60, which prohibit national restrictions on "freedom to provide services within the Community" in the areas of industry and commerce.

The Court, in its most significant decision on transborder advertising, said in 1990 that a Belgian supermarket's brochures that had been distributed to neighboring Luxembourg and were found to be illegal by Luxembourg law, could not be prevented from being distributed. Consumers, the Court said, should have the freedom to be informed, and the Luxembourg Court was wrong in subordinating Article 30, 59 and 60 to its domestic advertising regulation.[11]

Advertising is also addressed by Chapter I of the **Transfrontier Television Directive,** which provides definitions of terms, and Chapter IV addresses "television advertising and sponsorship."[12] Article 10 requires that television advertising be "readily recognizable" and "kept quite separate from other parts of the programme service." Isolated advertising spots and subliminal or surreptitious advertising are prohibited.

In principle, according to Article 11, advertisements are to be inserted between programs; within-program insertion is allowed if "the integrity and value of the programme" is maintained. In programs that provide natural breaks, advertisements are to be presented during those breaks. As a general rule, films (exclusive of documentaries and serials) that last longer than 45 minutes may be interrupted once every 45 minutes. "Advertisements shall not be inserted in any broadcast of a religious service." News, public affairs, documentary, religious and children's programs that are shorter than 30 minutes "shall not be interrupted by advertisements."

Article 12 requires that advertisements not "prejudice respect for human dignity," "include any discrimination on grounds of race, sex or nationality," "be offensive to religious or political beliefs," "encourage behavior prejudicial to health or to safety" and "encourage behavior prejudicial to the protection of the environment." Article 13 prohibits advertising of any tobacco products. Prescription medicine products and treatments are not allowed (Art. 14).

Alcoholic product advertising should abide by the rules of Article 15:

a. it may not be aimed specifically at minors or, in particular, depict minors consuming these beverages;

b. it shall not link the consumption of alcohol to enhanced physical performance or to driving;

c. it shall not create the impression that the consumption of alcohol contributes towards social or sexual success;

d. it shall not claim that alcohol has therapeutic qualities or that it is a stimulant, a sedative or a means of resolving personal conflicts;

e. it shall not encourage immoderate consumption of alcohol or present abstinence or moderation in negative light;

f. it shall not place emphasis on high alcohol content as being a positive quality of the beverages.

Article 16 addresses advertising to minors and requires that it not "cause moral or physical detriment" to them. More particularly:

a. it shall not directly exhort minors to buy a product or service by exploiting their inexperience or credibility;

b. it shall not directly encourage minors to persuade their parents or others to purchase the goods or services being advertised;

c. it shall not exploit the special trust minors place in parents, teachers or other persons;

d. it shall not unreasonably show minors in dangerous situations.

Program sponsorship restrictions are addressed in Article 17, which prohibits the sponsor from exercising any influence on the content or scheduling of the sponsored program. Sponsor identification must be clear and presented at the beginning and end of each sponsored program. The sponsored program "must not encourage the purchase or rental of the products or services of the sponsor or a third party, in particular by making special promotional references to these products and services." "News and current affairs programmes may not be sponsored."

Article 18 limits advertising time to 15 percent of the total daily transmission time of the station and requires that "the amount of spot advertising within a given one-hour period shall not exceed 20%." Article 19 allows member states to introduce their own stricter rules, as long as they take into consideration public needs, the protection of pluralism and the role of television as an informational, educational, cultural and entertainment medium. Article 21 requests member states to provide appropriate legal and punitive means to enforce the directive.

Finally, the **European Court of Human Rights** and the European Commission of Human Rights have over the years reinforced the increasing importance of commercial speech by reviewing several cases dealing with advertising regulations of member states.

These cases, according to Prof. Dirk Voorhoof, a veteran observer of Article 10's impact on freedom of expression issues in Europe, present "a clear and explicit interpretation towards the protection of commercial information or commercial speech under the scope of Art. 10 ECHR."[13] The trend toward such protection started with the 1979 *Church of Scientology v. Sweden*, in which the commission ruled that "commercial 'speech' as such does not fall outside the protection" of Article 10, but that

the level of protection must be less than that afforded to the expression of "political" ideas, in the broadest sense, with which the values underpinning the concept of freedom of expression in the Convention are chiefly concerned.[14]

The commission reiterated its stand in the 1983 *Ingemar Liljenberg v. Sweden* case, in which it said that "commercial advertisements and promotional campaigns are as such protected by Art. 10, paragraph 1," but that the test of a speech restriction's necessity in a democratic society "should be a less strict one when applied to restraints imposed on commercial ideas."[15]

Another significant decision on commercial speech protection was made by the European Court of Human Rights in 1989 when it decided that "information of commercial nature cannot be excluded from the scope of Art. 10, paragraph 1."[16] Finally, the Court in a more detailed ruling declared its authority over domestic advertising regulation against the spirit and letter of ECHR's Article 10, as it ruled in the 1994 case of the Spanish Bar Association's reprimand of a lawyer for advertising his services. The Court said:

For the citizen advertising is a means of discovering the characteristics of goods and services offered to him. Nevertheless, it may sometimes be restricted, especially to prevent unfair competition and untruthful or misleading advertising. In some contexts, the publication of even objective, truthful advertisements might be restricted in order to ensure respect for the rights of others or owing to the special circumstances of particular business activities and professions. Any such restrictions must, however, be closely scrutinized by the Court, which must weigh the requirements of those particular features against the advertising in question; to this end, the Court must look at the impugned penalty in the light of the case as a whole.

However, the Court said, the legal profession's "special status ... in the administration of justice" makes advertising by lawyers a legitimate concern for the bar associations in all member states and because of each state's "cultural traditions" and "changes in their respective societies and in particular the growing role of the media in them," the local bar authorities and courts are

in a better position than an international court to determine how, at a given time, the right balance can be struck between the various interests involved, namely the requirements of the proper administration of justice, the dignity of the profession, the right of everyone to receive information about legal assistance and affording members of the Bar the possibility of advertising their practices.

Therefore, the Court ruled, the Spanish Bar's reaction to the lawyer's advertisements "could not be considered unreasonable and disproportionate to the aim pursued"—in short, Article 10 had not been violated.[17]

As is evidenced in the following discussion, these central decisions and directives have had great impact on advertising regulations of the E.U. member states, and similarities are plentiful.

National Frameworks

Advertising restrictions in **Austria** center mostly around broadcasting, where tobacco and hard liquor cannot be advertised. Other alcoholic beverages may be advertised, if they meet certain restrictions, such as not appealing to minors, drivers, etc. A public policy debate about a total ban on tobacco advertising is currently being held. Pharmaceuticals advertising is very limited. Advertising by lawyers and tax consultants has been held unconstitutional by the Constitutional Court, especially since the Court declared, three years before the European Court did, that commercial speech comes under the purview of the ECHR's Article 10.

Probably the most controversial advertising regulation, however, has been the one addressing comparative advertising. In the early 1980s, for example, comparative advertising was impermissible, with the courts' blessings, but a decade later and in view of the European Court's decisions, Austrian courts began changing their opinions.[18] Since a 1990 Constitutional Court decision, comparative advertising is allowed if its superiority claims are based on "verifiable and objective data," must not "be misleading and must not violate the requirement of objectivity, either by making disparaging remarks or by making unnecessary disclosures of competitors or in some other manner."[19]

The Law Against Unfair Competition, Paragraph 1, guides the strict regulations that require honest price displays and the truthful use of "list," "manufacturers suggested retail" prices and price "reductions" or "special offers." The law (Para. 1) says that "Any person who, in the course of business activity for purposes of competition, commits acts contrary to honest practices, may be enjoined from these acts and held for damages."

This wording is shared by the same law in **Germany** as is the Deceptive Advertising section, Paragraph 3:

Any person who, in the course of business activity for purposes of competition, makes deceptive statements concerning business matters, in particular concerning the nature, the origin, the manner of manufacture, or the pricing of individual goods or commercial services or of the offer as a whole, concerning the possession of awards, concerning the occasion or purpose of the sale, or concerning the size of the available stock may be enjoined from making such statements.

Furthermore, the laws in **both** Austria and Germany, caution specifically about the use of claims concerning a product's impact on the environment, a company's longevity in business, a company's leadership in a certain area or type of product and of a geographic origin of a product. It should be noted that European courts have repeatedly upheld the Commissions' trademark decisions that have restricted certain products and their names to certain countries—Roquefort cheese and Champagne can come only from France, Scotch can be only from Scotland, feta cheese and Kalamata olives can be only from Greece, etc.[20]

In addition to its compliance with the E.U.'s Transfrontier Television Directive, Germany, the first E.U. country to allow television commercials (20 minutes daily) to complement its income from the television-set fee,[21] has its own Broadcasting Agreement of 1987, which requires clear identification of advertising, allows program sponsorship as long as the sponsors' products are not promoted and allows coverage of sponsored events as long as the program's content is not influenced by the sponsor.

As in Austria, price advertising in Germany is a sensitive issue, especially for a country that is so commercially driven. In addition to their having to be truthful and clearly marked, prices have to include all taxes and must be the final prices. Strict laws regulate sales periods and pricing, "going out of business" sales and, as in Austria, geographic origin claims, the company's age, environmental impact, etc. All comparative claims must be based on truthful and objective proof.

Within the limits of the E.U. directives, alcoholic products may be advertised, but tobacco products may not be advertised on radio and television. Physicians are not allowed to endorse products, and pharmaceuticals may be advertised only without making unprovable claims. Advertisements disguised as newspaper stories are forbidden by the press law, and comparative advertising is allowed only when the public's welfare requires it and when claims can be proven.

In **Belgium**, misleading advertising is the regulatory target. Advertising "that could mislead the public regarding the identity, nature, composition, origin, quantity, availability, method and date of manufacture or the characteristics of products or the environmental impact" is prohibited by the Law on Commercial Practices and Consumer Protection. As in all E.U. member states, claims on geographical origin, company age and leadership, environmental impact, product performance tests, etc., are carefully regulated. Comparative advertising is prohibited as is advertising of illegal or immoral activity (i.e. massage parlor advertisements).

Advertising for alcohol, tobacco, cosmetics, education providers, financial consultants, travel agencies and doctors/dentists is strictly controlled. Pharmaceuticals cannot be advertised on radio and television, on billboards or in children's magazines and may promote themselves only with verifiable claims and without a "before" and "after" treatment presentation or patient product endorsement. Food advertisements may not use such words as "hygienic, medicinal, ill, illness" or their synonyms, may not depict ill people, promise weight loss, show health care professionals or include statements that may alarm the public.[22]

The regulation of advertising in **Luxembourg** is very similar to that of Belgium. The most important relevant regulation emanates from the 1986 Unfair Competition Act, which forbids comparative advertising and selling goods below their cost.

In **Denmark**, a product is defective if it does not meet the promises of its advertisement, and the authorities are strict in enforcing consumer protection and sales laws. Any misleading references to another product, place of origin, product quality, environmental impact, etc., are prohibited. Comparative advertising is allowed but only if it uses provable, accurate and fairly and understandably presented data. Prices must be clearly presented, and "former" prices or "manufacturer recommended," etc., must be truthful.

One of the unique characteristics of the main **French** law on advertising (Law 75-1349, December 31, 1975) is its requirement that the French language be used in all advertisements and transactions that take place in France. Another law requires the clear identification of all advertising, including advertisements disguised as newspaper stories, and allows sponsorships or endorsements. Advertised prices must include all taxes, price promotion must be clear and truthful (i.e., sales, discounts, etc.) and selling below cost is strictly forbidden (except in cases of perishable and seasonable or outdated goods).[23]

The sweeping 1973 law on misleading advertising, Law 73-1193, December 27, 1973, Article 44, requires complete truthfulness in advertising. It defines misleading advertising as "assertions, information or representations which are false or apt to give rise to errors" when addressing

the existence, the nature, the composition, essential properties, content or mode of operation, kind, origin, quality mode and time of production, advantages, price and conditions of sale of the goods and services to which the advertising refers, conditions of use, advantages to be expected from the use, reasons for and methods of the sale or the services, content of the obligations assumed by the advertiser, identity, characteristics and skills of the producer, the advertiser or the performer of the services.

Statutes governing comparative advertising do not exist, but court decisions have found such advertisements to be inappropriate. However, the French Supreme Court has ruled that comparisons provided by competent, non-competing third parties are permissible.

Beverages containing more than 1 percent alcohol cannot be advertised on television, children's magazines or in sports facilities. Alcohol advertising, in general, must include text and/or visuals that appeal to moderation and not promise any positive results through the use of alcohol. Product endorsement by people not related to the manufacturing of the alcoholic product is prohibited.

Educational institution advertisements must have the approval of the Ministry of Education and pharmaceuticals advertisements must have the approval of the Ministry of Public Health. Prescription drugs may be advertised only in physicians' periodicals. Car performance claims must abide by measuring units set by law. Tobacco may be advertised only in the print media, as may firearms, which must include a clear identification that they are meant for hunting or other sports activities.

Children receive special attention by the law. In addition to the E.U. directives' limitations, children are not supposed to be used in advertisements of products that may be harmful to them or in promoting products whose value children cannot fully assess. Advertising that promotes a children's product as a status symbol is prohibited.[24]

The French Electoral Code governs political advertising during campaign periods and access by politicians to public broadcasting services. Print or broadcast paid advertisements by politicians or parties are prohibited during the last three months of a campaign.

In **Greece**, freedom to advertise may be traced to the country's constitution which, in Article 5.1, guarantees each person

the right to freely develop his/her personality and to participate in the social, economic and political life of the Country, as long as he/she does not insult the rights of others, and does not violate the Constitution and accepted morals.

Truthfulness and fairness are demanded of all advertising components, such as pricing, discounts, sales and advertisements disguised as news. Misleading advertising is prohibited, but the prevailing interpretation of that provision rests on the behavior of the average member of the target audience—if such a person "effortlessly recognizes" the incorrect nature (via exaggeration, for example) of the advertisement, then it is not misleading. Comparative advertising is allowed only for a company's or a product's defense, and scientific evidence or endorsement through scientific evidence is allowed only if it is true and provable.

The 1995 law on private television, Law 2338, Chapter A, Article 3.4, prohibits the advertising of "tobacco or other tobacco products, prescription pharmaceuticals or therapies, as well as telecommunication services of sexual nature."

The Netherlands is the only E.U. country that specifically *excludes* advertising from constitutional protection through Article 7.4, which says that its provisions guaranteeing freedom of expression and to publish "do not apply to commercial advertising."

However, the 1988 Media Act has deemed that this provision does not extend to promotions of political, scientific, cultural, spiritual or philanthropic causes because they normally do not represent a commercial product or service for sale.

Political advertising is regulated only during campaign periods, during which the Advertising Code requires that the advertisements be clearly labeled as such, include sponsor identification, not injure the reputation of the advertising profession and abide by the generally accepted decency and taste standards. Refusal to publish offensive advertisements is acceptable, and if the Advertising Code Commission recommends it, refusal is obligatory. Court rulings have indicated that rejection of advertisements that promote political ideas should be done only in extreme circumstances.

The main law that regulates advertising is the 1980 Misleading Advertising Act that covers grounds very similar to those referred to earlier—pricing honesty and clarity, including all special discounts, sales periods, advertisement identification, claim substantiation, geographic origin truthfulness, etc. Tobacco, alcohol, candies and several foods are some of the products whose advertisements are specially regulated to prevent the use of claims that might be injurious to public health. Pharmaceutical advertising has to be reviewed by special boards before it runs.

Comparative advertising is allowed as long as it utilizes only similar products or services, does not mislead or attack the other product/service and does not use the other company's trademark. Advertising addressed to children must not exploit children's gullibility.

Although advertising is not explicitly protected by the constitution of **Spain**, it is widely interpreted that Article 38 encompasses it. It recognizes "free enterprise" as the "framework of a market economy" and guarantees state protection to "its exercise and the safeguarding of productivity in accordance with the demands of the economy in general. ... " The General Advertising Act of 1988 and the Protection of Consumers and Users Act of 1984 are the country's main regulatory instruments of the advertising industry. Their aim is to promote true representations and fair competition.

Advertisements are required to be clearly identified and use honest prices and claims. Comparative advertising is allowed unless it is unfair or hurts market competition by utilizing claims that put a competitor in a bad light—comparisons must be provable and relevant to the products' purpose. Prescription drugs cannot be advertised to the general public unless permitted by the government. Foods and services that promote cures are not allowed. Lawyers are not allowed to advertise, but doctors and dentists are permitted if they receive permission from their professional associations. Real estate advertising is specifically regulated by a 1989 Royal Decree that encourages revelation of all pertinent facts about a particular piece of real estate. Tobacco and products with more than 20 percent alcohol are not allowed to advertise on television.

Political advertising is allowed during campaign periods only. Print media and private radio are allowed to accept paid political advertisements during campaign periods, but television, private and public, and public radio are to grant to all political parties *free* air time, the length of which is based on the party's performance in the previous elections.

In **Sweden,** the Freedom of the Press Act, Chapter 1, Article 9, permits "bans on commercial advertising inasmuch as it is used to market alcoholic beverages or tobacco products," on advertising that may affect "the protection of health or the environment" and advertising that "improperly infringes the personal integrity of a private subject or which contains incorrect or misleading statements." Political advertising is free unless it violates the E.U. directives or the national laws that protect one's honor.

Advertising in the **United Kingdom** is primarily regulated by the Advertising Standards Authority (ASA), a private organization independent of the advertising industry. Its job is to oversee the Committee of Advertising Practice (CAP), a committee whose members come from advertising-related organizations and which publishes the British Code of Advertising Practice (BCAP). ASA is responsible for dealing with complaints from consumers (it receives about 6,000 annually), and CAP is responsible for complaints from competing advertisers. ASA is "happy to give advice about the content of an advertisement prior to its publication to ensure compliance with the Code."[25] Media do not run advertisements if the ASA or CAP determines they have violated the BCAP. The Independent Television Commission and Radio Authority, as well as their complaints agencies (see Chapter 6), control private radio and television advertising. Other laws that govern the advertising industry are the 1987 Consumer Protection Act and the 1968 Trade Descriptions Act.

There are regulations in the United Kingdom addressing advertising methods (prices, special offers, discounts, sales, etc.) as well as content, i.e., any beverage containing more then 1.2 percent alcohol is not advertised on radio or television, advertisements should not appeal to minors, automotive advertisements are supposed to use government-approved measurements of performance and philanthropic institutions must be required by the media to prove their status as such. Claim truthfulness is required of advertisements of diet products, food product nutrition, loan services and travel and investment promotion. Prescription drugs cannot be advertised to the general public, and tobacco cannot be advertised on television. There are specific prohibitions on advertising medicines or foods for "medicinal purposes," which often creates confusion in categorizing such products as toothpaste, which may be "a cosmetic or toilet article" if its advertising claims it whitens the teeth, or a "medicinal product" if it is promoted as preventing tooth decay or gum disease.[26]

Comparative advertising is legal but heavily regulated. The BCAP, for example, says, in Part B.22,

1. Advertisers should not seek to discredit the products of their competitors by any unfair means.

2. In particular, no advertisement should contain inaccurate or irrelevant comments on the person, character or actions of a competitor.

3. Nor should an advertisement describe or show the products of a competitor as broken, defaced, inoperative or ineffective. The only exception to this rule is where the description or depiction is based upon the outcome of a fair comparative test to which the advertiser's product has been subjected and the results of such tests are stated.

Any misleading comparison (from price to content) or unfair attack may result in a "trade libel" suit. Utilization of test results in an advertisement requires permission from the testing agent.

Advertisements in the print media of political, religious, cultural or social issues are unrestricted as long as the advertisement is clearly identified as such, the advertiser is fully named and, during campaign periods, as long as the advertised person has given permission for the advertisement. Commercial broadcasters may be asked by their licensing authorities to run political party advertisements, but advertisements by lobbyists on behalf of political causes or institutions are not allowed.

Although the United Kingdom complies with the E.U. directive of advertising aimed at children, it has added restrictions that include warnings against unsafe practices with products that are legal, frequent snacking and sugar consumption.

The Advertising Standards Authority for Ireland (ASAI) and its Code of Standards are the main regulatory sources for advertising in **Ireland.** Like its sister association in the United Kingdom, ASAI is a media industry-sponsored organization, and its Code's provisions are very similar to those found in the United Kingdom. They basically require that advertisements be responsible, truthful, legal and in conformity with good taste and fair competitive practices.

Furthermore, the 1978 Consumer Information Act requires that a person

not publish, or cause to be published, an advertisement in relation to the supply or provision in the course or for the purposes of a trade, business or profession, of goods, services or facilities if it is likely to mislead, and thereby cause loss, damage, injury to members of the public to a material degree.

It also polices price quotations, testimonials, company longevity claims and exaggerations. Comparative advertising is allowed as long as it is truthful and fair to the other product or company. Use of test results requires the approval of the testing agency.

In **Italy,** the Code of Self-Control of Advertising is one of the main sources of advertising regulation in that country. It requires that advertising should be based on truthfulness, honesty and "susceptibility to proof." Indecency is to be avoided, as is "unethical comparative advertising" and "exploitation of superstition or gullibility."

Another law that governs advertising is the Regulation of Competition section of the Civil Code, which says, in Article 2595, that competition should not "harm the interests of national economy" and should abide by "the limits provided by law." Article 2598 calls a competitor unfair if he/she is "likely to create confusion with the names or distinctive signs legitimately used by others ... or closely imitates the products of a competitor"; disseminates information that is "likely to discredit" a competitor; or engages in acts that "do not conform with the principles of correct behavior in the trade and are likely to injure another's business." Exaggerated claims of product quality or performance are allowed only if they clearly can be interpreted as puffery.

Broadcasting regulations cover advertising as well. Since both newspapers and television stations started their own advertising agencies in order to cash in on the advertising explosion of the 1980s, that part of the economy has been faced with serious concentration and limited competition. The law naturally, therefore, aims at discontinuing the trend. It prohibits advertising agencies from selling commercial time to more than three national networks. If the agencies are owned by the networks themselves, they are not permitted to sell to newspapers amounts higher than 5 percent of the total agency sales. Commercial interruptions of movies, sporting events, religious services, etc., follow the E.U. guidelines of "natural breaks." Children's cartoon programs are not to be interrupted by advertisements. Prices, sales, geographic origin of products as well as test results and environmental claims require truthfulness and verification much in the way it is in the other countries.

Prescription drug advertisements to the general public are prohibited, but allowed in medical professionals' media. Advertisements of pharmaceuticals and therapeutic devices require prior government approval. Tobacco advertising is prohibited, and travel advertisements require truthful description of all details of the trip.

Portugal has an interesting angle to advertising regulation—its 1990 Advertising Law Regulation focuses primarily on controlling advertising that may influence consumer *safety*. The Portuguese Advertising Council therefore requires that "advertisers and advertising agencies (particularly their creative staff) must exercise the necessary caution whenever risks are involved in handling products advertised." Warnings and education should be used prominently.

The other key law affecting advertising is the 1981 Consumer Protection Law, which requires that the consumer be given complete and truthful information, requirements that cover all advertising claims in much the same fashion as in the other E.U. countries. Comparative advertising is allowed but carefully policed—comparisons must be based on verifiable standards and must not be demeaning to the other product or company. In order to protect children, in addition to the E.U. directives requirements, Portugal does not allow alcohol to be advertised on television until after 9:30 p.m. Minors may appear in commercials only if the product is relevant to them.

1. J.J. Boddewyn, "The Global Spread of Advertising Regulation," in *Current Issues in International Communication* (White Plains, N.Y.: Longman, 1990), p. 82.

2. Paul P. deWyn, "Regulation, Deregulation, Self-Regulation," speech delivered April 28, 1993, at the Advertising Colloquium of the European Institute for International Communication, Maastricht, The Netherlands.

3. 52 Stat. 111 (1938) and AMREP Corporation v. FTC, 768 F. 2nd (10 Cir. 1985).

4. Dwight L. Teeter, Jr., and Don R. Le Duc, *Law of Mass Communications*, (Westbury, N.Y.: The Foundation Press, Inc. 1995), pp. 477-478.

5. Emmanuel Paraschos, "The Corrective Ad Challenge," Freedom of Information Center Report No. 283 (Columbia, Mo.: School of Journalism, University of Missouri, 1972), p. 1.

6. Associated Press, "Seagram to Go Ahead with Whiskey Ads," *The Boston Globe,* Sept. 24, 1996, Section A, p. 8.

7. Peter Gosselin, "Liquor Industry Ends TV Ad Ban," *The Boston Globe,* Nov. 8, 1996, Section A, p. 1.

8. 84/450/EEC.

9. DRAFT E.C. Directive on Comparative Advertising, COM(94) Final-COD 343, 21/4/94.

10. 96/C 219/02, OJ C 219/14, March 19, 1996.

11. GB-INNO-BM v. Confédération du Commerce Luxembourgois, European Court of Justice, 362/88, 7/3/90.

12. 89/552/EEC.

13. Dirk Voorhoof, "Restrictions on Television Advertising and Article 10 of the European Convention on Human Rights," *International Journal of Advertising,* 1993, No. 12, p. 199.

14. *Church of Scientology v. Sweden,* decision of May 5, 1979, D.R. 16, No. 7805/77.

15. *Ingemar Liljenberg v. Sweden,* decision of March 1, 1983, No. 9664/82.

16. *Markt intern Verlag GmbH and Klaus Beermann v. the Republic of Germany,* ECHR judgment of 20 November 1989, Series A No. 165.

17. *Casado Coca v. Spain,* ECHR judgment of 24 February 1994, Series A No. 285.

18. Article XIX, *Press Law and Practice* (London, U.K.: Article XIX, 1993), p. 36.

19. Karl Preslmayer, "Austria," in James R. Maxeiner and Peter

Schotthoffer (Eds.), *Advertising Law in Europe and North America* (Deventer, The Netherlands: Kluwer Law and Taxation Publishers, 1992), p. 7.

20. Fred Barbash, "Europe's Fetaful Ruling: It's Only Greek to Them," *The Washington Post,* March 10, 1996, Section A, p. 1. (A good discussion of cases and implications of geographical origin of products can be found in Howard Johnson's "Elderflowers and Champagne," *Media and Law Practice,* Vol. 15, No. 4, 1994, pp. 54–56.)

21. Timothy Green, *The Universal Eye: The World of Television* (New York, N.Y.: Stein and Day, 1972), p. 103.

22. Christina De Keersmaeker, "Belgium," in James R. Maxeiner and Peter Schotthoffer (Eds.), *Advertising Law in Europe and North America* (Deventer, The Netherlands: Kluwer Law and Taxation Publishers, 1992), p. 25.

23. Campbell Philippart & Associés, "France," in Wedlake Bell (Ed.), *Marketing Law That Matters* (London, U.K.: Pittman Publishing, 1994), p. 139.

24. F.O. Ranke, "France," in James R. Maxeiner and Peter Schotthoffer (Eds.), *Advertising Law in Europe and North America,* (Deventer, The Netherlands: Kluwer Law and Taxation Publishers, 1992), p. 136.

25. Tom Crone, *Law and the Media* (Oxford, U.K.: Focal Press, 1995), p. 205.

26. Ivor H. Harrison, "Advertising Medicinal Products," *Media Law and Practice,* June 1992, p. 194.

CHAPTER 8

Pluralism, Competition and Concentration

Until the 1980s, world media owners, academics and experts, such as journalists, news directors or editors, considered European media more responsive to pluralism than American media, although European media never operated in such a diverse society as the American "melting pot." The European media's commitment to pluralism emanated mainly from their multi-party political systems that required multiple media voices to satisfy the informational needs of the various audiences that sustained these systems.

In the 1980s, however, the European media scene was hit by the communications technology revolution and, fueled by the end of Communism, capitalism's response—corporate competition. The electronic media began to expand their presence and role in the European industrial democracies, and it was not long before deregulation, privatization and eventually commercialization arrived. America's colonization of the European media market had ended, and its domesticated Americanization had just begun.

The process started with imitating production values—from *USA Today*'s style of content selection, writing and appearance to the introduction of game shows, talk shows, actuality-driven news programs and American-inspired radio formats. The changes added new life to the normally staid, politics-dominated, party-driven and primarily government-run electronic media. Commercial funding generated new programs that found new audiences and infused these media with an energy, enthusiasm and talent unseen before in Europe.

At the same time, advertising francs, lire, marks and drachmas abandoned the print media in traumatic ways. Even countries that traditionally and proudly had subsidized their print media had to reassess the new reality. At the same time, the E.U. countries faced the dilemma of having to tame the untamable—electronic media technologically capable of bypassing all government gatekeeping and gaining by the day more usefulness, power and popularity. To make matters worse, whatever regulation was to take place had to be done with due respect to the European countries' traditional commitment to and constitutionally protected right of free expression and without injury to the rights of a free press system. The challenge was so large that both the European Union and the Council of Europe eventually had to take collective positions on media regulation of, for example, broadcasting and advertising, as discussed in the previous chapters.

However, the challenge was not over. A new media "disease" was born by the new competitive environment, and it begged for a cure—that of media concentration. Large corporations, some communications related, some not, entered the picture and acquired considerable numbers of newspapers, as well as some television and radio stations or networks, in the name of saving from extinction weakening media or improving others. The European Union's commitment to the free movement of services, capital, goods and people facilitated the growth of many inter-European media conglomerates, such as Germany's Bertlesmann A.G. and Italy's Fininvest. Just as in the United States, the corporate mentality, for better or for worse, had started to penetrate media organizations, their goals, their methods and their principles.

The great American media critic Ben Bagdikian in his classic *The Media Monopoly,* first published in 1980, wrote about the American scene:

The problem is not one of universal evil among the corporations and their leaders. Nor is it a general practice of constant suppression and close monitoring of the content of their media companies. There is, in the output of the dominant fifty [media owning corporations], a rich mixture of news and ideas. But there are also limits, *limits that do not exist in most other democratic countries with private enterprise media.*

The limits are felt on open discussion of the system that supports giantism in corporate life and of other values that have been enshrined under the inaccurate label of "free enterprise." (Italics added.)[1]

Bagdikian was right at the time, of course, but he is right no longer. Media concentration is one of the most important problems faced by both the media and the governments of most world nations, including those of the European Union. Very much as in the United States, the concerns with media concentration in Europe are about diminishing pluralism and an increasing preoccupation with corporate goals, such as bottom lines, circulation and ratings, or as Bagdikian puts it, "no longer City Hall but the shopping mall."[2] The latter, of course, usually results in layoffs that can upset the balance of most of the European welfare states at a time that competitive and fiscal forces from the United States and the Far East are putting tremendous pressures on the traditional, socially conscious European economies.

Some of the E.U. countries, such as France and Germany, have reacted to the concentration trend with strict laws against certain levels of concentration while others, such as France, Greece and Spain, have restrictions on foreign ownership. The Netherlands, Spain and the United Kingdom test proposed mergers against their anti-monopoly laws.

This is the main weapon used in the United States, as well, where antitrust laws have been judged as applicable to the press in spite of its being protected by the First Amendment. As Justice Hugo Black, one of the staunchest supporters of press freedoms under the First Amendment, said in *Associated Press v. United States*, the 1945 landmark case on this issue, that the Associated Press (AP) had no right to refuse its services to media that wanted them just because they happened to be in the same locality as other AP subscribers.

Freedom to publish is guaranteed by the Constitution, but freedom to combine to keep others from publishing is not. Freedom of the press from governmental interference under the First Amendment does not sanction repression of that freedom by private interests. The First Amendment affords not the slightest support for the contention that a combination to restrain trade in news and views has any constitutional immunity.[3]

Although several other decisions since have supported the spirit of the AP case, economic pressures kept leading many newspapers to cooperative publishing ventures that eventually were found to violate antitrust laws in the 1969 *United States v. Citizen Publishing Co.* case.[4] One year later, however, Congress passed the "Failing Newspaper Act," which legalized the combination of the advertising, business, circulation and printing operations of two newspapers in the same locality, while the editorial and news operations of the two newspapers remained independent.[5] Because the act's goal was to help save weak newspapers and thus preserve voice diversity in American communities, it soon became known as "The Newspaper Preservation Act."

The emergence in America of the electronic media as powerful and profitable institutions created another from of concentration—cross-ownership, the ownership of more than one type of medium. The trend started in the 1950s, but the Federal Communication Commission (FCC) in 1953 limited ownership, by one person or company, to seven AM and seven FM radio stations and seven television stations. By 1994 the gradual relaxation of the rule had resulted in allowing a single owner to have 20 AM and 20 FM stations. In a large market, a single owner could own up to two AM and two FM radio stations, but no one could own more than one type of medium (a radio station, a television station or a newspaper) in the same market. Furthermore, in 1992 the FCC allowed each television network to also own cable companies that serve no more than 10 percent of the national market and no more than 50 percent of a single local market.[6]

Finally, although only U.S. citizens may own American broadcasting stations, favorable monetary conditions and trade balances have allowed foreign owners to expand considerably their holdings of U.S. print, film and recording media. Germany's Bertlesmann, Australia's News Corp. (owned by Rupert Murdoch), Canada's Thomson and Dutch-British Reed Elsevier are some of the largest.

The trend toward global media concentration into the hands of few international companies presents a formidable challenge. In the words of Anthony Smith, president of Oxford's Magdalen College and former director of the British Film Institute,

The end of the 20th century ought to be witnessing a transformation of the media industries into hundreds and hundreds of small companies. ... It was supposed to be the end of "mass" society. ... At present we can see—often in the same societies at the same time—a process of Hollywood style cultural homogenization on the one hand, and on the other a paradoxical determination by governments to encourage new competitive enterprises. To some extent the proliferation is indeed taking place. While the new giants are gobbling up the smaller giants from Buenos Aires and Hollywood to Paris and Tokyo an army of small-scale entrepreneurs are also establishing themselves.[7]

Other observers are more alarmed at recent developments. Leo Bogart, the former executive vice president and general manager of the Newspaper Advertising Bureau, for example, complains that the 1996 U.S. Telecommunication Act, designed to "unbridle the free forces of the market," may end up "accelerating the concentration of media power." Although many economists, he says, support the notion that corporate mergers "work in the best social interest—by attracting investments to those enterprises that show the greatest promise," the work of media conglomerates "must be judged in social, political, moral and aesthetic terms as well as by its economic efficacy." Media concentration, he adds, "may affect not only the merit of mass communications but the vital political function embodied in their news-gathering and opinion-forming activities."[8]

The current wave of concentration, capped by three U.S. mergers of titanic proportions in 1995, Capital Cities/ABC with Disney, CBS with Westinghouse and Time Warner with Turner, is changing the media landscape globally. This, warns Gene Roberts, managing editor of *The New York Times*, allows for news coverage to be "shaped by corporate executives at headquarters far from the local scene," and,

[through] the appointment of a pliable editor, by a corporate graphics conference that results in a more uniform look or by the corporate research director's interpretation of reader surveys that seek simple common denominators solutions to complex coverage problems.

It is high time, Roberts says, that newspaper corporations were held "accountable for covering the communities they serve," and stopped "managing their newspapers like chain shoe stores, with no sense of being important community institutions with highly important responsibilities to the public."[9]

The purpose behind all of the E.U. initiatives regarding merger regulation has been to ensure pluralism by encouraging the development of new media and by saving existing media from extinction. Those initiatives thus far show that the Europeans are prepared to be more restrictive in allowing media concentration to continue than the U.S. government has been. However, the willingness, at least by some countries, to interfere *only* after concentration has reached a certain level might indicate what is to come—much as in the United States, a government temptation to continue stretching the limits of allowable concentration to safeguard failing media, thus ironically, encouraging more concentration.

Finally, although the debate over the merits of media concentration is continuing energetically on both sides of the Atlantic, it is the European Union and the Council of Europe that remain vigilant and clearly outspoken on the subject, arguing that the trend must be kept in check. U.S. governmental, consumer, cultural and academic institutions, on the other hand, appear paralyzed by the realization that this country has no effective legal weapons with which to combat the practice. In the words of Todd Gitlin, a New York University professor of journalism, sociology and culture,

The point is that the mergers are taking place amid a deafening silence. Trusts with the capacity for overbearing power are being merged and acquired into existence as if there were nothing at stake but stock values. Today's deals may weigh on the culture for decades. The potential for harm is at least as impressive as the potential for good. If the country believed in the countervailing authority of the government, the recourse would be obvious. It's time for the sheriff to step in and say, Not so fast. But the sheriff has been disarmed—at least politically. It suits the parties in power to collect impressive sums from the titans while proclaiming the virtues of self-regulation. If the issue were street crime, conservatives would be crying out against this abject surrender. They would be declaring that we must take the country back, city by city, newsstand by newsstand, frequency by frequency.[10]

Perhaps there is more than symbolic significance to the 1991 signing of a bilateral cooperation agreement between the European Union and the United States, which calls for information exchanges on anti-trust enforcement cases and notification of mergers or other activities that may affect competition on either side of the Atlantic. Furthermore, the agreement requires the U.S. FTC and the E.U. Commission to coordinate enforcement activities relevant to both parties.

The E.U. Framework

Competition in the European Union is regulated by several articles of the Treaty of Rome. Article 85 prohibits as "incompatible with the common market" all agreements, decisions or practices among member states that "have as their object or effect the prevention, restriction or distortion of competition." Article 86 prohibits "unfair purchase or selling prices," "limiting production, markets or technical development to the prejudice of consumers," "applying dissimilar conditions to equivalent transactions" and adding extraneous requirements at the end of a contract.

Article 90 applies the rules (especially those concerning fair trade practices) of the treaty to all "public undertakings to which member states grant special or exclusive rights" and those that are "entrusted with the operation of services of general economic interest or having the character of a revenue-producing monopoly."

The 1990 Community Merger Regulation made these articles applicable to concentrations or mergers of "community dimension." A merger is considered to be of "community dimension" if the total world sales of all its members is more than 5 billion European Currency Units (ECUs) (approximately $3.5 billion) or if its E.U.-wide sales are more than 250 million ECUs ($175 million). If each of the merger participants obtains more than two-thirds of its community net sales from one member state, these limits do not apply. Community-dimension mergers require the approval of the commission, which may not grant it if it concludes that the merger is against the public interest or is not "compatible with the common market." Interestingly, the commission has gone on record as favoring reduction of the worldwide sales level to 2 billion ECUs ($1.4 million) so that it can have approval rights over more mergers. The regulation has been applied to resolve inter-media conflicts; the most significant media-related case of the recent past concerned the rights of television companies to limit access of their program schedules to publications affiliated with them. The commission and eventually the Court of Justice in 1991 held that the practice was violative of Article 86.[11]

The E.U. Transfrontier Television Directive (see Ch. 6) in a limited way includes some provisions aimed at facilitating pluralism and minimizing concentration of voices. Articles 5 and 6 of the directive require that 10 percent of a member state's broadcaster's budget be reserved for "European works created by producers who are independent broadcasters. ... " Article 23 requires each state to provide for a legal "right of reply."

In another initiative, the European Union addressed with some specificity the problem of media concentration in a 1992 Green Book entitled *Pluralism and Media Concentration in the Internal Market: An Assessment of the Need for Community Action.* The book recommends, as one of the possible solutions to the problem, that citizens encourage their countries to legally require greater transparency of media ownership and control. The Union's Economic and Social Committee in 1993 supported another option that called for E.U.-wide *specific limits* on media ownership both within one country and transnationally with other Union countries.[12] The commission has not taken a position on these proposals and may not in the near future because it wants to avoid authoring media-specific competition rules that will require harmonization among all member states, a tedious, contentious and time-consuming task.

The Council of Europe expressed its concern over media concentration in Resolution 1 of the Third European Ministerial Conference on Mass Media Policy held in 1991. In the resolution's preamble, the ministers referred to the need for a resolution because of the critical role media play in the lives of citizens, and although it recognized the positive role mergers play by enabling media to "operate more competitively in national and international markets," it found the pace of concentration to be such that it was "prejudicial to freedom of information and pluralism of opinions, as well as to the diversity of cultures." The resolution called on member states to develop policies to deal with "the specific problems raised by media concentrations," while guaranteeing "the independence and the development of the media," including their competitiveness, when adopting such policies.

Furthermore, the resolution called on the Council's Committee of Ministers to monitor media concentration at the transnational level, with particular emphasis on the "problems which transnational media concentrations might raise for those European countries and cultural or linguistic entities with a limited geographic area."

In the conference's final declaration, the Council of Ministers decided to take appropriate measures to promote "the establishment, consolidation and functioning of a plurality of independent and autonomous media reflecting a diversity of opinions and ideas and which meet the interests and expectations of the public." This includes, the Council said, "policies which are conducive to the diversification of sources of financing of the media as one means of promoting media plurality in the increasingly competitive environment in Europe" and " ... if necessary, take action to counter media concentrations harmful to pluralism and independence of the media."

National Frameworks

An accurate summary of the status of national legislation concerning media concentration is given by Anton Lensen, an administrator in the European Parliament's Research Service and advisor to several parliamentary committees on media legislation.

Anticoncentration laws for the media are not new in Europe, but they differ substantially from country to country in their effectiveness and in the imperatives they address. Some countries emphasize support mechanisms; others combine such mechanisms with restrictive legal positions either based upon generic competition law or specifically adapted to the media. Some countries consider concentration case by case, while others refer to general regulation. The result is a regulatory patchwork which may not be sufficient to the challenge of the international aspects of media concentration.[13]

The countries with the most concentrated media environments in the European Union are Italy and Austria. Ireland and Greece appear to be on the second tier.

Although it is hard to measure accurately media concentration's impact on **Italy's** media pluralism, two things are clear: (a) four companies own media that share about half of the country's television audiences and newspaper daily circulation and three-quarters of the advertising lire (the four are Giovanni Agnelli's Instituto Finanziano Italiano [IFI], Silvio Berlusconi's Fininvest, Carlo DeBenedetti's Compagnia Finanzaria De Benedetti [CFDB] and Raul Gardini's Feruzzi); and (b) of these four only one, Fininvest, might qualify as a company whose primary business is truly media-related. The primary business of IFI is Fiat automobiles, space and weapons technology, department stores and financial services; Fininvest owns film and video-production facilities, advertising agencies, financial services institutions, department stores and construction companies; CFDB owns Olivetti office machines, financial services institutions and real estate, and Feruzzi's primary business is Montedison Chemicals and agricultural products manufacturing.

After the profound changes within the media and political landscapes of the 1970s and 1980s and because of the domination of these four companies and their political party affiliates, the Italian Parliament approved the Law of 1990 that addressed ownership and concentration issues. Unfortunately, the law's provisions ended up being more cosmetic than substantive because it grandfathered the existing media empires and did not go into effect until three years later, thus allowing more time for the media emperors to solidify old holdings or make appropriate, law-abiding adjustments.

The law says that no one company can own more that three national networks, thus dividing the Italian network system into two parts—one belonging to the Italian state and the other to Berlusconi. Three-network owners cannot own newspapers, but two-network owners can own newspapers that control up to 8 percent of the national daily newspaper circulation. One-network owners can control up to 16 percent of the national daily newspaper circulation. Non-media-related companies are not allowed network ownership but may control up to 20 percent of national daily newspaper circulation, while companies that make two-thirds of their income from their media holdings may control up to 25 percent of daily national circulation.

Finally, the law regulated television advertising much in the vein of the U.N. Directive: RAI, the public network, may allow advertising to occupy only 12 percent of its daily air time or 4 percent of its weekly programming, while advertising in the national commercially funded networks may run up to 18 percent of hourly programming or 15 percent of daily programming. The allowances for local commercial stations are slightly higher. Films, operas and other similar productions may not be interrupted by commercials more than four times. No advertisements are allowed during children's cartoon programs. Policing of the law is entrusted to the parliamentary Watchdog's Office, which is responsible for enforcing all media laws and has been given appropriate powers to do so.

The only bright spot among Italy's battles for media and advertising concentration is the small, local Italian newspapers, which have been prospering in the last decade. This seems to go against the grain of the international trends in the newspaper industry. Sylvia Poggioli, the Central and Eastern Europe correspondent of the U.S. National Public Radio, describes the Italian situation this way:

If the local press succeeds in attracting local advertisers, creating a new market of classified ads that cannot be controlled by the large advertising agencies, its independence and autonomy will be guaranteed. This could result in another great revolution for the Italian press: a national press highly concentrated in the hands of a small oligarchy counterbalanced by a freer local press. The result could be another Italian anomaly: readers of newspapers in Treviso, Perugia or Foggia may soon be better informed than those in Milan, Turin or Rome where many issues are increasingly off-limits to the big national newspapers.[14]

The opposite seems to be happening in **Austria,** where smaller newspapers have been dying and fewer and fewer companies seem to control more and more of the circulation figures, in spite of a generous government subsidies system that approximates $10 million annually.[15] Half of the country's daily circulation and more than three-quarters of the circulation in Vienna belong to three newspapers, two of which are half owned by WAZ, the German chain. The German publishing giant Springer also owns controlling interest in two other influential Austrian daily newspapers and a weekly news magazine.

Austria's regulatory instrument safeguarding pluralism against excessive concentration has been its anti-trust legislation, and it is expected that Austria's recent entry to the European Union would automatically bring the Union's supervisory instruments into operation, thus ensuring protection of "the public interest."

The competition provisions of the Treaty of Rome (see above), which were incorporated into **Irish** law through the 1991 Competition Act, were used by Competition Authority to assess how the Irish media might be affected by the 25 percent ownership acquisition by the British Independent Newspapers group of the Irish Press newspapers. The authority concluded that although the British group, which already owns several cable and commercial broadcasting properties in Ireland, was not involved in predatory practices, its decision to acquire was made in order to stop others from buying the Irish Press and to prevent competition from increasing—in short, its aim was to injure its competitors. Although the authority's decision seems to fit well within the competition safeguards of the Union, it may backfire: there is a strong likelihood that if Independent Newspapers is asked to sell its Irish Press shares, the press may not survive the current competitive environment.[16]

Greece addressed the concentration issue in the 1995 Private Television Law. The law's Chapter A, Article 1.9, limits non-E.U. owners to no more than 25 percent ownership of a station. Article 10 says that a person can own interest in only "one company that has a broadcasting station license and up to 25 percent of the capital stock." There are strict and detailed rules about relatives of owners wishing to invest in the same companies. Ownership in more than one type of medium (television, radio or newspapers) is prohibited. Those who wish to own more than 2.5 percent of a television station may not have been convicted of a criminal offense.

Finally, Article 11 says that those who are investors in or manage a company that conducts business with the state

may not have their own company or be shareholders in or administer a company that has a television or a radio station license or publishes a daily or a weekly newspaper of national circulation, or [publishes] a daily or non-daily regional newspaper. ...

The **United Kingdom** is another country notorious for its media concentration. Media mergers are being controlled by the 1973 Fair Trading Act, which, in the Secretary of State for Trade office, set up the Monopolies and Mergers Commission (MMC) to assess proposed newspaper mergers of newspapers with 500,000 daily circulation. The act's main aim is to ensure that mergers are in the public interest and will not harm the "accurate presentation of news and free expression of opinion." Although in the period between 1990 and 1994 there have been 25 applications for newspaper mergers, only nine merited MMC assessment, and of those only two were found to be not in the public interest. The others were excused from MMC supervision because they met the act's "exception" requirements, which allow the secretary of state's office to give merger permission without MMC consultation if the merging newspaper has a daily circulation smaller than 25,000 copies or if the newspaper is not economically viable and will not survive alone.[17]

The 1990 Broadcasting Act requires that the public interest govern any media concentration and control issue. More specifically, the act regulates ownership of electronic and cross-ownership of the main types of media. The act is superseded by the 1996 Broadcasting Act, which also updates the 1994 Media Ownership Rules. The act's main concern is "to protect the traditionally impartial broadcasters from undue influence from traditionally partisan newspapers."[18]

The 1996 Media Ownership Rules allow newspaper groups with less than 20 percent of national circulation to control television stations that have up to 15 percent of the total television market. No group can control more than 15 percent of the radio market. Regional monopolies, including dominant local newspapers, are not allowed to control local radio stations. The act also sets strict requirements for assigning digital television channels.

Sweden has one of the world's highest readership rates and one of the lowest newspaper concentration rates of the European Union. The only national newspapers are evening tabloids, while morning newspapers circulate mainly in well-defined local areas. Although the number of independent newspaper owners has decreased, the concentration is not yet a major concern. For that reason, Sweden has no specific regulations concerning media ownership concentration. The only applicable laws are those dealing with competition practices and there have been criticisms aimed at the various governments of the past decade for allegedly trying to find loopholes to satisfy major media holders.

What might have helped the relatively low level of media concentration is Sweden's widely respected system of government subsidies that has traditionally worked well to promote pluralism. Subsidies go mainly to the second or third local or regional newspapers, although there have been instances of monopoly newspapers receiving aid, and they are intended to shore up advertising revenue deficiencies.[19] However, Professor Karl Erik Gustafsson of the School of Economics of the University of Göteborg says that although the subsidies managed to "put a stop to the concentration process" and kept newspapers "competing in the industry even though they were unprofitable," they "have not provided any sort of counterweight" to the Bonnier Media Group, Sweden's largest media chain.[20] In fact, it is the continued growth in the number of holdings of Bonnier that has resulted in recent proposals to limit cross-ownership.[21]

In **France**, where media laws are based on "at least three fundamental principles"—freedom of communication, pluralism and transparency—media concentration is carefully monitored. In fact, transparency itself aims at identifying those who have authority over a medium or a group of media in order to make a judgment about their impact on community diversity or pluralism.[22] The key monitoring instruments are the Law of August 1, 1986, and the Amendments of November 27, 1986, which were drawn, in order to pass constitutional muster, under the guidance of the French Constitutional Council. Article 11 of the act does not allow any company or person to control one general newspaper or a group of general newspapers whose circulation exceeds 30 percent of the total circulation of similar dailies in France. Fear of dilution of cultural values was behind the regulation that does not allow foreigners to own more than 20 percent of a media company. Furthermore, in order to increase the chances of survival of failing newspapers and thus maintain pluralism, the French government has been subsidizing general interest daily newspapers since 1974.

In the broadcast field, a person or a group may not own more than 25 percent of a television channel or more than 15 percent interest in any two channels. Detailed regulations govern the cross-ownership of newspaper, television, cable television and radio companies, and the ceiling beyond which they come into force is 6 million people. The dilemma French regulators have faced over the years, according to Professor Raymond Kuhn of the political studies department of Queen Mary and Westfield College of the University of London, is that

the national market is not large enough both to sustain a wide range of domestic media players and, at the same time, provide France with companies which can compete with the global giants on equal terms. The authorities feared that if ownership regulations to protect pluralism at the domestic level were too strict, then French companies might lose out in the international market place.[23]

However, France's largest media groups, Hachette, Havas and Hersant, have fared very well in international competition.

In **Germany**, media concentration is governed by the Federal

Cartel Law of July 27, 1956, as amended in 1976. The law normally requires that government approval be given in mergers of companies with sales of more than DM 500 million (approximately $300 million). However, the ceiling for press mergers has been set at DM 25 million (approximately $15 million). This effectively means that mergers of medium-sized newspapers with daily circulations of 60,000–80,000 must be approved by the Federal Monopolies Commission (FMC), whose decision is based on the potential for market dominance of the new entity. Approval of a merger requires an FMC finding that the benefits to competition outweigh the ills of the merger.[24]

The January 1, 1992, Broadcasting Act addresses broadcasting and cross-ownership concentration. It says, in Article 21, that one company can own up to two radio and/or television national channels, but only one "may be a full channel or a special interest channel focusing on information." National full-channel licenses will not be given to a company in which someone controls 50 percent or more of the interest. A person or a company that owns 25–50 percent of shares of a full national television channel

may only hold stakes in two further broadcasting companies transmitting corresponding programs, which must be less than 25 percent of the capital of voting rights, or not in any other way exercise decisive influence on these broadcasting companies.

The three major cross-media giants of Germany are Bertelsmann (Europe's largest), Springer-Verlag and Kirch.

Although the guiding force behind Germany's anti-concentration measures is its commitment to pluralism, German courts have found that government subsidies are unconstitutional because they may favor some media over others, and thus exercise undue influence on the content of communication.[25]

On the other hand, the constitutionality of the **Dutch** governments' subsidy to failing newspapers is accepted based on the fact that the support is temporary and aims only at compensating for advertising lost to the broadcast media. The subsidies are administered by the Press Fund, which was founded in 1974 and has been financed by taxing broadcast advertising. The Minister of Welfare, Health and Cultural Affairs appoints the fund's board and sets its annual budget.

Media ownership concentration is regulated by the Economic Competition Act but receives no special treatment from it. As in the other E.U. countries, at the heart of government approval for media concentration is its effect on voice pluralism. The Dutch Media Council, an advisory group of media representatives, academics and media experts, has repeatedly proposed specific concentration levels beyond which justice ministry approval should be required, but as of yet no law has been approved.

The **Spanish** Constitution's commitment, in Article 38, to "free enterprise" and a "market economy," has kept media concentration regulation at bay. However, Spain's reliance on foreign capital, especially when private television became an attractive investment in the late 1980s, necessitated the 1988 Private Television Act. The act limits foreign ownership of a television channel to 25 percent of the shareholders and prohibits any one person or group from owning, directly or indirectly, more than 25 percent of a broadcasting company. Although the French Canal Plus, Italy's Fininvest and Britain's Maxwell have seriously invested in Spanish private television, the largest single shareholder is the Spanish banking establishment. There have been no rules regulating print media ownership concentration since the 1984 repeal of the 1966 Press Law's provisions on ownership.[26]

In **Portugal** media concentration was first dealt with through foreign investment legislation, when it became apparent that Swiss, Italian, Brazilian and Spanish interests were moving into publishing and private television. Today the limit of foreign ownership in a television channel is 15 percent, and it is said that it has been reached on several occasions. Furthermore, supervision of media pluralism is entrusted to the Portuguese Press Council, known as the High Authority for Press and Broadcasting. Its charter says that its mission should be, among others, to "ensure that the media are independent of political and economic powers," guarantee that all current opinion may be expressed" and "see that the independence and pluralism of all state-owned programs of the press and broadcasting are guaranteed." However, the government is frequently seen as ineffective or unwilling to safeguard pluralism through rigorous enforcement of these regulations. One attempt at promoting pluralism is the small subsidies program, which aims almost exclusively at supporting technological innovation in existing newspapers.[27]

The situations in **Belgium** and **Denmark** are similar. Both countries have experienced reductions in the number of their newspapers and both safeguard pluralism through temporary government subsidies. Mergers are regulated by fair competition laws but, despite the existence of chains, neither country shows signs of excessive media concentration. In Belgium, in order for subsidies to go to more than one newspaper of the same chain, each newspaper must prove its total independence from the other units of the chain. In Denmark, on the other hand, arrangements similar to the U.S. Newspaper Preservation Act, requiring the combination of some aspects of the operations while keeping others independent, are becoming more popular.

Finally, it should be pointed out that all the E.U. countries require media to "register" either as corporations for tax and mail reasons or as informational media, in order to name a "responsible publisher" in case of litigation. Furthermore, some journalists' labor contracts include a "consciousness clause," which allows the journalist to refuse a request by management to perform a professional duty that violates his/her principles.

NOTES

1. Ben Bagdikian, *The Media Monopoly* (Boston, Mass.: Beacon Press, 1987), p. xxii.

2. Ibid, p. 220.

3. *Associated Press v. United States*, 326 U.S. 1, 65 S. Ct. 1416 (1945).

4. *United States v. Citizen Publishing Co.*, 394 U.S., 897 S. Ct. 927 (1969).

5. 15 U.S.C.A. 1801.

6. Warren K. Agee, Phillip H. Ault and Edwin Emery, *Introduction to Mass Communication* (New York, N.Y.: HarperCollins College Publishers, 1994), pp. 72-76.

7. Anthony Smith, "Media Globalism in the Age of Consumer Sovereignty," in *Gannett Center Journal* (New York, N.Y.: Gannett Foundation Media Center, Fall 1990), p. 5.

8. Leo Bogart, "What Does It All Mean," in *Media Studies Journal* (New York, N.Y.: Media Studies Center, Spring/Summer 1996), pp. 20-21.

9. Gene Roberts, "Corporate Journalism and Community Service," in *Media Studies Journal* (New York, N.Y.: Media Studies Center, Spring/Summer 1996), pp. 104-107.

10. Todd Gitlin, "Not So Fast," in *Media Studies Journal* (New York, N.Y.: Media Studies Center, Spring/Summer 1996), p. 6.

11. Regulation 4064/89.

12. Per Jauert and Ole Prehn, "Ownership and Concentration in Local Radio Broadcasting in Scandinavia," in *Nordicom Review* (Göteborg, Sweden: Göteborg University, 1996), No. 1, pp. 83-86.

13. Anton Lensen, *Concentration in the Media Industry* (Washington, D.C.: The Annenberg Washington Program, Communications Policy Studies, Northwestern University, 1992), p. 31.

14. Sylvia Poggioli, *The Media in Europe After 1992: A Case Study of La Republica* (Cambridge, Mass.: Joan Shorenstein Barone Center, Harvard University, 1991), p. 18.

15. Walter Berka, "Press Laws in Austria," in *Press Law and Practice* (London, U.K.: Article 19, 1993), pp. 26-27.

16. Marie McGonagle, *A Textbook on Media Law* (Dublin, Ireland: Gill & Macmillan, 1996), pp. 279-280.

17. Lesley Ainsworth and Daniel Weston, "Newspapers and UK Media Ownership Controls," in Tolley's *Journal of Media Law and Practice* (London, U.K.: A Tolly Professional Journal, 1995), Vol. 16, No. 1, pp. 2-4.

18. Simon Jones, "Lights, Camera, Action—A Review of the Proposed Changes to UK Broadcasting Law," in *Communications Law* (London, U.K.: Tolley Professional Publication, 1996), Vol. 1 No. 4, p. 160.

19. Karl Erik Gustafsson and Stig Hadenius, *Swedish Press Policy* (Stockholm, Sweden: The Swedish Institute, 1976), p. 85.

20. Karl Erik Gustafsson, "Origins and Dynamics of Concentration," in Karl Erik Gustafsson (Ed.), *Media Structure and the State* (Göteborg, Sweden: Göteborg University, 1995), p. 93.

21. Staffan Sundin, "Media Ownership in Sweden," in the *Nordicom Review* (Goteborg, Sweden: Nordic Documentation Center for Mass Communication Research, 1995), No. 2, pp. 65-71.

22. Nico van Eijk, "Legal and Policy Aspects of Community Broadcasting," in Nick Jankowski, Ole Prehn and James Stappers (Eds.), *The People's Voice: Local Radio and Television in Europe* (London, U.K.: John Libbey & Company, 1992), p. 238.

23. Raymond Kuhn, *The Media in France* (London, U.K.: Routledge, 1995), p. 193.

24. Hermann Meyn, *Mass Media in the Federal Republic of Germany* (Berlin, Germany: Wissenschaftsverlag Volker Spiess GmbH, 1994), p. 77.

25. Ulrich Karpen, "Freedom of the Press in Germany," in *Press Law and Practice* (London, U.K.: Article 19, 1993), p. 83.

26. Richard Maxwell, *The Spectacle of Democracy: Spanish Television, Nationalism, and Political Transition* (Minneapolis, Minn.: University of Minnesota Press, 1995), pp. 92-95.

27. Helle Nissen Kruuse, "Portugal," in (Marcel Berlins, Claude Grellier and Helle Nissen Kruuse (Eds.), *Les droits at les devoirs des journalistes dans les douze pays de l' Union Européenne* [The rights and responsibilities of journalists in the twelve countries of the European Union] (Paris, France: Centre de Formation et de Perfectionnement des Journalistes, 1994), pp. 192-3, 205.

Self-Regulation and Ethical Considerations

In addition to domestic and E.U.-wide legal controls, the media of the E.U. countries must abide by many rules that are made by the *media profession* itself, both at the national and international levels. Through these rules, the profession attempts to accomplish three goals: control excesses by its members, appease those in government who might want to place additional *legal* limitations on the press and, as much as possible, fill the void left in the law by unaddressed or unaddressable circumstances. As with the laws that have been discussed in the previous chapters, these self-regulations also reflect the cultural values of the society in which the journalists operate and are often difficult to enforce by colleagues on colleagues.

Self-regulation is mainly exercised through two mechanisms—the *Press Council* (sometimes known as the "disciplinary committee" of a journalists' union, if it addresses labor issues as well as ethical issues) and a code of ethics. Normally, the former uses the latter with which to assess the professional behavior of journalists. The *ombudsman* concept, an idea of Scandinavian origin that refers to an office or officer in charge of investigating and mediating public complaints against state institutions and/or the press, is another regulatory mechanism, but it normally falls in between government and self-regulation.

The most basic definition of a Press Council is a private, voluntary organization that assesses media performance. It consists of media representatives (journalists and/or publishers) and lay people (lawyers, judges, academics and/or members of the public un-related to the media) and has no punitive powers other than the moral clout carried by its decisions. It hears complaints mainly from the public but it also can offer its opinion on serious issues affecting the press. In many countries, the degree of its success determines the amount of government interference in media matters and it is often seen as a last resort before government legislation. Most press councils are funded by media organizations or by a combination of media organizations and the state.

The world's first Press Council was started as the Court of Honor in 1916 in Sweden and was followed by councils in Finland and Norway. Today 12 of the E.U. nations have Press Councils: Austria, Belgium, Denmark, Finland, Germany, Greece, Italy, Luxembourg, The Netherlands, Portugal, Sweden and the United Kingdom. France, Ireland and Spain have no self-regulatory bodies, although several Irish newspapers have had readers' representatives since 1986. The most notorious council in Europe was probably that of the United Kingdom, which met with considerable success for almost two decades after its establishment in 1953, but its ineffectiveness since then caused its demise and replacement by the Press Complaints Commission in 1991.

The National News Council, the U.S. version of a Press Council, was founded in 1973 with funding mainly from the Twentieth Century Fund. It was disbanded in 1984, after assessing 227 complaints, "many of them trivial" and leaving a "creditable record of achievements."[1] Its problems were both financial and philosophical. Although it reviewed many important cases and made some very incisive decisions, it never managed to generate enough support or interest among journalists or the public, and it soon atrophied. The early refusal of such major news organizations as *The New York Times* and the "exceedingly cool" reaction to it by all major print and broadcast news organizations of New York irreparably damaged its chances of success, especially at time when an omniscient American press was riding the wave of its successes over the Nixon administration.[2]

The most recent comprehensive study of Press Councils in Europe was made in 1994–95 by members of the Department of Journalism and Mass Communication of the University of Tampere, Finland.[3] Their survey followed the pioneer ethical codes collection and analysis conducted by the International Organization of

Journalists in the 1970s and showed that associations of journalists, editors and/or publishers were responsible for the establishment of the council in most countries.[4] Only in Belgium, Denmark, Greece and Portugal was the state the founder of the council and still is its main financial supporter.[5]

The common elements among the ethical codes (see The E.U. Nations' Journalistic Codes of Ethics, this chapter), the Finnish study found, center around six functions that the codes perform: (1) ensuring accountability to the public by requiring truthful, objective, clear reporting and serving as the public's watchdog over government, etc.; (2) preserving the integrity of the news source through fair presentation of the information received, respect of privacy, right of reply, etc.; (3) "showing accountability to the state" by respecting its institutions, laws and interests; (4) showing regard for the interests of the employers by avoiding misuse of the journalistic profession and fulfilling the work/labor contracts; (5) protecting the integrity of journalism by refusing gifts or benefits, fighting against censorship, protecting news sources, rejecting exploitation by employers, etc.; and (6) protecting the "status and unity of the profession" by following the code of ethics, respecting professional organizations, avoiding conflict of interest, etc.[6] The importance of these codes lies not only in their being the main measuring instrument of professionalism, but also in that in litigation courts normally consult these codes to assess professional journalistic behavior.

Media Ethics and the Council of Europe

As the deregulation, privatization and commercialization of the European broadcast media was expanding in the late 1980s and early 1990s, politicians began assessing the early impact of this new phenomenon. They apparently did not like what they saw, and for the first time they felt powerless to do anything about it; this most captivating, popular and potent of all media was no longer within their grasp. Apparently they thought its programming quality was decreasing, news/views were more inseparable than ever before, privacy boundaries were becoming thinner and, in general, the service element of the journalism profession was being replaced by more market-oriented agendas. Worse, yet, they saw a few European media barons easily enlarging their empires, thus increasing concentration, minimizing pluralism and gaining more power, even getting elected to high government office as Silvio Berlusconi, Europe's largest media owner, accomplished in Italy.

Their reservations reached the Council of Europe in the spring of 1993, and on July 1, 1993, the council's Parliamentary Assembly approved Resolution 1003, which was characterized by its austere and didactic tone toward journalists and their profession. It started by declaring that "the media have an ethical responsibility toward citizens and society" and the journalistic profession "comprises rights and obligations, freedoms and responsibilities." It called for "a clear distinction" between news and opinions, "making it impossible to confuse them." "News is information about facts and data, while opinions convey thoughts, ideas, beliefs or value judgments on the part of media companies, publishers or journalists," it said. "News broadcasting should be based on truthfulness. ... Rumor must not be confused with news," it continued.

The media's work is one of "mediation," providing an information service, and the rights which they own in connection with freedom of information depend on its addressees, that is the citizens. ...

The owner of the right is the citizen, who also has the related right to demand that the information supplied by journalists be conveyed truthfully, in the case of news, and honestly, in the case of opinions, without outside interference by either public authorities or the private sector. ...

When dealing with journalism it must be borne in mind that it relies on the media, which are part of a corporate structure within which a distinction must be made between publishers, proprietors and journalists. To that end, in addition to safeguarding the freedom of the media, freedom within the media must also be protected and internal pressures guarded against.

News organizations must consider themselves as special socio-economic agencies whose entrepreneurial objectives have to be limited by the conditions for providing access to a fundamental right.

News organizations must show transparency in matters of media ownership and management, enabling citizens to ascertain clearly the identity of proprietors and the extent of their economic interest in the media.

If we are to ensure that information is treated ethically, its target audience must be considered as individuals and not as a mass.[7]

The resolution later focused on the need to respect the truth, human dignity, privacy, right of reply and journalistic independence. It also called on journalists to avoid sensationalism and the glorification of violence, sex and consumerism.

On the same day, the assembly passed Resolution 1251, which recommended to the member states that the ethical behavior of the media be safeguarded through national legislation ensuring "neutrality of information, plurality of opinions and gender balance, as well as a comparable right of reply to any individual citizen who has been the subject of an allegation." Furthermore, it recommended the formation of a "European mechanism for information verification, taking the form of a European media ombudsman."

Western media reaction was swift and overwhelmingly critical. Typical of the criticism aimed at the resolutions was the reaction of the president of the International Federation of Newspaper Publishers (FIEJ), who called the resolutions "singly and together one of the most profound assaults on the freedom and independence of the press which we have witnessed on the part of democratic countries in recent years."[8] A Finnish delegate said that some of the recommendations "appear very alien not only to Finland's but all Western systems of freedom of speech and the press."[9] An article in *The Wall Street Journal Europe* said that the Council of Europe was replacing "Communist censors as the bogeyman for the free press."[10] Journalism's trade journal, *Editor and Publisher,* called the ombudsman idea "tantamount to putting a KGB office in every news office."[11] FIEJ further complained that the council was attempting to unnecessarily divide the profession. The resolutions, it said, "cannot protect journalists against publishers or employees against employers."[12]

In March 1994, the council's Committee of Ministers refused to accept the assembly's recommendations and was "particularly opposed to the idea of a 'European Media Ombudsman,'" but did approve a resolution (Resolution No. 2) that was based largely on the language of Article 10 of the European Convention on Human Rights. Its tone was not as condescending as the one found in the Assembly resolutions, but the message was clear—shape up or be regulated. Principle 4 of the Resolution says:

Bearing in mind the fundamental role of journalistic freedom of expression in a genuine democracy, any interference by public authorities in the practice of journalism must:

    a. be foreseen in the complete and exhaustive list of restrictions set out in para-

graph 2 of Article 10 of the European Convention on Human Rights;
   b. be necessary in a democratic society and reply to a pressing social need;
   c. be laid down by law and formulated in clear and precise terms;
   d. be narrowly interpreted;
   e. be proportional to the aim pursued.

The resolution also reiterated the importance of the principles already included in most national codes of ethics: the public's right to accurate information, fair means of information collection, fair comment, correction of erroneous information, source confidentiality and avoidance of promotion of "any violence, hatred, intolerance or discrimination based, in particular, on race, sex, sexual orientation, language, religion, politics or other opinions, national or regional origin, or social origin."

The resolution was greeted with similar skepticism by Western media. The World Press Freedom Committee, for example, said that the reasons for restrictions "are so broadly stated that you could drive a truck through the openings ... and they merely echo the excuses commonly cited whenever the press is hemmed in."[13]

Although that was the last major pronouncement by the Council on journalistic ethics, the subject still is very controversial. It is important, however, to note that the Ministerial Resolution has not elicited any major changes within the European media performance or structure.

National Frameworks

In **Sweden,** the oldest Press Council in Europe underwent a serious transformation in the 1960s because of its perceived ineffectiveness due to lack of a punitive procedure. At that time, the Union of Journalists, the Newspaper Publishers Association and the National Press Club proposed the establishment of the office of the Press Ombudsman for the General Public and a new membership structure that included three media representatives and three media-unrelated representatives of the public, including a judge from one of the high courts of the country that normally serves as a chair of the group. The current council membership includes four representatives of the publishers, two representatives of the journalists, four lay persons and four lawyers, one of whom serves as the chairperson. The main focus of both the ombudsman and the council seems to be the protection of the individual's privacy through enforcement of the ethics code. The council is funded by the media industry associations.

The ombudsman receives written complaints from the public, companies or even the government, seeks media responses, assesses the two sides and decides if a complaint rejection, media retraction or a censuring opinion is appropriate. In serious cases where none of the above remedies is appropriate or feasible, the complaint is referred to the Press Council. If the council censures a newspaper, it is obligated to publish the decision and may have to pay a fine to the council to help defray its expenses. Voluntary compliance with this system is very high, as is acceptance by the public. The only drawback is that it could be pursued in court after it has been addressed by the council. In those rare cases, media that have been found in the wrong by the council find themselves at a disadvantage because the plaintiff's lawyers already have had access to the council's decision and the media's defenses.

Inconsistency, lack of enforcement power and general ineffectiveness were the main reasons for the disbanding of the **British Press Council** in 1991. Its replacement, the Press Complaints Commission (PCC), was the result of a proposal made by the Committee on Privacy and Related Matters under David Calcutt at the request of the Secretary of State for National Heritage. The committee mainly was charged with recommending solutions to two key problems: privacy protection and the right of reply. The Calcutt committee's report, released in 1990, did not recommend a statutory solution to the problems. It said, "The press should be given one final chance to prove that voluntary self-regulation can be made to work." It recommended the end of the Press Council, the establishment of the PCC and the development of a means of effectively dealing with press excesses.

The press's bad image among vast numbers of both the public and the government was responsible for a quick press compliance with the spirit of the committee's recommendations. The Press Standards Board of Finance (Presbof) was formed, consisting of representatives from all the print media associations in the United Kingdom. Presbof is responsible for financing the PCC and overseeing the Appointments Commission that appoints members to the PCC, and the Code Committee that reviews and amends the Code of Practice. Currently the PCC consists of seven editors and nine public representatives, one of whom serves as the chairperson. Plaintiffs write to the commission directly, and if the complaint is deemed worthy of acceptance, the commission will ask the editor for comment and then make a decision. If the decision is in favor of the plaintiff, the offending medium is required to publish the commission's finding. Complaints are judged against the Code of Practice.

Since 1981, the United Kingdom has had the Broadcasting Complaints Commission (BCC), empowered by the Broadcasting Act 1981 and amended by the Broadcasting Act 1990. It is to assess unfair treatment and privacy violations in radio and television programs of people who appeared in them or have a direct interest in them. The BCC complaint procedure is similar to that of the PCC, with the major exception that the BCC can mandate when and how its decision will be broadcast by the offending station. Finally, the Broadcasting Standards Council (BSC) hears complaints about sex and violence and operates similarly to the BCC. Neither body has had a major impact on the broadcasting industry.

Journalists, editors and publishers were responsible for the formation of the **Dutch** Press Council in 1960. Its goals are to protect privacy, prevent journalistic excesses and safeguard press rights. Its membership includes eight journalists and eight lay people, including the president, who is a professional jurist. It reviews complaints about all media (print and broadcast), and its membership includes journalists from all media. Its decision is published in the country's trade journal *De Journalist,* and it is recommended, although not legally required, that the media involved in the case also report on it (about half of them do). The council hears cases in small panels that may invite people to comment on the case. The council does not require journalists to appear before it, but the journalists' union does. The council hears complaints against journalists, unless the complaint is against the institutional opinion of the medium in question. Its aim is to assess if the journalist has exceeded the "boundaries of what is socially acceptable ... in view of the demands of journalistic responsibility." The council has eight weeks within which to reach a decision. It is funded by the professional associations that compose it.

In order to manage conflict between the media and the law enforcement and judicial authorities, these three groups in 1980 formed The Consultative Body, whose main responsibility is to hear press complaints with these authorities. The amount of freedom granted the press in the reporting of these issues has been defined by guidelines provided by the ministers of justice and internal affairs. Dutch journalists, however, said that "the body has not lived up to expectations" and complained that "police and justice [officers] too often used press material to chase criminals."[14]

The **Austrian** Press Council was established in 1961 by the Austrian journalists' and publishers' unions, which still fund it. The council's main goals are to safeguard the rights, reputation and interests of the press before the public and the state and to prevent abuses by the press. The council, which has 12 volunteer members from each of the two founding unions, addresses complaints (initiated by an individual or an entity or by itself) that deal with media fairness, accuracy, privacy, decency, etc., as outlined in the Code of Ethics. The council has no legal punitive powers—it can recommend corrective actions and can request that media publicize a negative decision about them, but it cannot force them to run it, although the vast majority of them do.

The **Finnish** Press Council, founded in 1927, is Europe's second oldest. It was reconstituted in 1968 as the Council for Mass Media, and it is financed equally by media organizations and the state.[15] It consists of five journalists, five publishers and five lay members of the public. The council's decisions must be run by the offending media (print or broadcast), but the council will not assess cases that are already being litigated.

The **German** Press Council was established in 1956 by the German journalists' and publishers' unions, and its main task is to enforce the 1973 Code of Professional Ethics, which promotes, like most of the other codes, respect for privacy, accuracy, fairness, press freedom and rights, cultural diversity, pluralism of ideas and honest methods of reporting. The council consists of ten journalists and ten publishers and is funded both by press associations and the state. Although it is not legally mandatory, the council's findings thus far have been published by the newspapers that have been found in error. State laws provide for the creation of broadcasting councils, but those in existence have minimum power and visibility.

In a sharp departure from Scandinavian tradition, **Denmark** in 1992 approved the Media Liability Act, which requires, in Article 34, that "mass media shall be in conformity with sound press ethics." It is the Press Council's job to judge complaints against the National Code of Conduct to measure if media performance falls within the parameters of "sound press ethics." The council was founded in 1964 and today is financed by the publishers' union and the Ministry of Justice. The eight council members include the following: two lawyers, appointed by the President of the Supreme Court, serving as chairperson and vice chairperson; two members of the journalists' union; two members of the print or broadcast media management; and two members come from the public at large. The only punishment the council can extract is to request that the offending medium allow the plaintiff a reply or that the offending medium run the council's decision in as prominent a manner "as may reasonably be demanded."

The **Belgian** Press Council, which was founded in 1985, consists of a 30-member assembly in which all types of media institutions are represented, a ten-member committee of experts, consisting of print and broadcast editors, trade unions, news agencies and political authorities and a chairperson. The council is funded by the state's Flemish budget.

Greece's National Radiotelevision Council, founded in 1989 by an act of parliament, which funds it, consists of nine members: four are appointed by the government in power, four are appointed by the opposition parties and one is appointed by the president of the parliament; five of the nine must be journalists. It is charged with evaluating applications for private broadcast station licenses, assessing the implementation of Greek and E.U. regulations on advertising and programming and hearing public complaints. It does have the right to order a reply.[16]

Portugal's High Authority for Press and Broadcasting was approved in 1990 by the parliament, which is responsible for its funding. It has 13 members: a chairperson who is a judge and is appointed by the state's High Court, five members who are appointed by the parliament, three who are appointed by the government and four who are appointed by the already-appointed members but are to be members of the public at large. The authority's tasks are to "ensure the right of access to information and freedom of the press," to protect the media's independence from political and economic interests, to guarantee impartiality in private television station licensing and to protect pluralism of ideas, news accuracy, the right of reply and diversity of opinion among the state-owned media. The Union of Journalists has disagreed with the composition of the authority and has started its own Court of Honor, whose task is to enforce the union's 1993 code of ethics.

The **Italian** Press Council was founded in 1995 by two journalists' unions, which still fund it. Its task is to see that journalists and media perform according to the 1993 Charter of Duties of Journalists. The council consists of a judge, who serves as a chairperson, a professor of private law, two journalists and a representative of the advertising industry. The charter and the council were the result of a wave of journalist corruption scandals that shook the media industry in the 1980s.

The Press Council of **Luxembourg** was established by the Law of December 20, 1979, and its main job is to supervise the issuing of licenses to journalists. The council comprises seven journalists and seven editors.

The E.U. Nations' Journalistic Codes of Ethics

The press councils mentioned in the previous section rely, formally or informally, on the ethical (or deontological, as some countries prefer) codes of the professional organizations that give authority to, recognize and/or fund the councils. Some councils have their own rules of proper journalistic behavior in addition to the codes, but it is the journalists' codes that eventually must be interpreted if the councils' decisions are to have any clout among working professionals.

The translated codes of ethics of the professional journalistic associations in the E.U. member countries, which follow alphabetically, have been edited for clarity.

Austria: *The Code of Honor of the Austrian Press*

Adopted on 31 January 1983 in Vienna by the Austrian Press Council.

Introduction
Newspaper and other publishers, radio and television companies and the journalists together bear the responsibility for the freedom of the media life in a democ-

racy. Therefore the Austrian Press Council appeals to all whose work/mission is to inform about and comment on the current issues, to be conscious of their duty to truthfulness, purity and correctness. Continuing self-control is a good means of fulfilling this duty. That is why the Austrian Press Council has made the following basic principles for all persons involved in news gathering and editing, or in commenting.

1. Journalism involves the responsibility for the publicity, for the medium in question and for its own consciousness. Therefore the most important duties of the journalist in his work in information collection and editing are consciousness and correctness. The same goes also for the collection of news, photographs and other information material.

2. The interference of outsiders in the contents of the form of the information is unacceptable. Not only direct interference and the pressure but also bribes and other personal gains not directly connected to the profession are regarded as such. Nor can personal interests influence the work.

3. When dealing with the private sphere, the public interest for information and the interest of the individuals and his/her intimacy must be balanced. Reports of the "false steps" of the juveniles must not hinder or make more difficult their re-socialization. In such cases the names must be abbreviated.

4. Freedom in the writing and commenting is an important part of the freedom of the press. The defamations of private persons, slander and libel are, however, a misuse of that freedom and a violation of the journalistic ethos. This goes also for the "single" accusations or defamations towards persons or groups of persons. All discrimination on the basis of race, religion, national or other reasons is inadmissible. The conscious publication of unrepresentative and hurtful pictures is also impermissible.

5. The journalists of newspapers who speculate with the fears of people in order to make money are regarded guilty of one of the biggest misuses of the freedom of the press.

Belgium: *Belgium's Code of Journalistic Principles*

Freedom of expression is one of the fundamental rights of people, an essential condition for public opinion to be enlightened and informed. In its concern to preserve the integrity and freedom of the press, the Belgian Association of Newspaper Publishers, the General Association of Professional Journalists of Belgium and the National Federation of the Information Newsletters have adopted the following code of principles of journalism in 1982.

1. Freedom of the Press

Freedom of the press is the main safeguard of freedom of expression without which the protection of other basic civil freedoms cannot be ensured. The press must have the right to collect and to publish information and commentaries without hindrance, to ensure the forming of the public opinion.

2. The Facts

Facts must be collected and reported on unbiased.

3. Separation of Information and Comment

The separation between facts reporting and commentaries must be clearly visible. This principle must not prevent the journal/newspaper from presenting its own opinion as well as the viewpoints of others.

4. Respect for the Diversity of Opinions

The press recognizes and respects the diversity of opinions, it defends the freedom of publishing different points of views. It opposes all discrimination based on sex, race, nationality, language, religion, ideology, culture, class or conviction, provided that the convictions thus professed are not in contradiction with the respect of fundamental human rights.

5. Respect for Human Dignity

Publishers, editors-in-chiefs and journalists must respect the dignity of and the right to private life of individuals and avoid all intrusion in physical or moral suffering unless considerations related to the freedom of the press make it necessary.

6. Presentation of Violence

Crimes and terrorism as well as other cruel and inhuman activities must not be glorified.

7. Correction of Erroneous Information

Facts and information proved to be false must be corrected without restriction and without prejudice to the legal provision of the right to reply.

8. Protection of Sources of Information

Sources of confidential information cannot be revealed without the explicit authorisation of the informant.

9. Secrecy

Secrecy of public and private affairs as defined by law cannot prevent the freedom of the press.

10. Human Rights

Should the freedom of expression be in conflict with other fundamental rights, it is up to the editors (in consultation with the journalists concerned) to decide on their own responsibility to which right they will give priority.

11. Independence

Newspapers and journalists must not give in to any outside pressure.

12. Advertisements

Advertisements must be presented in a way they cannot be mixed with the factual information.

Denmark: *Denmark's National Code of Conduct*

The following is a legal code adopted by the Danish Parliament with the acceptance of the national Union of Journalists in 1992 and incorporated into the Media Liability Act.

Fundamental Points of View

The safeguarding of the freedom of speech in Denmark is closely connected with the free access of the press to collect information and news and to publish them as correctly as possible. The free comment is part of the exercise of the freedom of speech. In attending to these tasks the press recognizes that the individual citizen is entitled to respect for his personal integrity and the sanctity of his private life and the need for protection against unjustified violations.

Breach of good press practice comprises the withholding of rightful publication of information of essential importance to the public and compliance towards outsiders if this compliance can lead to doubts as to the freedom and independence of the mass media. It is also considered to be a breach of good press practice if tasks that are in conflict with these rules are placed upon a journalist.

A journalist ought not to be placed on tasks that are contrary to his conscience or convictions. The rules comprise all editorial materials (text and picture) published in the written periodical press, in radio, television and remaining mass media. The rules also comprise advertisements and publicity in the written periodical press, in radio, in television and remaining mass media. The rules also comprise advertisements and publicity in the written periodical press and the rest of the mass media to the extent, where no special rules have been established. The rules comprise persons mentioned and depicted, including deceased persons and also corporations and similar associations.

A. Correct Information

1. It is the duty of the press to bring correct and prompt information. As far as possible it should be controlled whether the information is correct.

2. The sources of news should be treated critically, in particular when such statements may be coloured by personal interest or tortuous intention.

3. Information which may be prejudicial or insulting to somebody or detract from other persons' opinion of the person concerned shall be very closely checked.

4. Attacks and replies should, in cases in which doing so is reasonable, be published consecutively and in the same way.

5. It shall be made clear what is factual information and what are comments.

6. Headlines and intermediate headlines shall as regards form and substance be substantiated by the article or publication in question. The same rule shall apply to the so-called contents bills.

7. Incorrect information shall be corrected on the editor's own initiative if and as soon as knowledge of errors of importance in the published information is received. The correction shall be given such as a form that the readers are given an easy possibility of noticing the correction.

B. Conduct Contrary to Good Press Practice

1. Information which may violate the sanctity of private life shall be avoided unless an obvious interest requires press coverage. The individual man is entitled to protection of his personal reputation.

2. Suicides or attempted suicides should not be mentioned unless an obvious public interest requires or justifies press coverage, and in such a case the mention should be as considerate as possible.

3. Victims of crimes or accidents should be paid the greatest possible regard. The same rule applies to witnesses and the relatives of the persons concerned. Collection and reproduction of pictorial material shall be made in a considerate and tactful way.

4. There should be kept a clear dividing line between advertising and editorial text. Text and pictures occasioned by direct or indirect mercantile interests should be used only if a clear journalistic criterion calls for publication.

5. Other people's confidence must not be abused. Special regard should be paid to persons who cannot be expected to realize the effects of their statements. Other people's feelings, ignorance, or failing self-control should not be abused.

C. Court Reporting

1. The general ethical rules for journalists mentioned under A and B should also apply to court reporting.

2. The rules for court reporting shall also apply to the preparatory steps of a lawsuit or a trial, including the preparation of criminal bases by the police and the prosecution.

3. Court reporting should be objective. At any stage of the preparation of lawsuits and trials and during the hearing by the court, the journalists should aim at a qualitatively equal representation of the points of view of the parties—in criminal cases the points of view of the counsel for the prosecution and the counsel for the defence, respectively. A mention of a criminal case should be followed up by an account of the end of the case, whether this takes place in the form of a withdrawal of the charge, acquittal, or conviction.

4. The mention of a person's family history, occupation, race, nationality, creed, or membership in organisations should be avoided unless this has something directly to do with the case.

5. As long as a criminal case has not been finally decided or the charge has not been withdrawn, no information must be published which may obstruct the clearing up of the case, nor must pronouncements to the effect that a suspect or an accused is guilty be published. When a criminal case is mentioned, it shall clearly appear from the report whether the suspect/accused has declared himself guilty or not guilty.

6. To the widest possible extent a clear objective line shall be followed in deciding which cases shall be mentioned and in which cases the names of the persons involved shall be mentioned. A suspect's or an accused's names or other identification should be omitted if no public interest calls for the publication of the name.

7. Caution should be exercised in publishing statements to the effect that the police have been informed about a crime committed by a person mentioned by name. Such information should as a rule not be published, until the information to the police has resulted in the intervention of the police or the prosecution. This rule shall not apply, however, if the conduct which the police have been informed about is beforehand known in wide circles or is of considerable public interest, or on the existing basis it must be assumed that the information to the police is solidly substantiated.

8. A suspect, accused, or convicted person shall be spared from having attention called to an earlier conviction if it is without importance in relation to the facts which he is suspected of, charged with, or convicted of. In connection with other news, the earlier criminal cases against a named person should, as a rule, not be mentioned.

Finland: *Finland's Guidelines for Good Journalistic Practice*

These guidelines, adopted by the Union of Journalists in Finland in November 1991, were entered into force on January 1, 1992.

Introduction

The basis of good journalistic practice is a citizen's right to collect all essential information by which he can form a realistic picture of the world and society around him. The professional ethics of a journalist involves the respect of basic human values, like human rights, democracy, peace and international understanding.

A journalist must recognize his responsibility for the environment and be aware of the environmental effects related to the questions he deals with. Good journalistic practice does not limit either the journalist's own or the public's freedom of expression. It aims at promoting discussion and information flow, and involves responsibility for the principles and policies of communication.

The guidelines for journalists concern all journalistic work, regardless of the medium. Nevertheless, they do not cover all situations arising in practice. The decisions and statements on principle of the Council for Mass Media interpret and complement these guidelines. Good practice also involves a journalist knowing the most important laws, regulations, international agreements and resolutions related to his work.

Professional Status

1. Decisions concerning the content of communications must be made on journalistic grounds. In no way must this authority be relinquished outside the editorial office.

2. A journalist is primarily responsible to his readers, listeners and viewers. He should not deal with subjects which might involve personal gain.

3. A journalist has the right and obligation to reject pressure or inducement with which someone might try to direct, prevent or limit communications.

4. A journalist must not misuse his own position or that of his medium nor accept benefits which might compromise his independence or his possibility to operate in accordance with the principles of his professional ethics.

5. A journalist must not act against his own convictions or good journalistic practice. He can refuse assignments which are inconsistent with this principle.

6. Good practice must be observed in using the work of another party. Although this might not involve material with copyright protection, it is good practice to mention the source when using information acquired and published largely by a second party.

7. Textual advertising in all its forms is to be avoided. Material which can be associated with commercial interests should be viewed critically. Such material can only be published if there are strong journalistic arguments for this. The line between advertising and editorial material must be kept clear.

Correct Information

8. In his work, a journalist must aim at truthful, essential and unbiased information.

9. Sources of information must be treated critically. This is particularly important in dealing with a controversial matter: the information source might have personal interests or the intention to cause damage.

10. Factual information must be checked as thoroughly as possible, including cases where the information has been published previously.

11. The public must be provided with the opportunity to distinguish facts from opinions and fictional material used to provide background. This principle does not restrict the choice of journalistic style or form.

12. Headlines, leads, cover and picture captions, sales-promotion posters for publications and other presentation material must be justified by the body of the story.

13. In addition, pictures and sound must be used truthfully. The recipient must be told whether the material is of a documentary or fictional nature.

Acquiring Information

14. Information must be acquired openly and by using honest means. Exceptional methods can only be resorted to if information of general public importance cannot be obtained by normal means.

15. A person being interviewed must have the right to know in which medium and in what connection his statements will be used. It is also good practice to tell whether the conversation is intended for publication or simply as background material.

16. If justified, a journalist should comply with an interviewee's request to check his statement before publication to ensure questions of fact are correct. However, journalistic authority cannot be relinquished outside the editorial office by such checking.

17. Sources of information must be protected. The identity of a person providing confidential information cannot be disclosed without permission. This is also the case concerning the identity of a person employing a pseudonym or pen name in the journalist's own medium.

Corrections and Right of Reply

18. Incorrect information must be corrected without delay, either on a journalist's own initiative or when the person concerned requests it.

19. Someone subjected to heavy criticism must be granted the right of reply if he has grounds for requesting this. Simply a difference of opinion does not necessarily give entitlement to the right of reply.

20. If the request for a right of reply is justified, the reply must be published in a form desired by the person making the reply without delay and in such a manner that those receiving the original information can notice the reply easily.

21. If the reply is not fit for publication as such, changes to it should be discussed with the writer. If he cannot be contacted within a reasonable time, it is advisable to publish the reply in amended form. However, its essential contents must not be changed.

22. If a certain person is strongly criticized in the medium, it is good journalistic practice to make his point of view known when possible in this connection.

Protection of the Individual

23. The human dignity and reputation of every individual must be protected. Skin colour, nationality, origins, religious or political convictions, sex or other personal characteristics must not be published if they are not related to the matter or in a derogatory way.

24. Detrimental facts related to the private life of a person or his family should not be published unless these are of considerable public interest.

25. Care must be observed in the publication of photographs. A picture cannot be used in a misleading way or in connection with something offensive to the party concerned. Particular care must be taken in publishing pictures of victims of accidents or crime.

26. The publication of a name or other identifying facts when dealing with crime can only be justified on the grounds that considerable public interest is served by this. The identity of a person should generally not be disclosed before court proceedings unless the nature of the crime or the position of the party concerned provide strong reasons for that.

27. No prior assumption of guilt should be made, nor should the decision of a court or an authority be anticipated.

28. If a news item on the report of an offence, arrest, imprisonment, charge or complaint has been published, it is good journalistic practice to follow the proceedings of the case right up to the final resolution.

29. The principles covering the protection of the individual also apply when information contained in public documents or other public sources is being used. The public availability of information does not necessarily imply that it can be freely published.

France: *Charter of the Professional Duties of French Journalists*

This charter was adopted by the National Syndicate of French Journalists in 1918 and revised and completed by the syndicate in 1938.

A journalist worthy of the name:

• assumes responsibility of all that he writes;
• considers the slander, unfounded accusations, alteration of documents, distortion of facts, and lying to be the most serious professional misconduct;

- recognizes the jurisdiction of his colleagues as the only one which is sovereign in matters of professional honour;
- accepts only such assignments that are compatible with his professional dignity;
- renounces to invoke an imaginary title of quality, use disloyal means to get information or take advantage of the good faith of anybody;
- does not receive money in a public service or a private enterprise where his status of journalist, his influence and his relations may be made use of;
- does not sign articles of commercial or financial advertising;
- does not commit any plagiarism;
- does not claim the position held by another colleague nor causes him to be dismissed by offering to work under inferior conditions;
- keeps the professional secrecy;
- does not make use of the freedom of the press with profit-seeking intentions;
- demands the freedom to honestly publish his information;
- respects justice and gives it top priority;
- does not confuse his role with a policeman's.

Germany: *The Press Code of Germany*

This code was drawn up by the German Press Council in collaboration with the press associations and presented to Federal President Gustav W. Heinemann on 12 December 1973 in Bonn. It was last updated February 23, 1994.

The freedom of the press guaranteed in the Basic Law of the Federal Republic of Germany embraces independence and freedom of information, expression of opinion and criticism. Publishers, editors and journalists pursuing their profession must remain constantly aware of their responsibility towards the general public and their duty to uphold the prestige of the press. They must perform their journalistic duties to the best of their ability and belief and must not allow their work to be influenced by personal interests or extraneous motives.

These journalistic principles are designed to preserve professional ethics; they do not constitute grounds for legal liability.

Article 1
Respect for the truth and accurate informing of the general public are the overriding principles of the press.

Guideline 1.1. Exclusive agreements

Public information about events or developments whose significance, import and implications make them of general interest and vital for the formation of political views and public opinion must not be restricted or impeded by exclusive agreements with informants or measures which screen such informants from the public domain. Anyone seeking to monopolize information prevents other members of the press acquiring important news and thus acts contrary to the principle of the freedom of the information.

Guideline 1.2. Election campaign reporting

In the interests of journalistic fairness, freedom of information for the public and equality of opportunity for the democratic parties, newspapers and magazines covering election campaigns should also publish views which they do not share themselves. A similar policy should be adopted towards advertising matter, which is also covered by the fundamental precept of press freedom.

Guideline 1.3. Press releases

Press releases issued by government agencies, political parties, associations, organizations or other representative bodies must be identified as such if they are published unedited.

Article 2

News and information accepted for text or pictorial publication must be checked for accuracy with all the thoroughness circumstances permit. Its meaning must not be distorted or falsified by editing, headings or captions. The content of documents must be faithfully reproduced. Unconfirmed reports, rumours and assumptions must be identifiable as such. Where a symbolic photograph is published, it must be made clear in the caption that it is not a documentary picture.

Guideline 2.1. Opinion polls

The German Press Council recommends that news agencies, newspapers and magazines publishing findings by opinion poll institutes should indicate the number of people interviewed, the dates on which the poll was conducted and the identity of the poll's sponsor. Where no sponsor is involved, reports should point out that the data was collected at the instigation of the opinion poll institute itself.

Guideline 2.2. Symbolic photographs

A non-documentary illustration—especially a photograph—which the casual reader might mistake for a documentary illustration must be marked accordingly.

The following must therefore be clearly identified or described in captions or accompanying text to ensure that they are not misinterpreted even by a casual reader:

– substitute or indicative illustrations (same motif on different occasion, different motif on same occasion, etc.)
– symbolic illustrations (reconstructed scenes, graphic representations, artists' impressions of events described in text, etc.)
– photomontages or other alterations.

Guideline 2.3. Advance reviews

Newspapers and magazines publishing advance reviews which summarize the contents of forthcoming publications and may be disseminated by news agencies are legally and professionally responsible for ensuring the accuracy of those reviews. Omissions or additions must not distort the basic tenor of the previewed publication or permit incorrect conclusions which could be detrimental to the legitimate interests of third parties.

Guideline 2.4. Interviews

An interview is always within the bounds of journalistic propriety if it is authorized by the interviewee or his proxy. Under circumstances of exceptional time pressure, it is also acceptable for comments to be published in unauthorized interview form as long as interviewees are aware of the intention to publish the wording or gist of their statements. Journalists should always identify themselves as such. An interview orally or in written form is not mere news material but a work protected by copyright, especially if it contains critical appraisals or comments which lend it a personal stamp. When such interviews are reproduced in full or in part, the publishing newspaper or magazine must indicate the source. Even where the essence of the thoughts expressed is paraphrased, journalistic propriety requires that the source should be indicated. Where interviews are announced in resume form, it must be borne in mind that interviewees, as co-authors, are protected against distortions or detractions which could jeopardise their legitimate personal or copyright interests (see also Guidelines 2.3 and 11.4).

Guideline 2.5. Release deadlines

Release deadlines postponing the publication of specific news items are only justifiable if they are in the interests of objective and accurate reporting. Their observance is basically a matter for voluntary agreement between informants and media. Release deadlines should only be observed if there is a legitimate reason for doing so, as in the case of the text of a speech which has not yet been delivered, advance copies of corporate annual reports or information about events scheduled for a future date (meetings, resolutions, award ceremonies, etc.). Release deadlines imposed for mere advertising purposes should not be entertained.

Guideline 2.6. Readers' letters

(1) Periodicals should publish readers' letters—of appropriate form and content—to give readers an opportunity to air their views and help form public opinion. In this way, a newspaper can promote discussion of its own editorial line, stimulate public debate and foster personal initiative.

(2) Correspondence addressed to publishers or editorial departments of a newspaper or magazine can be published as readers' letters if it is evident from the form and content that this is in accordance with the sender's wishes. The sender's consent can be assumed if a letter refers to articles published by the newspaper or magazine concerned or to matters of general interest. Readers have no legal right to have their letters published.

(3) It is both proper and common practice to publish reader's names along with their letters. By the very act of sending a letter, a reader gives tacit consent to the publication of his or her name.

(4) Only in exceptional cases can a different name be appended at the author's request.

(5) The obligation of the press to take care not to publish material of punishable content also applies to readers' letters. Under press laws, editors are co-responsible for readers' letters which contain derogatory allegations about an identifiable third part.

(6) The publication of fictitious readers' letters represents deception of the public and is irreconcilable with the duty of the press. If there is any doubt about the origin of the letter, it is incumbent on the editor to check its authenticity.

(7) Where a reader's letter contains factual claims about a third party, that party is entitled under press law to reply to the allegations in print.

(8) The right of the press to refuse to give evidence also extends to the writers of reader's letters. A reader's letter published in a periodical is classified as editorial matter and privileges its author to refuse to give evidence.

(9) The laws protecting the general right of the individual basically prohibit the alteration or abridgment of letters from named correspondents without their consent. This also applies to letters which do not bear an "individual stamp" and are thus not protected by copyright. Letters can be shortened only if the "Reader's Letters" column contains a standard reference to the publisher's right to print letters in edited form. If the author of a letter expressly forbids alteration or abridgment, the editorial department addressed must either comply with the writer's wishes or

refuse publication even if it has retained the edit reader's letters.

(10) All reader's letters arriving on an editor's desk are to be treated as confidential documents. Under no circumstances may they be passed on to third parties.

Article 3

Published news reports or assertions subsequently found to be incorrect must be promptly and appropriately corrected by the publication concerned.

Guideline 3.1. Editorial corrections

An editorial correction must draw the reader's attention to the fact that the preceding report was wholly or partially incorrect. It must therefore contain not only the correct facts but also a reference to the incorrect report in question. Publication of the correct facts is required even if the error has already been publicly acknowledged elsewhere. The duty to rectify an incorrect report lies with the editorial department. This duty is not fulfilled by merely prompting and publishing readers' letters.

Article 4

Dishonest methods must not be employed to acquire news, information or pictures.

Guideline 4.1. Research

Research is a legitimate tool of journalistic work but must be conducted within the bounds of the constitution, the law and respect for human dignity. As a matter of principle, a researching journalist who makes untruthful statements about his identity or the identity of the publication he represents is guilty of conduct incompatible with the dignity and role of the press. Covert research can be justified in individual cases if it brings to light information of special public interest which could not be obtained by other means. In the case of accidents and disasters, the press shall bear in mind that rescue operations for victims and persons in jeopardy take precedence over the public's right to be informed. Nor does the public's interest in being informed justify any unlawful acts committed by journalists to acquire news material.

Article 5

As a general principle, confidentiality agreed to at briefings and background interviews must be observed.

Guideline 5.1. Confidentiality

Where an informant agrees to supply information for publication only on condition that he or she remains unidentified and protected as a source, that stipulation shall be respected. A bond of confidentiality may only be broken where the information in question relates to the planning of a criminal act, in which case the journalist has a duty to report the matter to the authorities. Nor need confidentiality be observed if, after careful consideration of material and other interests, important reasons of state are deemed predominant. This situation can arise, in particular, if constitutional order is likely to be affected or endangered. Reporting on plans and activities which are designated secret is permissible if, after careful consideration, the need to inform the public is found to outweigh the stated reasons for secrecy. This does not, however, justify the committing of unlawful acts to acquire information (see also Guideline 4.1).

Article 6
All members of the press shall maintain professional confidentiality, exercise their right to refuse to give evidence and refrain from disclosing the identity of informants without their explicit consent.

Guideline 6.1. Intelligence service
Any journalist or publisher engaging in intelligence work damages the credibility of the press and undermines the trust placed in the profession.

Guideline 6.2. Separation of press and government duties
If a journalist enters the service of a government or government agency, all parties should take care to ensure that his or her press and official duties are kept strictly separate, especially where those official duties relate to media activity. The same applies to government officials who take up posts in journalism. The clear separation—anchored in contracts of employment—is needed to avoid any semblance of divided loyalties or professional compromise which could damage the reputation and credibility of the media.

Article 7
The responsibility of the press towards the general public precludes the publication of editorial matter which is influenced by the private or business interests of third parties. Publishers and editors must resist any attempts at such influence and ensure that editorial and advertising matter are kept clearly separate. Advertising announcements, advertising photographs and advertising drawings should be identifiable as such.

Guideline 7.1. Separation of editorial material and advertising matter
Advertisements resembling editorial material must be printed in a script, position and form which clearly distinguish them from the editorial contents of a newspaper or magazine so that they are identifiable as advertising even to the casual

reader. They must be clearly marked with the word "Advertisement". If the sponsor is not clearly identified in the text of the advertisement, his name must be printed in a clearly visible position. The same applies to advertising inserts and any other special publications financed by individuals, corporate bodies or institutions with a personal, commercial or political interest in their contents. Where an insert or special publication contains articles of specialists who themselves have a vested interest in its dissemination, this must be indicated by references to their respective role. PR texts, which are intrinsically connected with advertising, must be labeled accordingly or laid out in a way which distinguishes them from the editorial contents of the host publication to ensure that they do not mislead the reader.

Guideline 7.2. Surreptitious advertising in editorial matter

The publication of editorial matter referring to companies or their product, services or activities must not overstep the boundary between editorial freedom and surreptitious advertising. This boundary is patently transgressed, in particular, where the information published does not cater to a legitimate public interest or the reader's interest in being informed.

To maintain the credibility of the press as a source of information, editors must exercise special care when handling PR texts and phrasing editorial references. Special publications are subject to the same rules of editorial responsibility as all published editorial material.

Article 8

The press shall respect the private life and personal sphere of the individual. If a person's private behaviour touches on public interests, however, it may be discussed in the press. In such cases, care must be taken to ensure that publication does not violate the personal rights of individuals who are not involved.

Guideline 8.1. Publication of names/photographs

As a general rule, there is no justification for publishing the names and photographs of offenders or victims in reports on accidents, criminal offences, criminal investigations or court proceedings. In all such cases, care must be taken to weigh the public's right to be informed and the personal rights of the individual concerned. Victims of accidents or crime are entitled to special protection from disclosure of their names. The identity of the victim is irrelevant for understanding the events surrounding an accident or crime unless it involves a person of contemporary history or occurs in circumstances touching on issues of wider public interest. In the case of relatives who have nothing to do with the incident, respect for their legitimate personal rights must, as a matter of principle, take precedence over the public's right to be informed. The names of individuals concerned and their families should also be protected in portrayals of criminal cases published after the death of the persons involved. In these cases, it is necessary to check whether the incident can be considered part of criminal history and the perpetrator a person of contemporary history (see also Guidelines 13.2 and 13.3).

Guideline 8.2. Anniversaries
Before publishing details of anniversaries involving persons not normally in the public eye, editors must first check whether the individuals concerned agree to publication or wish to be protected from publicity.

Guideline 8.3. Illness
Physical and mental illnesses and disorders fall within the confidential sphere of the person concerned. Out of respect of the privacy for that person and his family, the press should refrain from publishing names and photographs in such cases and avoid using disparaging names for medical conditions or medical institutions even if such names are found in common parlance. Individuals (including persons of contemporary history) have a right to be protected from discriminating revelations both during their lifetime and after their death.

Guideline 8.4. Suicide
Restraint must be exercised when reporting on cases of suicide. This applies particularly to the publication of names and detailed descriptions of circumstances. Exceptions are only justifiable where the incident in question is of contemporary historical significance and general public interest.

Guideline 8.5. Political opposition and refugees
When reporting on countries where opposition to the government entails a risk to life and limb, journalists must always consider whether publishing names or photos could lead to the identification and persecution of the persons concerned. The same applies to reports on refugees. The publication of details identifying refugees, their escape routes and the manner in which they prepared and executed their escape might endanger the families and friends those refugees left behind or close escape channels for other refugees.

Article 9
It is contrary to journalistic decorum to publish unfounded allegations, especially allegations of a defamatory nature.

Article 10
The publication of text or pictures whose form or content could deeply offend

the moral or religious sensibilities of a particular group of persons is incompatible with press responsibility.

Article 11

Violence and brutality should not be sensationalized. Reporting must take due account of the need to protect young people.

Guideline 11.1. Threats and acts of violence

When reporting on threats or acts of violence, the press must carefully weigh the public's interest in information against the interests of the victims and persons concerned. Reports on such events must be unbiased and authentic but the press must not become the tool of criminals or make any unauthorized attempt to mediate between criminals and police.

Guideline 11.2. Accidents and disasters

The bounds of acceptable reporting on accidents and disasters are exceeded where the suffering of victims and the feelings of their families cease to be respected. Those hit by misfortune must not become victims for a second time because of the tactless media coverage.

Guideline 11.3. Collaboration with authorities/news blackouts

Without neglecting its fundamental duty to inform, the press should exercise restraint in reporting on threats of violence of any kind. Collaboration between media and police should only occur if the lives and health of victims or other persons involved can be protected or saved by journalists' actions.

Where requests are received from criminal prosecution authorities for a temporary, complete or partial cessation of reporting in the interests of crime detection, the press will comply with such requests provided they are backed by cogent arguments and are not connected with news blackouts by official agencies.

Guideline 11.4. Criminal memoirs

The publication of criminal memoirs can give alleged or convicted criminals a degree of publicity which is not warranted by the need to inform the public. The detailed description of criminal acts from the exclusive viewpoint of their perpetrator, who may still be in prison, is not compatible with the journalistic responsibilities of the press. Interviews must not be held with persons who are in the process of committing a crime.

Article 12

There must be no discrimination against anyone on grounds of sex, race, ethnic background, religion, social group or nationality.

Guideline 12.1. Crime reporting

In crime reports, the fact that a suspect or offender belongs to a particular religious, ethnic or other minority should only be mentioned if the information is important for understanding the reported events.

Article 13

Reports on cases under criminal investigation or subjudice must be devoid of all preconceived opinion. Before and during such proceedings, therefore, the press shall avoid making any comment in the heading or body of a report which could be construed as partisan or prejudicial to the issue. An accused person must not be presented as a guilty party before legal judgment has been pronounced. Wherever possible in the case of minor offences committed by juveniles, names and identifying photographs should not be published out of consideration for the young persons' future. Court rulings should not be reported prior to their official announcement without sound legal justification.

Guideline 13.1. Criminal investigations and court proceedings,
prejudgment of issues and follow-up reporting

The purpose of reporting on official investigations and court proceedings is to provide the general public with a thorough and unbiased account of the commission, prosecution and judgment of crimes. Until a court pronounces judgment, an accused person is presumed innocent. Portrayals and assertions which prejudge a legal issue are in violation of the constitutional rules protecting human dignity, which also applies in full to offenders. In the wording of reports, a clear distinction must be made between suspicion and proven guilty. The portrayal of a suspect as a guilty party prior to the pronouncement of judgment is also prohibited in cases where a confession has been made. Even if the identity of the person responsible for a crime is obvious to the general public, the person concerned must not be presented as the guilty party until a court verdict is announced. Where the press reports on an appealable conviction and names or identifies the person concerned to a wide readership, it must also report on any subsequent appeal resulting in final acquittal or a significant quashing of charges, provided this does not conflict with the legitimate interests of the person concerned. This recommendation also applies to reports on criminal investigations which are subsequently discontinued. Critical reports and commentaries on legal proceedings should be clearly distinguished from trial reports.

Guideline 13.2. Publication of names and photographs of
suspects, offenders and victims

When publishing names and photographs of suspects, offenders, victims and other persons affected by a crime, great care must be taken in weighing up the public's interest and the personal rights of the individuals concerned. Legitimate public interest, however, does not justify sensationalism. The publication of the full names and/or photographs of suspects charged with a capital offence is only justified if this is in the interests of crime detection and the requirements for issuing a warrant of arrest are satisfied. In any case where there are indications that the suspect may not be guilty, names and photographs should not be published. As a matter of principle, it is not permissible to publish names and photographs of relatives or other affected persons who have nothing to do with a crime. In the interests of resocialization, names and photographs must not appear in reports published after the conclusion of criminal proceedings (see also Guideline 8.1).

Guideline 13.3. Persons of contemporary history

Certain exceptions to the principles stated at 13.2. apply in the case of persons of contemporary history (including public office-holders and individuals with a public mandate) who are suspected, accused or convicted of an offence.

In the case of persons in public office or with a public mandate, the publication of names and photographs is admissible if there is a connection between their office or mandate and the offence in question. In the case of persons of contemporary history who do not hold a public office or mandate, the publication of names and photographs may be justified if the offence with which they are charged is in contradiction to their public image.

Guideline 13.4. Juvenile crime

When reporting on juvenile crime and juvenile court proceedings, the press should exercise restraint out of consideration for the future of the young people concerned. This recommendation also applies to reports on juvenile victims of crime. As a general rule, there is no objection to the publication of photographs and names of missing young persons. These should only be published, however, with the agreement of the relevant authorities.

Article 14

In reports on medical issues, care must be taken to avoid undue sensationalism which could arouse baseless fears or hopes in the reader. Early research findings should not be presented as though they were conclusive or almost conclusive.

Guideline 14.1. Medical or pharmaceutical research

In reporting on alleged successes or failures of medical or pharmaceutical research aimed at controlling disease, the press should exercise circumspection and responsibility. In both text and presentation, care must be taken to ensure that such reports do not convey a distorted image of the actual state of medical research and that undue hopes of a cure in the foreseeable future are not aroused in the sick and their families. Conversely, care must be taken to ensure that victims of disease are not disconcerted and the possible success of therapeutic measures called into question by critical or one-sided reports on controversial views.

Article 15

The acceptance or granting of any kind of privilege which could impinge on publishing or editorial discretion is not compatible with the concept of a respectable, independent and responsible press. Anyone accepting bribes for the dissemination or suppression of news is guilty of dishonourable and unprofessional conduct.

Guideline 15.1. Invitations and gifts

Publishing and journalistic discretion can be impaired if editors and editorial staff accept invitations or gifts whose values exceeds the bounds of social convention and professional etiquette. (See also German Press Council statement of 21 February 1961 calling upon all press and business associations to take appropriate steps to uphold this principle. See corresponding agreements between the German Journalists' Association and the Federal Association of German Newspaper Publishers of 17 October 1961 and the association of German Magazine Publishers of 9 January 1961.)

Article 16

In the interests of fair reporting, public reprimands by the German Press Council should normally be published in the publication concerned.

Guideline 16.1. Publication of reprimands

The publication concerned must ensure that the reader is informed of the circumstances which gave rise to the reprimand and the publicistic principle they violated.

Greece: *Principles of Deontology of Greek Journalists*

Approved on October 31, 1988, by five Greek journalists' unions: the Union of Journalists of Daily Newspapers of Athens, the Union of Journalists of Daily Newspapers of Macedonia-Thrace, the Union of Journalists of Daily Newspapers of Peloponissos, Epirus and Islands, the Union of Journalists of Daily Newspapers of Thessaly, Sterea, Evia and the Union of Journalists of Periodical Press.

1. Journalism is a public service.

2. Truth and its presentation constitute the main concern of the journalist.

3. The journalist defends everywhere and always the freedom of press, the free and undisturbed propagation of ideas and news, as well as the right to opposition.

4. The religious convictions, the institutions, the manners and customs of nations, peoples and races, as well as citizens' private and family life are respected and inviolable.

5. Primary task of the journalist is the defence of people's liberties and of the democratic regime, as well as the advancement of social and state institutions.

6. Respect for national and popular values and the defence of people's interests should inspire the journalist in the practice of his function.

7. The journalist while practicing his function rejects any intervention aimed at concealing or distorting the truth.

8. The access to sources of news is free and undisturbed for the journalist, who is not obliged to reveal his information sources.

9. The function of journalism may not be practiced for self-seeking purposes.

10. The journalist does not accept any advantage, benefit or promise of benefit offered in exchange for the restriction of the independence of his opinion while practicing his function.

Ireland: *Irish Journalists' Code of Conduct*

Adopted on June 29, 1994, by National Union of Journalists.

1. A journalist has a duty to maintain the highest professional and ethical standards.

2. A journalist shall at all times defend the principle of the freedom of the press and other media in relation to the collection of information and the expression of comment and criticism. He/she shall strive to eliminate distortion, news suppression and censorship.

3. A journalist shall strive to ensure that the information he/she disseminates is fair and accurate, avoid the expression of comment and conjecture as established fact and falsification by distortion, selection or misrepresentation.

4. A journalist shall rectify promptly any harmful inaccuracies, ensure that correction and apologies receive due prominence and afford the right of reply to persons criticised when the issue is of sufficient importance.

5. A journalist shall obtain information, photographs and illustrations only by straight-forward means. The use of other means can be justified only by over-riding considerations of the public interest. The journalist is entitled to exercise a per-

sonal conscientious objection to the use of such means.

6. Subject to the justification by over-riding considerations of the public interest, a journalist shall do nothing which entails intrusion into private grief and distress.

7. A journalist shall protect confidential sources of information.

8. A journalist shall not accept bribes nor shall he/she allow other inducements to influence the performance of his/her professional duties.

9. A journalist shall not lend himself/herself to the distortion or suppression of the truth because of advertising or other considerations.

10. A journalist shall only mention a person's age, race, colour, creed, illegitimacy, disability, marital status (or lack of it), gender or sexual orientation if this information is strictly relevant. A journalist shall neither originate nor process material which encourages discrimination, ridicule, prejudice or hatred on any of the above-mentioned grounds.

11. A journalist shall not take private advantage of information gained in the course of his/her duties, before the information is public knowledge.

12. A journalist shall not by way of statement, voice or appearance endorse by advertisement any commercial product or service save for the promotion of his/her own work or of the medium by which he/she is employed.

Italy: *Charter of Duties of Italian Journalists*

This charter was adopted by the National Federation of the Italian Press and National Council Order of Journalists in Rome on July 8, 1993. Translated by the Federation.

Introduction

The journalists' job is based on the principles of freedom of information and of opinions. It is confirmed by the Italian law n. 69 dated 3 February 1963. "Freedom of information and of criticism is a right of journalists which cannot be suppressed. It is limited by observing the rules of law protecting the personality of others. Journalists commit themselves to respect the substantial truth of facts, while at the same time observing the duties imposed by loyalty and good faith. Inaccurate information must be corrected and possible errors put right. Journalists and publishers must respect professional secrecy pertaining to their sources of information, as required by their confidential character. They must promote a spirit of collaboration between colleagues, co-operation between journalists and publishers and trust between the press and its readers." A relationship of trust between the organs of information and the public is the basis of the work of journalists. In order to promote and settle this relationship, all Italian journalists undersign the following:

Principles

A journalist has to respect, cultivate and defend the right of information of all people; for these reasons he researches and diffuses every piece of information that he considers of public interest in observance of truth and accuracy.

A journalist researches and spreads news of public interest in spite of the obstacles which can arise in his work; he makes every effort to guarantee to people knowledge and control of all public documents.

A journalist's responsibility towards people always prevails over any other thing.

A journalist can never subordinate his responsibility to other people's interest and particularly to the publishers' interest, governments' interest or of the other organizations of the State.

A journalist has to respect people, his dignity and his right of secrecy and he never discriminates against anyone according to his race, his religion, his sex, his mental and physical condition, his political views.

A journalist rectifies, quickly and with accuracy, his mistakes or his imprecisions in conformity with the duty to rectify and with what is established by law.

A journalist always respects the right of presumption of innocence.

A journalist has to observe professional secrecy when it is required by the fiduciary character of his sources. In any other cases a journalist has to respect the transparency of the sources.

A journalist can not adhere to secret associations that in any way contrast with Article 18 of the Italian Constitution.

A journalist cannot accept benefits, favours or tasks that make dependent his autonomy and his professional credibility.

A journalist cannot omit facts or essential details for a complete reconstruction of events. Titles, summaries, photos and subtitles must not either distort reality or the news.

A journalist must not publish images and photos of people involved in daily episodes particularly terrifying or however prejudicial to people's dignity, he must neither dwell upon details of violence or brutality, unless it prevails over preeminent reason of social interest. He must not intervene on reality to create artificial images. Comments and opinions belong to the right of speech and criticism and, therefore, they have to be absolutely free from any obligation, except for the constraint set by law against offence and violence on people.

A Journalist's Responsibility

A journalist is responsible for his job towards people, he has to favour their dialogue with ombudsman. He has to create proper instruments (reader's guarantee, pages for readers, spaces for reply, etc.), giving a wide diffusion to their activity.

A journalist only accepts suggestions and instructions from the editorial hierarchy of his newspaper, as long as the dispositions are not against the professional law, against the national Italian journalist's work contract (CNLG) and the Ethic Code (Carta dei Doveri).

A journalist cannot discriminate against people according to race, religion, mental and physical conditions, political opinions. Circumstances that are not extenuating, references that are not insulting or denigratory of people and their privacy are only accepted when they are of relevant public interest.

A journalist respects the right of secrecy of every person and he cannot publish news on their private life, unless they are transparent and of relevant public's interest; however, he makes always known his own identity and profession when he collects such news. Names of people involved in such daily events cannot be published, unless they are of relevant public interest; they can be neither made known in case of danger of people's safety nor they can publish other elements that can make clear people's identity (photos, images).

Names of victims of sexual violence can be neither published nor can details be given details that can lead to their identification, unless it is required by the victims themselves for relevant general interest.

A journalist has to proceed with great caution when publishing names or elements that can lead to the identification of members of the legal team or of the police, when they can provoke the risk of calamity for themselves or of his family.

Rectification and Reply

A journalist respects the inviolable right of people by rectifying incorrect news or news that is wrongly considered prejudicial to people's interests.

A journalist makes rectification, therefore, with timeliness and appropriate emphasis, also in case of a lack of a specific requirement that all news [items], after their wide diffusion, seem to be incorrect or erroneous, especially when the mistakes can damage people, organizations, categories, associations and communities.

A journalist does not make charges against people, and does not spread news damaging person's reputation or person's dignity without giving the opportunity of reply to the charged person. If it is impossible (because the person is impossible to find or he doesn't want to reply), he has to inform the readers and the public. In any case, before publishing a piece of news concerning the investigations' warning by a judge, he has to determine if the charged person is aware of it.

The Presumption of Innocence

In all the process and investigations, a journalist must always remember that every person charged with an offence is innocent until the final judgment, and he may not imply his guilt in news stories.

A journalist may not publish images that present deliberately or artificially as offenders people that have not been judged as guilty persons in a process.

In case of the accused's acquittal, a journalist must always give an appropriate journalistic emphasis to this piece of news, while also making reference to all news and articles previously published.

Sources

A journalist has to observe the maximum caution in spreading news, names and images of people charged with habitual offences and received slight punishment, except in cases of particular social interest.

A journalist has to check all information obtained by his sources; he must accept the reliability and determine the origins of what he says; he must always safeguard the substantial truth of facts.

The case in which the sources must be kept secret, a journalist has to respect the professional secret and has to be able to inform the reader of such circumstance.

In any other case a journalist must always respect the principle of more transparency of the sources of information, giving the the readers or the audience the maximum possible attention. The fulfillment of an obligation to the quotation of a source is particularly important when a journalist uses a piece of news from a press agency or from any other source of information, unless the piece of news is not correct or widely spread by its own means, or unless it is modified in meaning and content. In all the other cases a journalist accepts the conditions derived from the sources for the publication or the abolition of a piece of information.

Information and Advertising

All people have the right to receive correct information, always distinct from an advertising message and not prejudicial to everyone's interests. The advertising message must be always and in any cases recognizable from journalistic documents through clear indications.

A journalist has to observe all principles signed in the Protocol's Agreement on Transparency of Information and of the national Italian journalists' work contract (CNLG); he has to make known the advertisement, however, he has to enable people to distinguish a journalistic job from a promotional message.

Incompatibility

A journalist cannot in any case subordinate for his personal benefit economic or financial information that he knows, he cannot disturb moreover the state of the stock market, spreading news and events that are referable to his own advantage.

A journalist cannot write articles or news concerning actions on which the trend of the market has a direct or indirect financial interest, he cannot sell or buy stock with which he is professionally involved or he is going to be concerned with in short time.

A journalist refuses payments, refund of expenses, donations, free holidays, duty travels, pleasure trip gifts, facilities, that may, depending on his job and activity, damage his credibility and professional dignity.

A journalist can neither accept tasks and responsibility in contrast with the independent discharge of his own duties, nor lend his name, voice or image for advertising enterprises that are incompatible with the safeguarding of professional journalists' autonomy. It is allowable instead, however, for a journalist to perform such services free of charge for social, humanitarian, cultural, religious or artistic organisations, or for trade union activities that are not speculative in character.

Children or Weak People

A journalist respects all principles confirmed in the ONU Convention dated 1989 on the right of children and their rules undersigned by the "Treviso Ethic Code" (Carta di Treviso) to protect children, their character and their personality, both as an active protagonist and a victim of a common-law offence and particularly:

a) a journalist doesn't publish a name or any other element that can lead to the identification of people involved in the daily episodes or events;

b) he has to avoid eventual utilization by adults to represent exclusively his own interest;

c) however, he values the dissemination of news about children if it is in the interest of the children themselves.

A journalist protects the rights and dignity of people with mental or physical handicaps in analogy with what is confirmed by the Treviso Ethic Code (Carta di Treviso) about children.

A journalist protects the rights of invalids, avoiding sensational publication of news on medical arguments that can bring fear and groundless hopes.

a) He doesn't spread news that is not controlled with important scientific sources;

b) he doesn't quote the names of commercial drugs and products so that consumption will increase production;

c) he quickly spreads the commercial names of pharmaceutical products that are withdrawn or suspended from circulation because they damage the health of people.

A journalist pledges, however, to use the maximum respect towards subjects of daily life that for social, economic or cultural reasons have little self-protection.

The Netherlands: *The Dutch Declaration of*
Principles on the Conduct of Journalists

The declaration was adopted by the Second World Congress of
the International Federation of Journalists at Bordeaux on April
25–28, 1954, and amended by the 18th IFJ World Congress in Hels-
ingör on June 2–6, 1986.

1. Respect for truth and for the right of the public to truth is the first duty of
the journalist.

2. In pursuance of this duty, the journalist shall at all times defend the principles of freedom in the honest collection and publication of news, and of the right of
fair comment and criticism.

3. The journalist shall report only in accordance with facts of which he/she
knows the origin. The journalist shall not suppress essential information or falsify
documents.

4. The journalist shall use only fair methods to obtain news, photographs and
documents.

5. The journalist shall do the utmost to rectify any published information
which is found to be harmfully inaccurate.

6. The journalist shall observe professional secrecy regarding the source of information obtained in confidence.

7. The journalist shall be aware of the danger of discrimination being furthered
by the media, and shall do the utmost to avoid facilitating such discrimination
based on, among other things, race, sex, sexual orientation, language, religion, political or other opinions, and national or social origins.

8. The journalist shall regard as grave professional offences the following:

- plagiarism
- malicious misrepresentation
- calumny, slander, libel, unfounded accusations
- the acceptance of a bribe in any form in consideration of either publication or suppression.

9. Journalists worthy of that name shall deem it their duty to observe faithfully
the principles stated above. Within the general law of each country the journalist
shall recognize in professional matters the jurisdiction of colleagues only, to the ex-
clusion of every kind of interference by governments of others.

Portugal: *The Portuguese Deontological Code of Journalists*

The code was adopted by the Syndicate of Journalists in May 1993.

1. The journalist has a duty to report the facts with accuracy and in exact manner, and to interpret them honestly. The facts are confirmed by hearing the parties with particular interests in the case.

2. The journalist has to fight censorship and sensationalism and to consider accusations without proof and plagiarism as serious professional mistakes.

3. The journalist has to resist restrictions on access to the information sources, and against the attempts to limit the freedom of expression and the right to inform. It is the obligation of the journalist to announce such offences to those rights.

4. The journalist has to use loyal means in obtaining the information, pictures or documents, and to avoid abusing anyone's good faith. Identifying oneself as a journalist is a rule, the breaking of which is permissible only on the grounds of an unquestionable public interest.

5. The journalist has to bear responsibility for all his/her work and professional acts, and to correct the information proved to be false or inexact. The journalist has to refrain from acts/behavior that violate his/her conscience.

6. Identification of sources is an essential criteria for the journalist. The journalist must not reveal, not even in the court, his/her confidential sources except when he has been abused by giving false information. The opinions shall always be attributed—separated as such.

7. The journalist has to guarantee the presumption of innocence until the case is finished. The journalist must not identify, directly or indirectly, the victims of sexual crimes or juvenile criminals nor may he/she humiliate people or aggravate their pain.

8. The journalist must resist treating people in a discriminatory way, based on their colour, race, nationality or sex.

9. The journalist has to respect the private life of the citizens except when the public interest demands the revelation or when the behaviour of the person in question is contradictory to the values and principles of the public, which he/she defends.

10. The journalist has to reject demands, functions, and benefits that could question his/her independent status and the professional integrity. The journalist must not use his professional status in order to get personal benefits.

Spain: *Spanish Catalonia's Deontological Code*

This code is an initiative of the Catalan Journalists Association. Its aim is to reassert the ethical principles of the journalism profession. This declaration has been elaborated in the last three years by an ad hoc commission constituted by it. In this process, a relevant participation has been assumed by the Consultative Council of the association where all Catalan media, press, radio and television are represented. The final draft of the text has been approved by the board of the association at its meeting of October 22, 1992, and, further, it has been presented in the second conference of Catalan journalists, held in Barcelona in November 1992.

Principles

1. A sheer difference between facts and opinions or interpretations has to be always observed, avoiding any deliberate confusion or distortion of both. The same criterion must be applied to any guess or rumour.

2. Diffuse only information duly founded; avoid making assertions or offering non-concrete and baseless data which may hurt or disdain the dignity of persons. Also, do not originate unjustified damage or discredit to institutions and to public and private agencies, or employ outrageous expressions or assessments.

3. Rectify with diligence appropriate to the circumstances, all information and opinions derived from it, whose falsity has been proved and which has damaged the rights and legitimate interests of people and/or institutions concerned. If it is necessary, apologise independently of what is prescribed by the legislation.

4. Use proper methods to obtain information or images without resorting to unlawful procedures.

5. Respect off-the-record information, if such a criterion is claimed by the source, according to customary use in a free society.

6. Recognize the individual and/or institutional right not to provide information or answer questions, though it may be the duty of journalists to find the information, taking into consideration their right as citizens. As far as the affairs of public agencies, the fundamental right to know must prevail over any type of limitation that seriously affects, with any kind of justification, the principle of information transparency, which must be respected.

7. Do not accept any kind of remuneration or compensation from third parties in order to promote, orient, influence or to have published news or opinions. It is never acceptable to act simultaneously as a journalist with other professional activities which are not compatible with the deontology of information, such as adver-

tising, public relations and image consultancy, either in the field of public institutions or agencies, or in private institutions.

8. Do not use to one's own benefit privileged information that has been confidentially obtained by a journalist in the performance of his duty.

9. Respect the rights of persons to privacy, principally in those cases or events which cause feelings of sadness or pain. Also avoid the gratuitous interference and unnecessary speculation related to their feelings or circumstances, especially when those persons concerned make it explicit.

10. Observe in a very scrupulous way the principle of presumption of innocence regarding information and opinions connected with the juridical process.

11. Use special care with all news concerning children. Do not identify them when they are victims (except in the case of murder), witnesses or accused in criminal prosecutions, especially in cases of great social repercussion such as sexual offences. Avoid identifying, against their will, those related people or innocent relatives of persons accused or convicted in criminal trials.

12. Behave with a definite sense of responsibility and harshness when it concerns information or opinions that may provoke sex, race, beliefs, social class or cultural discrimination. By the same token, [behave responsibly when dealing with information which tends] to incite the use of violence, and thus avoid expressions or manifestations that are degrading or harmful for the personal condition of individuals and their physical or moral integrity.

Sweden: *The Swedish Code of Conduct for Press, Radio and Television*

The code was originally adopted by the Co-operation Council of the Press in August 1994 in 1978. The Co-operation Council consists of Publicistklubben (Publishers' Club), Svenska Journalistförbundet (Swedish Journalists' Association), Svenska Tidningsutgivareföreningen (Swedish Newspaperpublishers' Union), Sveriges Radio (Sweden's radio), Sveriges Television (Sweden's Television), Utbildningsradion (educational radio) and Radioutgivareförening (Radiobroadcasters' Union).

Preamble
Press, radio and television shall have the greatest possible freedom within the framework of the press law and the constitutional law on freedom of expression. This is necessary in order for the media to be able to serve as news-intermediary and as a watchdog of the public life. In this connection, nevertheless, individuals should be protected against the unnecessary suffering through publicity.

I. Publicity Rules

Give accurate news

1. The role played by the mass media in society and the confidence of the general public in these media demands accurate and unbiased news.

2. Be critical towards news sources. Check facts as carefully as possible even if they have been published earlier. Give the reader/listener/viewer the possibility of distinguishing between a statement of fact and a commentary.

3. Newspaper placards (newsbills), headings and introductions must have coverage in the text.

4. Use care with documentary pictures/photographs. Make sure that the photos and graphic illustrations are correct and not exploited/manipulated in a misleading way.

Give space for replies

5. Factual errors are to be corrected when necessary. Anyone with a legitimate reason to reply to a statement has to be given the opportunity to do so. Corrections and replies are to be published in appropriate form without delay in such a way they will be noticed by those who have received the original information. Note that a reply does not always call for an editorial comment.

6. Publish without delay the Press Council's statements concerning your own newspaper.

Respect personal integrity

7. Consider carefully publishing information that can constitute an infringement of privacy. Refrain from such publicity unless an undeniable public interest demands it.

8. Observe great caution when publishing information about suicide and attempted suicide. Consider particularly the relatives and the sacredness of private life.

9. Always show the greatest consideration when dealing with the victims of crimes and accidents.

Consider carefully the publishing of names and pictures in such cases

10. Do not emphasize race, sex, nationality, profession, political affiliation or religious views if it is irrelevant to the story or causes disrespect to some groups of people.

Apply caution to the use of pictures

11. The rules given in this code are also applicable to pictures.

12. Photomontage, retouching by electrical means or captures must not be for-

mulated in a way that might mislead or fool the reader. Always mention it next to the picture if it has been changed through montage or retouching. This goes also for filing of the pictures.

Hear both sides

13. Endeavour to give people who are being criticized in factual material the opportunity to reply to the criticism at the same time. Endeavour also to express the views of all parties concerned. Bear in mind that sometimes the only purpose of reports/notices is to injure the person being reported.

14. Remember that a person suspected of a crime is, according to the law, innocent until something else is proved. The final outcome of a reported court case must be showed.

Apply caution to the publication of names

15. Refrain from publishing names if it can injure the persons in question. The names can be published only if an obvious public interest requires it.

16. If the name is not published, do not publish a picture or information about the person's profession, title, age, nationality, sex or anything else that makes his/her identification possible.

17. Observe that the entire responsibility for the publication of names and pictures lies with whoever represents the material.

18. Scrutinize critically particulars of persons wanted for police enquiries.

19. Bear in mind that the entire responsibility for the publication of names and pictures lies with whoever publishes the material.

Commentary to Part I

The Swedish Press council is primarily responsible for defining the concept of good journalistic practice, and in matters not referred to the Council, the Press Ombudsman for the General Public is responsible for its interpretation. It should be noted that the Swedish Press Council and the Press Ombudsman for the General Public do not make decisions on cases of divergence from the rules governing radio or television programmes. The National Broadcasting Council is responsible for scrutinizing the content of these programmes. Decisions of the Swedish Press Council are published not only in the censured newspapers but also in the *Press Journal* and in *The Journalist*.

II. Professional Rules
The integrity of the journalist

1. Do not accept an assignment from anyone outside the editorial staff leaders.

2. Do not accept an assignment or an invitation, a free trip or any other benefit either in or outside of your job, that could bring into question your status as a free and independent journalist.

3. Do not use your position as a journalist in order to exert pressure for your own or someone else's profit or in order to acquire personal benefits.

4. Do not utilize for your own or someone else's profit unpublished news concerning economic conditions or measures by state, municipalities, organizations, companies or private persons.

5. Bear in mind the provision in the Collective Agreement for Journalists according to which a journalist cannot be ordered to write against his/her conviction or to carry out humiliating assignments.

Obtaining of material

6. Comply with reasonable wishes from the persons interviewed to find out beforehand how and where their statements will be published.

7. Show particular consideration of people not used to being interviewed. Inform him/her about whether the conversation is intended for publication or only for information.

8. Do not falsify interviews or pictures.

9. Show consideration in taking photographs and in procuring them, especially in connection with accidents and crimes.

10. Do not give in to outside pressure intended to prevent or restrict justified publishing.

11. Observe copyright as well as quotation rules and rights to photographs.

12. Indicate the source when the published material is mainly based on information from other parts.

Time of press releases

13. Respect the agreed times of releases.

III. Rules Against Editorial Advertising
Main rule

Protect the public trust of the press, radio and television as well as their integrity. Do not let the general public suspect that anybody might improperly influence the content of a program/text. Therefore, do not publish or present among editorial material something that is not motivated by journalism. Published information must have news or information qualities or be motivated by entertaining or artistic reasons, and must not have an advertising purpose.

General regulations

1. Frame the material only in accordance with journalistic and/or program-re-

lated decisions. The intention must never be to give publicity to any products or services; neither can the presentation of the material be such that the audience thinks it is commercial by nature. Watch that the commercial cannot be mixed with editorial material even by "a quick look."

2. Dismiss ideas and proposals of articles and programs if they include a favour in return containing advertisement in any form. As a principle, also dismiss offers about free or heavily subsidised trips. Refuse gifts and other benefits. Never promise beforehand that you are going to publish something.

3. Consumer-informing articles and programs put particularly heavy demands on the journalistic integrity. Therefore, show how the choice of the products/services in the article/programme has been made. Tell clearly how the products/services have been compared or tested. Be particularly careful and critical when dealing with reviews of products. Do not inform one-sidedly only about limited groups of products or only about one producer of products/services, warehouses, shops, restaurants, etc.

4. Put information about theatre shows, concerts, films, art exhibitions, sport events and likewise through a normal journalistic evaluation to determine the value of the news. Look critically through the material and make sure that it is given in a journalistically motivated form. Consider carefully if information and pictures about new companies and shops or likewise have journalistic news value.

5. Only mention companies and organizations that donate or deliver prices, or take part in any other way, for example, as a sponsor at parties, competitions, carnivals, charity balls and such, if there are very strong journalistic reasons to do so. Concerning such sponsoring that is refered to in Article 6 in Radio Law as well as in broadcasting companies treaties with the state, those rules apply.

6. Do not publish/present in editorial space information about the rights and obligations of individuals and other public messages that state or municipal authorities demand/wish to get published. Broadcasting companies are subject to the rules on government messages that may exist in agreements between the broadcasting company and the state and in internal instructions in connection to that. Reject from the editorial space the facts about companies and organizations, such as opening hours, product demonstrations, prize competitions or other arrangements that are not journalistically motivated.

7. Newspapers'/broadcasting companies' advertisements for their own products and services as well as own arrangements shall be presented as advertisements.

8. When using material (cars, boats, clothing, furniture, kitchen equipment, etc.) for photographing purpose, the names of the producers, the re-sellers or retailers can be mentioned only if there are journalistic motives for that.

9. Editorial special pages and supplements in newspapers must be journalistically motivated. Overviews as "jobmarket," "boatmarket," "cottagemarket," "carmarket" and likewise, which might be considered as advertisements or which imply

that the products and services are offered for sale, must be presented as commercials.

10. Lists of entrepreneurs and suppliers at building companies presented in the newspaper must take a form of an advertisement.

United Kingdom: *Code of Practice*

The Press Complaints Commission is charged with enforcing the following Code of Practice, which was framed by the newspaper and periodical industry and ratified by the Press Complaints Commission in April 1994.

All members of the press have a duty to maintain the highest professional and ethical standards. In doing so, they should have regard for the provisions of this Code of Practice and for safeguarding the public's right to know.

Editors are responsible for the actions of journalists employed by their publications. They should also satisfy themselves as far as possible that material accepted from non-staff members was obtained in accordance with this code.

While recognizing that this involves a substantial element of self-restraint by editors and journalists, it is designed to be acceptable in the context of a system of self-regulation. The code applies in the spirit as well as in the letter.

It is the responsibility of editors to co-operate as swiftly as possible in PCC enquiries. Any publication which is criticised by the PCC under one of the following clauses is duty-bound to print the adjudication which flows in full and with due prominence.

1. Accuracy

i) Newspapers and periodicals should take care not to publish inaccurate, misleading or distorted material.

ii) Whenever it is recognized that a significant inaccuracy, misleading statement or distorted report has been published, it should be corrected promptly and with due prominence.

iii) An apology should be published whenever appropriate.

iv) A newspaper or periodical should always report fairly and accurately the outcome of an action for defamation to which it has been a party.

2. Opportunity to reply

A fair opportunity for reply to inaccuracies should be given to individuals or organizations when reasonably called for.

3. Comment, conjecture and fact

Newspapers, whilst free to be partisan, should distinguish clearly between comment, conjecture and fact.

4. Privacy

Intrusions and enquiries into an individual's private life without his or her consent including the use of long-lens photography to take pictures of people on private property without their consent are not generally acceptable and publication can only be justified when in the public interest. Note: Private property is defined as any private residence, together with its garden and outbuildings, but excluding any adjacent fields of parkland. In addition, hotel bedrooms (but not other areas in a hotel) and those parts of a hospital or nursing home where patients are treated or accommodated.

5. Listening devices

Unless justified by public interest, journalists should not obtain or publish material obtained by using clandestine listening devices or by intercepting private telephone conversations.

6. Hospitals

i) Journalists or photographers making enquiries at hospitals or similar institutions should identify themselves to a responsible executive and obtain permission before entering non-public areas.

ii) The restrictions on intruding into privacy are particularly relevant to enquiries about individuals in hospitals or similar institutions.

7. Misrepresentation

i) Journalists should not generally obtain or seek to obtain information or pictures through misrepresentation or subterfuge.

ii) Unless in the public interest, documents and photographs should be removed only with the express consent of the owner.

iii) Subterfuge can be justified only in the public interest and only when material cannot be obtained by any other means.

8. Harassment

i) Journalists should neither obtain nor seek to obtain information or pictures through intimidation or harassment.

ii) Unless their enquiries are in the public interest, journalists should not photograph individuals on private property (as defined in the note to Clause 4) without their consent; should not persist in telephoning or questioning individuals after having been asked to desist; should not remain on their property after having been asked to leave and should not follow them.

iii) It is the responsibility of editors to ensure that these requirements are carried out.

9. Payment for articles

Payment or offers of payment for stories, pictures or information should not be made directly or through agents to witnesses or potential witnesses in current criminal proceedings or to people engaged in crimes or to their associates—which includes family, friends, neighbours and colleagues—except where the material concerned ought to be published in the public interest and the payment is necessary for this to be done.

10. Intrusion into grief or shock

In cases involving personal grief or shock, enquiries should be carried out and approaches made with sympathy and discretion.

11. Innocent relatives and friends

Unless it is contrary to the public's right to know, the press should generally avoid identifying relatives or friends of persons convicted or accused of crimes.

12. Interviewing or photographing children

i) Journalists should not normally interview or photograph children under the age of 16 on subjects involving the personal welfare of the child, in the absence or without the consent of a parent or other adult who is responsible for the children.

ii) Children should not be approached or photographed while at school without the permission of the school authorities.

13. Children in sex cases

1) The press should not, even where the law does not prohibit it, identify children under the age of 16 who are involved in cases concerning sexual offences, whether as victims, or as witnesses or defendants.

2) In any press report of a case involving a sexual offence against a child

i) the adult should be identified

ii) the term "incest" where applicable should not be used

iii) the offence should be described as "serious offences against young children" or similar appropriate wording

iv) the child should not be identified

v) care should be taken that nothing in the report implies the relationship between the accused and the child

14. Victims of crime

The press should not identify victims of sexual assaults or publish material likely to contribute to such identification unless, by law, they are free to do so.

15. Discrimination

i) The press should avoid prejudicial or pejorative reference to a person's race, colour, religion, sex or sexual orientation or to any physical or mental illness or handicap.

ii) It should avoid publishing details of a person's race, colour, religion, sex or sexual orientation, unless these are directly relevant to the story.

16. Financial journalism

i) Even where the law does not prohibit it, journalists should not use for their own profit, financial information they receive in advance of its general publication, nor should they pass such information to others.

ii) They should not write about shares or securities in whose performance they know that they or their close families have a significant financial interest, without disclosing the interest to the editor or financial editor.

iii) They should not buy or sell, either directly or through nominees or agents, shares or securities about which they have written recently or about which they intend to write in the near future.

17. Confidential sources

Journalists have a moral obligation to protect confidential sources of information.

18. The public interest

Clauses 4, 5, 7, 8 and 9 create exceptions which may be covered by invoking the public interest, such as

i) detecting or exposing crime or a serious misdemeanour

ii) protecting public health and safety

iii) preventing the public from being misled by some statement or action of an individual or organization.

In any cases raising issues beyond these three definitions the Press Complaints Commission will require a full explanation by the editor of the publication involved, seeking to demonstrate how the public interest was served.

United Kingdom: *The Journalists' Code of Conduct in the United Kingdom*

Adopted on June 29, 1994, by the British National Union of Journalists (NUJ).

1. A journalist has a duty to maintain the highest professional and ethical standards.

2. A journalist shall at all times defend the principle of the freedom of the press and other media in relation to the collection of information and the expression of comment and criticism. He/she shall strive to eliminate distortion, news suppression and censorship.

3. A journalist shall strive to ensure that the information he/she disseminates is fair and accurate, avoid the expression of comment and conjecture as established fact and falsification by distortion, selection or misrepresentation.

4. A journalist shall rectify promptly any harmful inaccuracies, ensure that correction and apologies receive due prominence and afford the right of reply to

persons criticised when the issue is of sufficient importance.

5. A journalist shall obtain information, photographs and illustrations only by straightforward means. The use of other means can be justified only by over-riding considerations of the public interest. The journalist is entitled to exercise a personal conscientious objection to the use of such means.

6. Subject to the justification by over-riding considerations of the public interest, a journalist shall do nothing which entails entrusion into private grief and distress.

7. A journalist shall protect confidential sources of information.

8. A journalist shall not accept bribes nor shall he/she allow other inducements to influence the performance of his/her professional duties.

9. A journalist shall not lend himself/herself to the distortion or suppression of the truth because of advertising or other considerations.

10. A journalist shall only mention a person's age, race, colour, creed, illegitimacy, disability, marital status (or lack of it), gender or sexual orientation if this information is strictly relevant. A journalist shall neither originate nor process material which encourages discrimination, ridicule, prejudice or hatred on any of the above-mentioned grounds.

11. A journalist shall not take private advantage of information gained in the course of his/her duties, before the information is public knowledge.

12. A journalist shall not by way of statement, voice or appearance endorse by advertisement any commercial product or service save for the promotion of his/her own work or of the medium by which he/she is employed.

1. Patrick Brogan, *Spiked: The Short Life and Death of the National News Council* (New York, N.Y.: Priority Press Publications, 1985), p. 89.

2. Ibid., pp. 27-31.

3. Two other significant studies on ethical codes and press councils in the world were Lars Bruun (Ed.), *Professional Codes in Journalism,* (Prague, Czechoslovakia: International Organization of Journalists, 1979) and Clement Jones, *Mass Media Codes of Ethics and Councils: A Comparative International Study on Professional Standards* (Paris, France: UNESCO Press, 1980).

4. Lars Bruun (Ed.), *Professional Codes in Journalism* (Prague, Czechoslovakia: International Organization of Journalists, 1979).

5. Päivi Sonninen and Tiina Laitila, "Press Councils in Europe," in Kaarle Nordenstreng (Ed.), *Reports on Media Ethics in Europe* (Tampere, Finland: Department of Journalism and Mass Communication, 1995), Series B 41, pp. 11-13.

6. Tiina Laitila, "Codes of Ethics in Europe," in Kaarle Nordenstreng (Ed.), *Media Ethics in Europe* (Tempere, Finland: Department of Journalism and Mass Communication, 1995), pp. 40-43.

7. Parlimanetary Assembly, The Ethics of Journalism (Strasbourg, France: Council of Europe, 1993), pp. 3-5. (Resolution 1003: Arts. 7-16.)

8. "Europe's Sneak Attack on the Press," *Wall Street Journal Europe,* Nov. 6, 1993, p. 6.

9. Ibid.

10. Ibid.

11. "European Code," *Editor and Publisher,* April 30, 1994, p. 6.

12. "Comments of FIEJ on the Eight Preliminary Draft Principles Laid Down by the MM-S-JF," memo to FIEJ Members, Jan. 25, 1994.

13. "Council of Europe Ministers Back Limits on Press," *World Press Freedom Committee Newsletter,* Dec. 16, 1994, p. 1.

14. Helle Nissen Kruuse, "The Netherlands," in Marcel Berlins, Claude Grellier and Helle Nissen Kruuse (Eds.), *Les droits et les devoirs des journalistes dans les douze pays de l'Union Européenne* [The rights and responsibilities of journalists in the twelve countries of the European Union] (Paris, France: Centre de Formation et de Perfectionnement des Journalistes, 1994), p. 181.

15. Robert G. Picard, *The Ravens of Odin* (Ames, Iowa: Iowa State University Press, 1988), p. 49.

16. Thimios Zaharopoulos and Manny E. Paraschos, *Mass Media in Greece: Power, Politics and Privatization* (Westport, Conn.: Praeger, 1993), p. 139.

Postscript

When Alexis de Tocqueville returned to France from his reconnaissance mission to the United States in 1831, he wrote not only about the political and legal systems of the "old" and the "new" worlds, but also about the new phenomenon of the press—its identity, role and relative power in the United States and France. In his *Democracy in America,* first published in 1835 in Paris, de Tocqueville complained about several things he found lacking in each country's newspapers. For example, he criticized the American press for being too commercially minded and profit driven, and he chastised the French press for being concentrated in too few and elite hands. He then addressed the issue of press criticism and how it might be regulated:

Many persons in France think that the violence of the press originates in the instability of the social state, in our political passions and the general feeling of uneasiness that consequently prevails; and it is therefore supposed that as soon as society has resumed a certain degree of composure, the press will abandon its present vehemence. For my own part, I would willingly attribute to these causes the extraordinary ascendancy which the press has acquired over the nation; but I do not think that they exercise much influence on its language. The periodical press appears to me to have passions and instincts of its own, independent of the circumstances in which it is placed; and the present condition of America corroborates this opinion.

America is perhaps, at this moment, the country of the whole world that contains the fewest germs of revolution; but the press is not less destructive in its principles there than in France, and it displays the same violence without the same reasons for indignation. In America as in France it constitutes a singular power, so strangely composed of mingled good and evil that liberty could not live without it, and public order can hardly be maintained against it. ... In this question, therefore, there is no medium between servitude and license; in order to enjoy the inestimable benefits that the liberty of the press ensures, it is necessary to submit to the inevitable evils that it creates.[1]

What is chronicled in the preceding chapters is the almost two-centuries-old evolution of this seemingly unattainable "medium" between "servitude and license," the effort of both Europeans and Americans to legally protect freedom of the press (and its corollary, freedom of expression) in recognition of the "inestimable benefits" it provides, while they try to safeguard legally against the "evils" that it inevitably creates.

The examination of the specific components of this legal balancing act, as described in the preceding chapters, shows that despite changing media and societies over time, and despite different historical, social, economic and political origins and circumstances, the media regulatory environments in the E.U. countries and the United States possess more similarities than differences.

For example, both the E.U. member nations and the United States view in very similar terms the worth of personal honor and reputation and its protection from media abuse. Thus, on **defamation,** the prevailing thinking of both sides seems to be that private citizens deserve more legal protection than those citizens who seek the public eye. Even E.U. countries that have had a long legal tradition of protecting public officials from media criticism are turning around, with the full blessing of the European Court of Human Rights, and are making it more difficult for public servants legally to limit or punish media or expression, in general. Furthermore, the protection of individual **privacy** and of **minors** is finding more and more significant common ground, and electronic data protection is currently being "harmonized" to ensure the codification of similar practices on both sides of the Atlantic.

Even official **secrecy,** for years an unchallenged tradition of many European countries, has come into disrepute in the current era of the information society and citizens' access to their government. In the last few years, for example, not only the E.U. central machinery but individual E.U. member states have institutionalized measures, reminiscent of the U.S. Freedom of Information regulation, to end government isolation and provide better access through transparency laws.

On national **security** issues, the commonalities may be fewer and more subtle, but they still exist: On the one hand is the United States, which, under its First Amendment, is legally obligated to tolerate anti-national expression, and on the other hand are most E.U. nations (some of which still have laws that protect symbols of the state, for example), which are choosing to interpret their laws more liberally or to enforce them sparingly out of deference to freedom of expression.

Obscenity seems to be not only equally elusive in the European Union and the United States, but also similarly less dependent on legal definitions and more on time, geography and enforcement personnel. Also, as media are becoming harder to track because of technology and proliferation, European and American parents are taking more monitoring functions away from government policing. It is safe to say, however, that Europeans have a more tolerant attitude than do Americans concerning what should be prosecutable as pornographic, and they prefer to view objectionable material in a more generic fashion, such as what is harmful to youth.

Professional journalistic practices, such as **source confidentiality, access to information** and **ethical limitations,** clearly are guided by the same principles in both the United States and the Union. In fact, even one of the key tenets of E.U. media philosophy, that of press subjectivity or partisanship, seems to be giving way to a more objective approach to news. This, perhaps not accidentally in the very competitive era of the 1990s, appears to make the capitalist press not only more widely acceptable but also more profitable. At the same time, American media seem to be less afraid to concede that their sacred objectivity is little more than a journalistic myth and honesty or fairness may be just as valuable a target in the pursuit of news. The only professional practice issue that seems to be viewed differently in the European Union and the United States is that of the **right of reply** or **correction,** which in the former enjoys almost universal, formal and legal recognition while in the latter it does not.

Cross-media ownership and **television programming** regulations also seem to have the same goal in both the European Union and the United States—diversity of opinion is an integral part of the democratic process and no one person or group should be allowed to monopolize access to significant segments of the citizenry.

But the coalescence of the two media systems is probably best evinced in the **commercialization** of their institutional sustenance. In the E.U. nations, the departure of the electronic media from the public payroll to private and eventually commercial funding sources has been nothing short of dramatic. Despite many national and E.U. collective efforts at some sort of control of the expansion in the numbers of new radio and television stations, the growth has been phenomenal. Such a growth has energized the advertising industry and created an almost hard-to-satisfy demand for programming. But most important, either by design or accident, the new commercial media seem to have created a new European media consumer, most likely a member of the *second* post–World War II generation youth who differ from their parents and grandparents in two significant ways: their de facto second language is English, largely imposed by global media, such as CNN and MTV, as well as pan-European or global advertising campaigns, and their primary entertainment standards (in music, films and videos) are American.

Such an Americanization is as lamented as it is welcome in the European Union and has served as a divisive force not only between the masses and the intellectuals, the capitalists and the socialists or laborites, but even among the cultural purists themselves. The best example of the disorienting power of this Americanization is the failure of the European Parliament in the fall of 1996 to tighten the "European works" requirement of the Television Without Frontiers Directive. In fact, in a stunning, as well as ironic, reversal of fortune and attitude, it was Jack Valenti himself and his Motion Picture Association of America that ended up lobbying hard to keep unaltered the directive they so strongly opposed seven years earlier![2] The reason: despite the directive's requirement that the majority of member states' programming was to be reserved for "European works," the European Union's trade deficit with the United States on audiovisual material increased by 3.88 percent in the 1990–94 period.[3] That, of course, was due to the dramatic increase in the number of commercial broadcasters who were always in need of programming. Most of the private broadcasters, especially in smaller nations, allied with the U.S. lobby in Brussels and opposed any amendments that might have made it more difficult for them to present non-European programming.

Official Eurocrats were bitter at the failure of the Union to tighten the directive's language and reverse the trend that had resulted in eight out of ten movies shown on European screens and six out of ten on television being American (see also Ch. 6). Luciana Castellina, head of the E.U. Parliament's Culture Committee, decrying the "McDonaldization" of European culture, said that cultural issues should not be left to the mercy of market forces as though they were commodities to be traded. She charged "the Hollywood oligopoly" with creating the potential of depriving "the children of the world of their fantasies, their images and their heroes." This will cause children to "become totally alienated," she said, and "there is a risk that when someone becomes alienated they become socially irresponsible."[4] This is an issue that will not go away any time soon.

There are differences to be sure. In clear divergence from U.S. practice, the E.U. member nations have stayed the course in legally restricting **violence** in their electronic media programs as well as **tobacco** and **alcohol** in their advertising. Also **truth-in-advertising** laws, at least for the time being, seem to be more vigorously enforced by the European Union and its member states than by the United States.

Furthermore, **racist** messages and **blasphemy** are viewed differently by both sides, but could come closer in the near future. Those kinds of expressions still find considerable protection under the U.S. First Amendment, while evidence in the European Union suggests that some of its member states, especially those dominated by strong religious communities and those that recently experienced domestic violence against immigrants, may tend to give through their courts considerable protection to those communities and minorities even at the occasional expense of free speech. However, the thinking of the European Court of Human Rights in several instances has echoed that of the U.S. Supreme Court and clearly recognized the importance of guaranteeing freedom of controversial expression in an open and democratic marketplace of ideas. Therefore, to the delight of libertarians and journalists in Europe, a European version of a U.S.-type "hate speech" protection may emerge out of the Court sooner rather than later.

Finally, there are signs in the United States that legislative and judicial institutions may be reconsidering the generous protections afforded by the First Amendment. The proposed congressional limitations on campaign financing of political speech, the "indecent" communications part of the 1996 Communications Decency Act, the government-sought 1997 television show rating system and the huge monetary awards ordered by juries against media are some of the indicators that the breadth of the First Amendment is undergoing a subtle re-examination. It *cannot* be a coincidence that this reassessment is taking place at a time when media have *penetrated* human life to an unprecedented degree while at the same time have managed to *distance* themselves significantly from their consumers through increasing chain ownership, corporate diversification, global conglomeration and a redirected emphasis on profitability.

The fact that this is as true of the United States as it is of the European Union points, again, to the similarities of their media systems. But such similarities in media practice and law cannot fully be attributed to the common cultural roots of the peoples of the European Union and the United States, especially in view of the fact that these are two fiercely competitive and often chauvinistic parts of the world. Much is owed to the abstruse effects of the technological revolution.

As the communications media reduce distances and eliminate borders to create the "global village," villagers, either as individuals or as institutions, *actively* seek to bypass artificial barriers and power elites to communicate directly with and learn from others. In a more *passive,* but no less informative, way other villagers may simply watch, absorb and learn from those cultures that are capable of participating in transnational communication processes. In either case, one inescapable result of this new knowledge seems to be the gradual shift from a villager's national culture to an environment that represents the "marriage" between his/her culture and the one he/she just discovered through the communication process. This new global culture, dreaded by some and celebrated by others, seems to be a more homogenized, composite entity that possesses some attributes from both cultures but also one unique characteristic: Its members subconsciously but constantly search for a third value system that would encompass only the *best* of what experience has taught in the two original systems. It is a search that is destined never to end, so that the villagers can constantly look for ways to adjust to the new realities that their generation and those of others in other parts of the world may be able create.

From this perspective, too, the continual interaction between the legal or press philosophies of the European Union member nations and the United States can be expected to converge more in the future, especially in the regulation of **new media, advertising truthfulness** and **government data access.**

The implication of this continued convergence, however, takes on special significance when added to the other global phenomenon of increasing numbers of media being owned by decreasing numbers of people. They are likely to operate out of a removed and ambiguous global administrative environment that is clearly beyond the reach of the vast majority of the consumers of these media.

If the regulation of these media also is based on a system of characteristics, values and needs that has global rather than local or national roots, the bond between the people and *their* media may be irreparably weakened. Although this may be a good omen for the future of global citizenship and the issues it must face, it can only be problematic for the sense of homeward *community* that has given purpose to media throughout their history.

NOTES

1. Alexis de Tocqueville, *Democracy in America* (New York, N.Y.: Vintage Books, 1945), pp. 190-192.

2. Tom Buerkle, "Parliament Calls Truce in Fight with Hollywood," *International Herald Tribune,* Nov. 13, 1996, Section A, p. 1.

3. "Audio-Visual Services/27," *Panorama of EU Industry 95-96,* European Commission, DG III, p. 3.

4. Untitled report by Janet McEvoy filed from Brussels for Reuters News Service online, Nov. 10, 1996, pp. 1-2.

Bibliography

Books

Agee, Warren K., Philip H. Ault and Edwin Emery. 1994. *Introduction to Mass Communication*. New York, N.Y.: HarperCollins College Publishers.

Alkema, Evert A. 1990. The Protection of the Freedom of Expression in the Constitution and in Civil Law—Netherlands. In *Netherlands Reports to the Thirteenth International Congress of Comparative Law*. The Hague, The Netherlands: T.M.C. Asser Instituut.

Bagdikian, Ben. 1987. *The Media Monopoly*. Boston, Mass.: Beacon Press.

Barendt, Eric. 1993. *Broadcasting Law—A Comparative Study*. Oxford, England: Clarendon Press.

The Basic Law. 1979. Wiesbaden, Germany: The Press and Information Office of the Federal Government of Germany.

The Belgian Constitution. 1994. Brussels, Belgium: Ministry of Foreign Affairs.

Berka, Walter. 1993. Press Law in Austria. In Sandra Coliver (Ed.), *Press Law and Practice*. London, England: Article 19, The International Centre Against Censorship.

Berlins, Marcel. 1994. Italy. In Marcel Berlins, Claude Grellier and Helle Nissen Kruuse (Eds.), *Les droits et les devoirs des journalistes dans les douze pays de l'Union Européenne* [The rights and responsibilities of journalists in the twelve countries of the European Union]. Paris, France: Centre de Formation et de Perfectionnement des Journalistes.

Berlins, Marcel. 1994. Luxembourg. In Marcel Berlins, Claude Grellier and Helle Nissen Kruuse (Eds.), *Les droits et les devoirs des journalistes dans les douze pays de l'Union Européenne.* [The rights and responsibilities of journalists in the twelve countries of the European Union]. Paris, France: Centre de Formation et de Perfectionnement des Journalistes.

Berlins, Marcel. 1994. The Republic of Ireland. In Marcel Berlins, Claude Grellier and Helle Nissen Kruuse (Eds.), *Les droits et les devoirs des journalistes dans les douze pays de l'Union Européenne.* [The rights and responsibilities of journalists in the twelve countries of the European Union]. Paris, France: Centre de Formation et de Perfectionnement des Journalistes.

Berlins, Marcel, Claude Grellier and Helle Nissen Kruuse. 1994. *Les droits et les devoirs des journalistes dans les douze pays de l'Union Européenne.* [The rights and responsibilities of journalists in the twelve countries of the European Union]. Paris, France: Centre de Formation et de Perfectionnement des Journalistes.

Boddewyn, J. J. 1990. The Global Spread of Advertising Regulation. In *Current Issues in International Communication.* White Plains, N.Y.: Longman.

Brogan, Patrick. 1985. *Spiked: The Short Life and Death of the National News Council.* New York, N.Y.: Priority Press Publications.

Browne, Donald R. 1989. *Comparing Broadcast Systems.* Ames, Iowa: Iowa State University Press.

Bruun, Lars (Ed.). 1979. *Professional Codes in Journalism.* Prague, Czechoslovakia: International Organization of Journalists.

Bunreacht na héireann (The Constitution of Ireland). 1978. Dublin, Ireland: Government Publications Sales Office.

Coliver, Sandra (Ed.). 1993. *Press Law and Practice.* London, England: Article 19, The International Centre Against Censorship.

Coliver, Sandra. 1993. *The Article 19 Freedom of Expression Manual.* London, England: Article 19, The International Centre Against Censorship.

Communication to the Council, the Parliament and the Economic and Social Committee, COM (93) 258.

Commission of the European Communities. 1993. *Openness in the Community.*

Commission of the European Communities. 1993. *Public Access to the Institutions' Documents.* Communication to the Council, the Parliament and the Economic and Social Committee, COM (93) 191.

Commission of the European Communities. 1994. *Communication from the Commission to the European Council and the European Parliament on the Application of Articles 4 and 5 of the Directive 89/552/EEC Television Without Frontiers.* COM (94) 57.

Commission of the European Communities. 1995. *Europe Without Frontiers.* OJC, 288, 1995.

Commission of the European Communities. 1995. *Television Without Frontiers: New Rules and Legal Framework for the Internal Market Information Society Services.* COM (95) 287.

Commission of the European Communities. 1996. *Proposals for Action Against Sex Tourism.* COM (96)1093.

Commission of the European Communities. 1996. *Communication to the Council, the European Parliament, the Economic and Social Committee and the Committee of the Regions.* COM (96) 487.

The Constitutional Act. 1977. Copenhagen, Denmark: Press and Cultural

Relations Department of the Ministry of Foreign Affairs of Denmark.

The Constitutional Law of Finland. 1992. Helsinki, Finland: Parliament of Finland, Ministry of Foreign Affairs and Ministry of Justice.

The Constitution of Sweden. 1989. Stockholm, Sweden: The Swedish Rijksdag.

The Constitution of the Grand Duchy of Luxembourg. 1980. Luxembourg: Ministry of State, Press and Information Service.

Constitution of the Portuguese Republic. 1989. Lisbon, Portugal: Directorate-General for Mass Communication.

The Constitution of the Republic of Italy. 1990. Rome, Italy: Presidency of the Council of Ministers, Information and Copyright Service.

Convention for the Protection of Human Rights and Fundamental Freedoms. 1950. 213 U.N.T.S. 221.

Council of Europe. 1995. *European Ministerial Conferences on Mass Media Policy: Texts Adopted.* Strasbourg, France: Directorate of Human Rights.

Council of the European Communities, Commission of the European Communities. 1992. *Treaty on European Union.* Luxembourg: Office for Official Publications of the European Communities.

Crone, Tom. 1995. *Law and the Media.* Oxford, England: Focal Press.

De Keersmaeker, Christina. 1992. Belgium. In James R. Maxeiner and Peter Schotthoffer (Eds.), *Advertising Law in Europe and North America.* Deventer, The Netherlands: Kluwer Law and Taxation Publishers.

Errera, Roger. 1990. Press Law in France. In Pnina Lahav (Ed.), *Press Law in Modern Democracies.* New York, N.Y.: Longman.

European Commission. 1994. *Access to Commission Documents: User's Guide.* Luxembourg: Office for Official Publications of the European Communities.

European Commission. 1994. *Audiovisual Policy of the European Union.* Brussels, Belgium: Directorate-General for Information.

Fauconnier, G. and Dirk De Grooff. 1988. Belgium. In Philip T. Rosen (Ed.), *International Handbook of Broadcasting Systems.* New York, N.Y.: Greenwood Press.

Finnish Press Laws. 1984. Helsinki, Finland: Ministry of Foreign Affairs, Press and Cultural Centre.

The French Constitution. 1987. New York, N.Y.: Ambassade de France.

Green, Timothy. 1972. *The Universal Eye: The World of Television.* New York, N.Y.: Stein and Day.

Grellier, Claude. 1994. Belgium. In Marcel Berlins, Claude Grellier and Helle Nissen Kruuse (Eds.), *Les droits et les devoirs des journalistes dans les douze pays de l'Union Européenne.* [The rights and responsibilities of journalists in the twelve countries of the European

Union]. Paris, France: Centre de Formation et de Perfectionnement des Journalistes.

Grellier, Claude. 1994. Spain. In Marcel Berlins, Claude Grellier and Helle
Nissen Kruuse (Eds.), *Les droits et les devoirs des journalistes dans les
douze pays de l'Union Européenne.* [The rights and responsibilities
of journalists in the twelve countries of the European Union].
Paris, France: Centre de Formation et de Perfectionnement des
Journalistes.

Gustafsson, Karl Erik. 1995. Origins and Dynamics of Concentration. In
Karl Erik Gustafsson (Ed.), *Media Structure and the State.* Göteborg,
Sweden: Göteborg University.

Gustafsson, Karl Erik and Stig Hadenius. 1976. *Swedish Press Policy.* Stockholm, Sweden: The Swedish Institute.

Head, Sydney. 1985. *World Broadcasting Systems.* Belmont, Calif.:
Wadsworth Publishing Company.

Jones, Clement. 1980. *Mass Media Codes of Ethics and Councils: A Comparative International Study on Professional Standards.* Paris, France: UN-
ESCO Press.

Karpen, Ulrich. 1993. Freedom of the Press in Germany. In *Press Law and
Practice.* London, England: Article 19.

Kingdom of the Netherlands: The Constitution. 1989. Rijswijk, The Netherlands: Ministry of Foreign Affairs.

Kommers, Donald P. 1989. *The Constitutional Jurisprudence of the Federal Republic of Germany.* Durham, N.C.: Duke University Press.

Kruuse, Helle Nissen. 1994. The Netherlands. In Marcel Berlins, Claude
Grellier and Helle Nissen Kruuse (Eds.), *Les droits et les devoirs des
journalistes dans les douze pays de l'Union Européenne.* [The rights
and responsibilities of journalists in the twelve countries of the
European Union]. Paris, France: Centre de Formation et de Perfectionnement des Journalistes.

Kuhn, Raymond. 1995. *The Media in France.* London, England: Routledge.

Laitila, Tiina. 1995. Codes of Ethics in Europe. In Kaarle Nordenstreng
(Ed.), *Reports on Media Ethics in Europe.* Tampere, Finland: Department of Journalism and Mass Communication.

Lahav, Pnina (Ed.). 1990. *Press Law in Modern Democracies.* New York, N.Y.:
Longman.

Lensen, Anton. 1992. *Concentration in the Media Industry.* Washington,
D.C.: The Annenberg Washington Program, Communications
Policy Studies, Northwestern University.

Leonard, Dick. 1988. *Pocket Guide to the European Community.* Oxford, England: Basil Blackwell Ltd. and The Economist Publications Ltd.

Mathijsen, P.S.R.F. 1990. *A Guide to European Community Law.* London,
England: Sweet and Maxwell.

Maxwell, Richard. 1995. *The Spectacle of Democracy.* Minneapolis, Minn.: University of Minnesota Press.

McGonagle, Marie. 1996. *A Textbook on Media Law.* Dublin, Ireland: Gill and Macmillan Ltd.

McNae, L.C.J. 1980. *Essential Law for Journalists.* London, England: Granada Publishing.

McNair, Brian. 1994. *News and Journalism in the UK.* London, England: Routledge.

Meyn, Hermann. 1994. *Mass Media in the Federal Republic of Germany.* Berlin, Germany: Wissenschaftsverlag Volker Spiess GmbH.

Nelson, Maria. 1993. Television Without Frontiers: The EC Broadcasting Directive. In Ralph H. Folsom, Ralph B. Lake and Ved P. Nanda (Eds.), *European Community Law After 1992.* Deventer, The Netherlands: Kluwer Law and Taxation Publishers.

Open Government. 1994. London, England: Office of Public Service and Science.

Ottaway, James H. and Leonard Marks. 1996. *Insult Laws: An Insult to Press Freedom.* Reston, Va.: World Press Freedom Committee.

Overbeck, Wayne and Rick D. Pullen. 1994. *Major Principles of Media Law.* Ft. Worth, Tex.: Harcourt Brace College Publishers.

Paulu, Burton. 1956. *British Broadcasting: radio and television in the United Kingdom.* Minneapolis, Minn.: University of Minnesota Press.

Petrogani, Roberto. 1982. Freedom of Information Italy: Restraints and Problems. In Dan Nimmo and Michael W. Mansfield (Eds.), *Government and the Media.* Waco, Tex.: Baylor University Press.

Philippart, Campbell & Associés. 1994. France. In Wedlake Bell (Ed.), *Marketing Law That Matters.* London, U.K.: Pittman Publishing.

Picard, Robert G. 1988. *The Ravens of Odin.* Ames, Iowa: Iowa State University Press.

Poggioli, Sylvia. 1991. *The Media in Europe After 1992: A Case Study of La Republica.* Cambridge, Mass.: Joan Shorenstein Barone Center, Harvard University.

Preslmayer, Karl. 1992. Austria. In James R. Maxeiner and Peter Schotthoffer (Eds.), *Advertising Law in Europe and North America.* Deventer, The Netherlands: Kluwer Law and Taxation Publishers.

Ranke, F.O. 1992. France. In James R. Maxeiner and Peter Schotthoffer (Eds.), *Advertising Law in Europe and North America.* Deventer, The Netherlands: Kluwer Law and Taxation Publishers.

Schlesinger, Philip. 1978. *Putting "Reality" Together: BBC News.* London, England: Constable and Company Ltd.

Sonninen, Päivi and Tiina Laitila. 1995. Press Councils in Europe. In Kaarle Nordenstreng (Ed.), *Reports on Media Ethics in Europe.* Tampere, Finland: Department of Journalism and Mass Communication.

Spanish Constitution. 1978. Madrid, Spain: Presidencia del Gobierno, Secretaría General Técnica.

Teeter, Dwight Jr. and Don R. Le Duc. 1995. *Law of Mass Communications.* Westbury, N.Y.: The Foundation Press, Inc.

To Syntagma tis Elladas (The Constitution of Greece). 1990. Athens, Greece: Pontiki Publications.

Traquina, Nelson. Portuguese Television: The Politics of Savage Deregulation. In *Media Culture and Society.* 1995. London, U.K.: Sage.

The Treaty of Rome. 1990. London, England: Blackstone Press Limited.

Tunstall, Jeremy. 1977. *The Media Are American.* New York, N.Y.: Columbia University Press.

Van Bol, Jean-Marie. 1976. *The Policy Surrounding Social Communications in Belgium.* Brussels, Belgium: Ministry of Foreign Affairs.

Van Dijk, Teun A. *Racism and the Press.* 1991. London, England: Routledge.

Van Eijk, Nico, 1992. Legal and Policy Aspects of Community Broadcasting. In Nick Jankowski, Ole Prehn and James Stappers (Eds.), *The People's Voice: Local Radio and Television in Europe.* London, Englnad: John Libbey & Company.

Voorhoof, Dirk. 1995. *Critical Perspectives on the Scope and Interpretation of Article 10 of the European Convention on Human Rights.* Strasbourg, France: Council of Europe Press.

Zaharopoulos, Thimios and Paraschos, Manny E. 1993. *Mass Media in Greece: Power, Politics and Privatization.* Westport, Conn.: Praeger Publishers.

Articles in Periodicals

Ainsworth, Lesley and Daniel Weston. Newspapers and UK media ownership controls. *Journal of Media Law and Practice,* Vol. 16, No. 1, 1995, p. 2.

Associated Press. "Seagram to Go Ahead with Whiskey Ads." *The Boston Globe,* September 24, 1996.

Audio-Visual Services/27. *Panorama of EU Industry 95-96,* DG III, p. 3

Banwell, Caroline. 1995. The courts' treatment of the broadcasting bans in Britain and the Republic of Ireland. In *Journal of Media Law and Practice,* Vol. 16, No.1, 1995, p. 29.

Barbash, Fred. 1996. Europe's fetaful ruling: It's only Greek to them. *The Washington Post.* March 10, 1966, A, 1.

Bogart, Leo. What does it all mean. *Media Studies Journal.* Spring/Summer 1996, p. 20.

Buerkle, Tom. "Parliament Calls for Truce in Fight with Hollywood." *International Herald Tribune*. November 13, 1996, A, 1.

Burkert, Herbert. 1990. An overview on access to government information legislation in Europe. *Journal of Media Law and Practice*, Vol. 11, No. 1, p. 12.

Choate, Roger. 1975. The public's right to know: Access to public documents. *Current Sweden*, No. 93, p. 1.

Cultural protectionism. Editorial. *The Boston Globe*, October 24, 1989, A 14.

Deckmyn, Veerle. La transparence et l'information européenne. *EIPAS-COPE*, No. 1994/2, p. 6 (Institut Européen d'Administration Publique).

European Code. Editorial. *Editor and Publisher*, April 30, 1994, p. 6.

Europeans step up co-productions among themselves. *Broadcasting*, February 19, 1990, p. 31.

"Europe's Sneak Attack on the Press." *Wall Street Journal Europe*. Nov. 6, 1993, p. 6.

Garneau, George. Reject rights treaty, journalism groups urge Senate. *Editor and Publisher*, December 7, 1991, p. 26.

Gosselin, Peter. "Liquor Industry Ends TV Ad Ban." *The Boston Globe*, November 8, 1996, A1.

Greenhouse, Steven. "Europe Reaches TV Compromise; U.S. Officials Fear Protectionism." *The New York Times*, October 4, 1989, A1.

Greenhouse, Steven. "The Television Europeans Love, and Love to Hate." *The New York Times*, August 13, 1989, 4, 24.

Gitlin, Todd. Not so fast. *Media Studies Journal*, Spring/Summer 1996, p. 6.

Harrison, Ivor H. Advertising medicinal products. *Journal of Media Law and Practice*, June 1992, p. 194.

"In the Courts: The Government vs. the Press." *Newsweek*, July 28, 1971, p. 27.

Itzin, Catherine. Pornography, harm and human rights—the European context. *Journal of Media Law and Practice*, Vol. 16, No. 3, 1995, p. 113.

Jauert, Per and Ole Prehn. "Ownership and Concentration in Local Radio Broadcasting in Scandinavia." *Nordicom Review*, No. 1, 1996, pp. 83-86.

Johnson, Howard. Elderflowers and champagne. *Media Law and Practice*, Vol. 15, No. 4, 1994, p. 54.

Jones, Simon. Lights, camera, action—a review of the proposed changes to UK broadcasting law. *Communications Law*, A Tolley Professional Publication, Vol. 1, No. 4, 1996, p. 160.

Joint Declaration. *Official Journal of the European Communities*, No. C 103. April 4, 1977, p. 1.

Laursen, Finn. Denmark's "Yes, But." *EIPASCOPE*, No. 1993/3, p. 12, (Institut Européen d'Administration Publique).

McConnell, Chris. Kids TV accord reached. *Broadcasting and Cable*, August 5, 1996, p. 5d.

McConnell, Chris. Three hours of kids TV. *Broadcasting and Cable*, August 12, 1996, p. 11.

Paraschos, Emmanuel (Manny). The Corrective Ad Challenge. University of Missouri's Freedom of Information Center Report, No. 283, 1972, p. 1.

Pedersen, Daniel. "A 'Grenade' Aimed at Hollywood." *Newsweek*, October 16, 1989, p. 58.

Press Laws. 1990. *Occasional Papers*. New York: Instituto Italiano di Cultura. p. 2.

"Rationing 'Dallas' in Europe." Editorial. *The New York Times*, October 24, 1989, A26.

Reuters News Service. "Food Lion Awarded $1,402 in ABC Case." December 30, 1996.

Roberts, Gene. Corporate journalism and community service. *Media Studies Journal*, Spring/Summer 1996, pp. 104-107.

Sack, Robert D. *Goodwin v. United Kingdom:* An American view of protection for journalists' confidential sources under UK and European law. *Journal of Media Law and Practice*, Vol. 16, No. 3, 1995, p. 93.

Single European Act. *Official Journal of the European Communities*, No. L 169. June 29, 1987, p. 2.

Smith, Anthony. Media globalism in the age of consumer sovereignty. *Gannett Center Journal*, Gannett Foundation Media Center, Fall 1990, p. 5.

Sundin, Staffan. Media ownership in Sweden. *Nordicom Review*, No. 2, 1995. p. 65.

Thompson, Estes. "Jury Finds ABC Guilty of Fraud." *The Boston Globe*, December 12, 1996 , D1.

Voorhoof, Dirk. Defamation and libel laws in Europe—the framework of Article 10 of the European Convention of Human Rights. *Journal of Media Law and Practice*, Vol. 13, No. 4, 1992, p. 260.

Voorhoof, Dirk. Restrictions on television advertising and Article 10 of the European Convention on Human Rights. *International Journal of Advertising*, 1993, No. 12, p. 199.

Wallace, Rebecca and David Goldberg. Television broadcasting: The Community's response. *Common Market Law Review*, 26:717-728 (1989), p. 717.

World Press Freedom Committee Newsletter. Council of Europe Ministers Back Limits on Press. December 16, 1994, p. 1.

Index

Abortion information, 39
Access to information, 113–26, 248–49
  Austria, 122
  Belgium, 124
  Denmark, 120–21
  European Union, 115–18
  Finland, 120
  France, 121
  Germany, 122–23
  Greece, 124
  Ireland, 126
  Italy, 123–24
  Netherlands, The, 40–41, 121–22
  Portugal, 123
  Spain, 123
  Sweden, 118–20
  United Kingdom, 124–26
  United States, 113–14
Action Committee for the United
  States of Europe (ACUSE), 8
Adenauer, Conrad, 9
Advertising, 153–71, 251
  Austria, 162–63
  Belgium, 164
  children and, 156, 159–60, 166–67,
    170
  children's programming and, 132,
    135–36, 171
  comparative, 155, 157–58, 162,
    164–71
  deceptive, 155, 163
  Denmark, 164–65
  ethical codes of press and, 207–9,
    211, 219–20, 230, 238–40
  European Union, 154–62
  France, 165–66
  Greece, 166
  Ireland, 170
  Italy, 170–71

  Luxembourg, 158–59, 164
  media concentration, 185, 189
  Misleading Advertising Directive,
    154, 156–58
  Netherlands, The, 166–67
  political, 154–56, 166–69
  Portugal, 171
  Spain, 167–68
  Sweden, 168
  Transfrontier Television Directive,
    154, 156, 159–60
  United Kingdom, 168–70
  United States, 155–56
African Charter on Human and Peo-
  ple's Rights (ACHPR), 32
Agricultural policy, European Community, 9–11
Alcohol advertising, 136, 154–55,
  159–60, 162, 164–65, 167–69, 251
American Declaration of the Rights
  and Duties of Man, 32
Animal cruelty, 104
Antitrust laws, 177, 180, 185. *See also*
  Media concentration
Associated Press v. United States, 177
Austria
  access to information, 122
  advertising, 162–63
  blasphemy, 107
  broadcast regulation, 145
  constitution, 36
  court coverage, 84
  defamation, 61
  demographics, 13
  ethical codes, 205–6
  freedom of expression, 36
  media concentration, 185
  national security, 99
  news source protection, 89

Austria (*continued*)
  obscenity, 104
  Press Council, 203
  privacy, 73
  racism, 107
  right of reply, 78
Autronic AG v. Switzerland, 46

Barford court case, 47
BBC (British Broadcasting Corporation), 137–38
Belgium
  access to information, 124
  advertising, 164
  blasphemy, 111
  broadcast regulation, 146
  constitution, 36
  court coverage, 84–85
  defamation, 67
  demographics, 13–14
  ethical codes, 206–8
  freedom of expression, 36
  media concentration, 191
  national security, 99–100
  news source protection, 207
  obscenity, 105
  Press Council, 204
  privacy, 74–75
  racism, 111
  right of reply, 79, 207
Benelux Union, 6
Black, Hugo, 177
Blasphemy, 106–11, 251
  Austria, 107
  Belgium, 111
  Denmark, 108
  Finland, 111
  France, 108
  Germany, 107–8
  Greece, 110
  Ireland, 110
  Italy, 110
  Netherlands, The, 108–9
  Spain, 110
  Sweden, 109
  United Kingdom, 109

  United States, 106
  Wingrove v. the United Kingdom, 55–56
Branzburg v. Hayes, 88
Bribes, 206, 225, 227, 231–32, 234, 244
Brind and others v. U.K., 149
British Broadcasting Corporation (BBC), 137–38
Broadcast regulation, 129–49, 249
  Austria, 145
  Belgium, 146
  Denmark, 146
  European Union, 133–40
  false, 155
  Finland, 144
  France, 146–47
  Germany, 141–42
  Greece, 142–43
  Ireland, 143–44, 148–49
  Italy, 144
  Netherlands, The, 145–46
  Portugal, 143
  Spain, 146
  Sweden, 145
  terrorism and, 148–49
  United Kingdom, 141, 148–49
  United States, 130–33

Cable News Network (CNN), 36, 149, 250
Cable television, 131, 133, 141, 146
Capital punishment, 45
Carlin, George, 132
Castells court case, 52
CBS, Inc., v. FCC, 131
Censorship. *See* Freedom of expression
Children's programs and advertising, 132, 135–36, 171
Children's Television Act, 132–33, 156
Churchill, Winston, 7
Church of Scientology v. Sweden, 161
CNN (Cable News Network), 36, 149, 250
Commercialization, media, 5, 249–50
Commission of Access to Administrative Documents, French (CADA), 121

Communications Act of 1934, U.S., 78
Communism, E.U. and, 6
Community Merger Regulation, 181
Competition, media. *See* Media concentration
Conference on Security and Cooperation in Europe, 32
Confidentiality. *See* News source protection
Confiscation of publications, 38
Consent and privacy, 71–77
Constitutions, 34–44
  Austria, 36
  Belgium, 36
  Denmark, 36–37
  Finland, 37
  Germany, 34, 38
  Greece, 38–39
  history of European, 34
  Ireland, 39
  Italy, 39–40
  Luxembourg, 40
  Netherlands, The, 40–41
  Portugal, 41
  Spain, 42
  Sweden, 42–43
  United Kingdom, 43–44
Contempt of court
  court coverage, 84, 86–87
  news source protection, 90
Correction. *See* Right of reply
Correctness of information. *See* Ethical codes
Council of Europe. *See also* European Convention of Human Rights
  access to information, 118
  freedom of expression, 30–31
  human rights, 44
  media concentration, 182
  media ethics, 198–200
Council of Ministers, 20–21
Court coverage, 83–84, 83–87
  Austria, 84
  Belgium, 84–85
  Denmark, 85, 209–10
  France, 85
  Germany, 85, 223
  Ireland, 87

  Italy, 87
  Netherlands, The, 85
  Spain, 86
  Sweden, 86
  United Kingdom, 86–87
  United Nations, 28
  United States, 83–84
Court of First Instance, 23
Court of Justice, 22–23, 158–59, 181
Cresson, Edith, 4
Cruelty, censorship and, 104
Culture
  Americanization, 250–51
  global, 252–53
  protection of, 4, 250–51
Custody and court coverage, 85–86

Data protection, 70–71, 73, 75, 77, 248
Death penalty, 45
Defamation, 59–70, 248. *See also* Ethical codes
  Austria, 61
  Belgium, 67
  of the dead, 69–70, 91
  defined, 60
  Denmark, 61
  Finland, 61–62
  France, 66–67
  Germany, 64
  of governmental officials, 61–63, 65–69, 97–101
  Greece, 62
  Ireland, 64
  Italy, 67–68
  Netherlands, The, 68–69
  Portugal, 69
  right of reply, 80, 82–83
  Spain, 64–65
  Sweden, 65–66
  unintentional, 63
  United Kingdom, 62–63
  United States, 59–60
de Gaulle, Charles, 9
Delors, Jacques, 4, 11
Democracy in America, 247
Demographics, European Union members, 13–18

Denmark
    access to information, 120–21
    advertising, 164–65
    blasphemy, 108
    broadcast regulation, 146
    constitution, 36–37
    court coverage, 85, 209–10
    defamation, 61
    demographics, 14
    ethical codes, 208–10
    freedom of expression, 36–37
    media concentration, 191
    national security, 53
    news source protection, 91
    Press Council, 203–4
    privacy, 72, 209
    racism, 108
    right of reply, 79
Deontological codes. *See* Ethical codes
de Tocqueville, Alexis, 247
Directorates-general, E.U., 19–20
Divorce and court coverage, 75, 85–87
D-notice, 126
Documents, access to. *See* Access to in-
    formation

Eavesdropping. *See* Privacy
EC (European Community), 8–11
ECU (European Currency Unit), 10
Engel and others court case, 46
England. *See* United Kingdom
Environment
    information, 115–16
    and press ethics, 210
    programming, 144
Ethical codes, 205–44
    Austria, 205–6
    Belgium, 206–8
    Denmark, 208–10
    Finland, 210–13
    France, 213–14
    functions of, 197
    Germany, 214–25
    Greece, 225–26
    Ireland, 226–27
    Italy, 227–31
    Netherlands, The, 232

    Portugal, 233
    Spain, 234–35
    Sweden, 235–40
    United Kingdom, 240–44
Euratom (European Atomic Energy
    Community), 8, 115
European Coal and Steel Community,
    8
European Community (EC), 8–11
European Convention of Human
    Rights, 44–45
    broadcast regulation, 149
    defamation, 60
    press regulation, 199–200
    privacy, 71–72, 74
European Council, 21
European Court of Human Rights,
    44–56
    abortion information, 39
    advertising regulation, 160–62
    court coverage, 86
    criticism of public officials, 248
    freedom of expression, 44–56, 251
    national security, 97
    news source protection, 87–88, 90
    obscenity, 101
    privacy, 73
European Court of Justice, 22–23,
    158–59, 181
European Currency Unit (ECU), 10
European Defense Community, 8
European Economic Community, 8,
    115
European Media Ombudsman, 199
European Monetary System, 10
European Monetary Union, 11
European Parliament, 21–22
European Regional Development
    Fund, 10
European Union. *See also specific mem-
    ber countries*
    access to information, 115–18
    advertising, 154–62
    broadcast regulation, 133–40
    freedom of expression, 32–34
    history, 6–12
    human rights conventions, 32–34
    legal instruments, 23–24

media concentration, 181–83
member demographics, 12–18
organization, 19–23
  commission, 19–20
  Council of Ministers, 20–21
  Court of Justice, 22–23
  European Council, 21
  European Parliament, 21–22
self-regulation, journalist, 195–200
Expression, freedom of. *See* Freedom of
  expression

Fairness Doctrine, 131
Fascism, 108
FCC (Federal Communication Commission), U.S., 130–32, 178
FCC v. Pacifica, 132
Federal Trade Commission (FTC), U.S.,
  155, 180
Finland
  access to information, 120
  blasphemy, 111
  broadcast regulation, 144
  constitution, 37
  defamation, 61–62
  demographics, 14
  ethical codes, 210–13
  freedom of expression, 37
  news source protection, 212
  Press Council, 203
  privacy, 72–73, 213
  racism, 111
  right of reply, 79, 212–13
France
  access to information, 121
  advertising, 165–66
  blasphemy, 108
  broadcast regulation, 146–47
  court coverage, 85
  defamation, 66–67
  demographics, 14–15
  de Tocqueville, Alexis, 247
  ethical codes, 213–14
  freedom of expression, 37–38
  history of European Union and, 6–10
  media concentration, 188
  national security, 98

news source protection, 88–89
obscenity, 104–5
privacy, 72
racism, 108
right of reply, 79–80
Saarland, 7
Freedom of expression
  African Charter on Human and Peo-
    ple's Rights, 32
  Austria, 36
  Belgium, 36
  Council of Europe, 30–31
  Denmark, 36–37
  European Court of Human Rights,
    44–56
  European Union, 32–34
  Finland, 37
  France, 37–38
  Germany, 38
  Greece, 38–39
  Ireland, 39
  Italy, 39–40
  Luxembourg, 40
  Netherlands, The, 40–41
  Organization of American States,
    31–32
  Portugal, 41
  Spain, 42
  Sweden, 42–43
  United Kingdom, 43–44
  United Nations, 27–29
Freedom of Information Act, U.S., 114,
  248
FTC (Federal Trade Commission), U.S.,
  155, 180

Gag orders, 84–85
Gannet Co., Inc., v. De Pasquale, 84
GATT (General Agreement on Tariffs
  and Trade), 10
GDP (Gross Domestic Product), European Union members, 13–18
Germany
  access to information, 122–23
  blasphemy, 107–8
  broadcast regulation, 141–42
  constitution, 34, 38

Germany (*continued*)
  court coverage, 85, 223
  defamation, 64
  demographics, 15
  ethical codes, 214–25
  freedom of expression, 38
  history of European Union and, 6–10
  media concentration, 188–89
  national security, 98–99
  news source protection, 89, 218–19
  obscenity, 105
  Press Council, 203
  privacy, 73–74, 220–21
  racism, 107–8
  right of reply, 80
Goodwin v. the United Kingdom, 54–55,
  88, 90
Government information access,
  113–26
Government in the Sunshine Act, U.S.,
  114
Great Britain. *See* United Kingdom
Greece
  access to information, 124
  advertising, 166
  blasphemy, 110
  broadcast regulation, 142–43
  constitution, 38–39
  defamation, 62
  demographics, 15
  ethical codes, 225–26
  freedom of expression, 38–39
  media concentration, 186
  national security, 47, 100
  news source protection, 92
  obscenity, 105–6
  Press Council, 204
  privacy, 76–77
  racism, 110
  right of reply, 83

Hadjianastasiou court case, 47
Hallstein, Walter, 9
Handyside court case, 46–47
Harassment, in the U.K., 241
High Authority, 8

Indecent materials. *See* Obscenity
Industrial secrets, 114, 118, 120–21, 124,
  126
Information access. *See* Access to information
Informationsverein Lentia and others
  court case, 52
Ingemar Liljenberg v. Sweden, 161
International Convention on Civil and
  Political Rights, 28–29
Internet and obscenity, 102
Ireland
  access to information, 126
  advertising, 170
  blasphemy, 110
  broadcast regulation, 143–44, 148–49
  constitution, 39
  court coverage, 87
  defamation, 64
  demographics, 16
  ethical codes, 226–27
  freedom of expression, 39
  media concentration, 185–86
  national security, 99
  news source protection, 92, 227
  obscenity, 104
  privacy, 74
  right of reply, 80
Irish Republican Army (IRA), 44. *See
  also* Sinn Fein
Italy
  access to information, 123–24
  advertising, 170–71
  blasphemy, 110
  broadcast regulation, 144
  constitution, 39–40
  court coverage, 87
  defamation, 67–68
  demographics, 16
  ethical codes, 227–31
  freedom of expression, 39–40
  media concentration, 183–85
  national security, 99
  news source protection, 90, 230
  obscenity, 106
  Press Council, 205
  privacy, 74

racism, 111
right of reply, 80–81, 229

Jenkins, Roy, 10
Jersild v. Denmark, 54
Journalist, self-identification of, 74,
    216, 233. *See also* Self-regulation,
    journalist
Judicial proceedings. *See* Court cover-
    age

Language, national
    advertising and, 165
    television and, 130, 141–44
Lawyers and advertising, 161–62, 168
Libel. *See* Defamation
Lingens court case, 49–50
Literacy rates, 13–18
Luxembourg
    advertising, 158–59, 164
    constitution, 40
    demographics, 16–17
    freedom of expression, 40
    news source protection, 92
    Press Council, 205
    right of reply, 81

Maastricht, Treaty of, 10–11
    governmental openness, 115–16
    human rights, 33
Mail privacy. *See* Privacy
Malice, defamation with, 60–63, 67–69
Marriage dissolution. *See* Divorce and
    court coverage
Media concentration, 131, 176–91,
    197–98, 249
    Austria, 185
    Belgium, 191
    Denmark, 191
    European Union, 181–83
    France, 188
    Germany, 188–89
    Greece, 186
    Ireland, 185–86

Italy, 183–85
Netherlands, The, 189–90
Portugal, 41, 190
Spain, 190
Sweden, 187–88
United Kingdom, 186–87
United States, 176–80
Medical records access, 121, 125. *See
    also* Access to information
Medical reporting, 224–25, 231
Mergers. *See* Media concentration
Miami Herald Publishing Co. v. Tornillo,
    78
Military information. *See* National se-
    curity
Miller v. California, 103
Minors, 248
    advertising and, 132, 135–36,
        159–60, 166–67, 170–71
    court coverage, 75, 85–86
    ethical codes of press and, 206,
        223–24, 231, 235, 242
    obscenity, 101–6
    television programs, 132–33, 136
Misleading Advertising Directive, 154,
    156–58
Monnet, Jean, 7–8
Monopolies. *See* Media concentration
Morality. *See* Obscenity
Murdoch, Rupert, 133

National security, 97–101, 248
    access to information, 120–26
    Austria, 99
    Belgium, 99–100
    Denmark, 53
    France, 98
    Germany, 98–99
    Greece, 47, 100
    Ireland, 99
    Italy, 99
    news source protection, 89–90
    Portugal, 100–101
    Sweden, 98
    United Kingdom, 51
    United Nations, 28

National security (*continued*)
  United States, 97
Nazism, 6, 37, 107–8, 111
Near v. Minnesota, 114
Nebraska Press Assn. v. Stuart, 84
Negligence, defamation and, 60, 67
Netherlands, The
  access to information, 40–41, 121–22
  advertising, 166–67
  blasphemy, 108–9
  broadcast regulation, 145–46
  constitution, 40–41
  court coverage, 85
  defamation, 68–69
  demographics, 17
  ethical codes, 232
  freedom of expression, 40–41
  media concentration, 189–90
  news source protection, 91
  obscenity, 104
  Press Council, 202–3
  privacy, 75
  racism, 108–9
  right of reply, 81
News
  CNN (Cable News Network), 36, 149,
    250
  media concentration and, 179
  programming, 137–38, 141, 143
Newspapers
  advertising, 176, 179
  government subsidy, 176, 187, 189,
    191
  media concentration, 131, 176–79,
    184–91
  Newspaper Preservation Act, 178
  per capita rates in European Union,
    13–18
News source protection, 87–92, 249
  Austria, 89
  Belgium, 207
  Denmark, 91
  ethical codes, 197
  Finland, 212
  France, 88–89
  Germany, 89, 218–19
  Goodwin v. the United Kingdom, 55

Greece, 92
Ireland, 92, 227
Italy, 90, 230
Luxembourg, 92
Netherlands, The, 91
Portugal, 91, 233
Spain, 91
Sweden, 89–90
United Kingdom, 90
  Journalists' Code of Conduct,
    243–44
United States, 88
Northern Ireland, 99, 148–49. *See also*
  United Kingdom

Oberschlick court case, 50
Obscenity, 101–6, 249. *See also* Free-
  dom of expression
  Austria, 104
  Belgium, 105
  broadcast regulation, 131–32
  France, 104–5
  Germany, 105
  Greece, 105–6
  Ireland, 104
  Italy, 106
  Netherlands, The, 104
  Portugal, 106
  Spain, 105
  Sweden, 105
  United Kingdom, 104
  United States, 103
Observer and Guardian Newspapers Ltd.
  court case, 51
Official Secrets Act, 125–26
Ombudsman, 195
  European media, 199
  Italian press, 228
  Swedish press, 200–201
Opinion, freedom of. *See* Freedom of
  expression
Opinion polls, 215
Organization of American States,
  31–32
Otto-Preminger-Institut court case,
  47–48

Pentagon Papers, 46, 49, 114
Pharmaceuticals
    advertising, 162, 164–69, 171
    reporting on, 224–25, 231
Photographs
    news source protection, 89
    privacy and, 71–77
    symbolic, 215–16
Physicians and advertising, 164, 168
Plagiarism, 214, 232, 238
Pluralism. *See* Media concentration
Politics
    advertising, 154–56, 166–68, 215
    candidates, 131, 215
    political parties
        European Parliament and, 22
        national security and, 98
        television and, 131, 140–45,
            148–49
Pornography, 101–6
Portugal
    access to information, 123
    advertising, 171
    broadcast regulation, 143
    constitution, 41
    defamation, 69
    demographics, 17
    ethical codes, 233
    freedom of expression, 41
    media concentration, 41, 190
    national security, 100–101
    news source protection, 91, 233
    obscenity, 106
    Press Council, 204
    privacy, 77–78, 233
    right of reply, 83
Prager and Oberschlick court case, 48
Press Councils, 200–205
    Austria, 203
    Belgium, 204
    defined, 195–96
    Denmark, 203–4
    Finland, 203
    Germany, 203
    Greece, 204
    history of, 196–97
    Italy, 205

Luxembourg, 205
Netherlands, The, 202–3
Portugal, 204
Sweden, 200–201
United Kingdom, 201–2
Press freedom. *See* Freedom of expression
Prior restraint, 52, 114
Privacy, 70–71, 70–78, 248
    Austria, 73
    Belgium, 74–75
    Denmark, 72, 209
    Finland, 72–73, 213
    France, 72
    Germany, 73–74, 220–21
    Greece, 76–77
    Ireland, 74
    Italy, 74
    Netherlands, The, 75
    Portugal, 77–78, 233
    Spain, 75–76, 235
    Sweden, 77, 235
    United Kingdom, 76, 201–2, 241
    United Nations, 28
    United States, 70–71
Privileged information. *See also* News
        source protection
    as defamation defense, 60–61, 63–64
Professional confidences, privacy of, 73
Public interest
    court coverage and, 84–87
    privacy and, 71–77
Purcell v. Ireland, 149

Racism, 106–11, 251
    Austria, 107
    Belgium, 111
    Denmark, 108
    Finland, 111
    France, 108
    Germany, 107–8
    Greece, 110
    Italy, 111
    Netherlands, The, 108–9
    Sweden, 109
    United Kingdom, 109

Racism (*continued*)
   United Nations, 28, 106–7
Radio
   per capita rates in European Union,
      13–18
   station ownership, 130, 178, 187, 189
Retractions. *See* Right of reply
Richmond Newspapers v. Virginia, 84
Right of reply, 78–83, 249
   Austria, 78
   Belgium, 79, 207
   Denmark, 79
   Finland, 79, 212–13
   France, 79–80
   Germany, 80
   Greece, 83
   Ireland, 80
   Italy, 80–81, 229
   Luxembourg, 81
   Netherlands, The, 81
   Organization of American States, 32
   Portugal, 83
   Spain, 81, 234
   Sweden, 81–82, 236
   television, 138, 145
   television programming, 136–38
   United Kingdom, 82–83, 201, 240
   United States, 78
Rome, Treaty of, 8–10, 19
   competition, 181
   human rights, 33–34

Saarland, dispute over, 7
Satellite television, 133
Schengen agreement, 71
Schuman, Robert, 7–8
Schwabe v. Austria, 50–51, 73
Secrecy. *See* Access to information
Security, national. *See* National secu-
   rity
Sedition. *See* National security
Seditious libel. *See* Defamation, of gov-
   ernmental officials
Self-regulation, journalist, 195–224. *See
   also* Ethical codes; Press Council

   European Union, 195–200
   United States, 196
Sexually explicit material. *See* Obscenity
Sheppard v. Maxwell, 84
Shield laws, 88
Single European Act of 1987, 10–11, 21,
   33
Sinn Fein, 148–49
Slander, 59–60, 62. *See also* Defamation
Source confidentiality. *See* News source
   protection
Spain
   access to information, 123
   advertising, 167–68
   blasphemy, 110
   broadcast regulation, 146
   constitution, 42
   court coverage, 86
   defamation, 64–65
   demographics, 17–18
   ethical codes, 234–35
   freedom of expression, 42
   media concentration, 190
   news source protection, 91
   obscenity, 105
   privacy, 75–76, 235
   right of reply, 81, 234
Speech, freedom of. *See* Freedom of Expression
Sponsorship, of E.U., 5, 160, 163
Spycatcher memoirs, 51–52
Stonehouse, John, 119
Subsidies, in E.U., 139
Suicide
   ethical codes of press and, 209, 221
   privacy and, 72, 77
Sunday Times and A. Neil court case, 51
Sunday Times court case, 48–49
Supreme Court, U.S.
   advertisement restriction, 156
   antitrust laws, 177
   candidate broadcast access, 131
   court coverage, 84
   defamation, 59
   news source protection, 88

Pentagon Papers, 46
prior restraint, 114
privacy, 70
right of reply, 78
Surveillance. *See* Privacy
Sweden
    access to information, 118–20
    advertising, 168
    blasphemy, 109
    broadcast regulation, 145
    constitution, 42–43
    court coverage, 86
    defamation, 65–66
    demographics, 18
    ethical codes, 235–40
    freedom of expression, 42–43
    media concentration, 187–88
    national security, 98
    news source protection, 89–90
    obscenity, 105
    Press Council, 200–201
    privacy, 77, 235
    racism, 109
    right of reply, 81–82, 236

Tax, value-added, 11
Telecommunications Act, U.S., 179
Telephone privacy, 70, 72–77, 241
Television. *See also* Advertising
    broadcast regulation, 129–49
    European Union
        advertising, 135–37, 139
        cultural protection, 129–30,
            133–35, 139–44
        European works quotas, 3–4, 135,
            137, 139–40, 250
        per capita rates, 13–18
    Greek constitution and, 38–39
    station ownership. *See* Media con-
        centration
    Transfrontier Television Directive
        advertising, 154, 156, 159–60
        pluralism, 3–4, 181–82, 250
    United States
        cable, 131

children's programming, 132–33
content regulation, 131–32
ownership of stations, 130–31
Terrorism and news source protection,
    90
Thorgeir Thorgeirson court case, 52
Tobacco products advertising, 136,
    154–55, 159, 162, 164, 166–69, 171,
    251
Tolstoy Miloslavsky court case, 53–54
Transfrontier Television Directive. *See
    also* Broadcast regulation
    advertising and, 154, 156, 159–60
    pluralism and, 3–4, 181–82, 250
Transparency, 115–16, 248. *See also* Ac-
    cess to information
    Italian press ethical code and,
        228–30
    media concentration, 188
    media ownership and, 182
    news organizations, 198
Treaty of Maastricht. *See* Maastricht,
    Treaty of
Treaty of Rome. *See* Rome, Treaty of
Trespassing, 71–73, 76
Trials. *See* Court coverage
Truth. *See also* Ethical codes
    as defamation defense, 60–64, 67–69
    as privacy invasion defense, 71–72
    right of reply and, 78–83

United Kingdom
    access to information, 124–26
    advertising, 168–70
    blasphemy, 109
    broadcast regulation, 141, 148–49
    constitution, 43–44
    court coverage, 86–87
    defamation, 62–63
    demographics, 18
    European Community and, 9–10
    freedom of expression, 43–44
    media concentration, 186–87
    national security, 51
    news source protection, 90, 243–44

United Kingdom (*continued*)
  obscenity, 104
  Press Council, 201–2
  privacy, 76, 201–2, 241
  racism, 109
  right of reply, 82–83, 201, 240
United Nations
  freedom of expression, 27–29
    International Convention on Civil
      and Political Rights, 28–29
    Universal Declaration of Human
      Rights, 27–28
  racism, 28, 106–7
United States
  access to information, 113–14
  advertising, 155–56
  blasphemy, 106
  broadcast regulation, 130–33
  court coverage, 83–84
  defamation, 59–60
  de Tocqueville, Alexis, 247
  media concentration, 176–80
  national security, 97
  news source protection, 88
  obscenity, 103
  privacy, 70–71

  right of reply, 78
  self-regulation, journalist, 196
  United States v. Citizen Publishing Co.,
    178
  Universal Declaration of Human
    Rights, (U.N.), 27–28

Valenti, Jack, 3, 250
Value-added tax (VAT), 11
*Vereinigung Demokratischer Soldaten
  Österreichs and Gubi* court case, 53
Vereniging Weekblad Bluf court case, 53
Versailles, Treaty of, 6
Violence, 101–6, 251
  ethical codes of press and, 207, 222,
    228
  racial, 107–8

Watergate, 114
Weber court case, 51
Whistleblowers, 125
Wingrove v. the United Kingdom, 55–56
Wire tapping. *See* Telephone privacy
Wright, Peter, 51

ISBN 0-8138-2807-4

9 780813 828077

90000>

Iowa State University Press

Orders: 1-800-862-6657
Office: 1-515-292-0140
Fax: 1-515-292-3348